Family Circle

Editorial Director   Arthur Hettich

Special Books Editor   Marie T. Walsh
Editor   Dick Demske

Art Director   Joseph Taveroni
Associate Editor   Gerri Hirshey

Art Associate   Walter C. Schwartz
Production Manager   Norman Ellers

Pennsylvania Dutch chair
and hooked cushion shown
on page 44.

DO-IT-YOURSELF PROJECTS

123 Things You Can Make for the Home

Created by Family Circle Magazine and published 1978 by Arno Press Inc., a subsidiary of The New York Times Company. Copyright © 1976 by The Family Circle, Inc. All rights reserved. Protected under Berne and other international copyright conventions. Title and Trademark FAMILY CIRCLE registered U. S. Patent and Trademark Office, Canada, Great Britain, Australia, New Zealand, Japan and other countries. Marca Registrada. This volume may not be reproduced in whole or in part in any form without written permission from the publisher. Printed in U. S. A. Library of Congress Catalog Card Number 75-42915. ISBN 0-405-06682-1.

Build this classic parson's table for less than $70. Page 46.

TABLE OF CONTENTS

BUYER'S GUIDE, pages 22-23

YOU CAN DO-IT

even with prices as out-of-sight as they are today, you can still get a lot for a little—a lot of things that make living more pleasant, more colorful, more convenient, more comfortable and generally easier—for a little (or no) cash outlay. The secret (and it's really no secret at all to millions of ambitious homeowners and apartment dwellers across the country) is called do-it-yourself. If you have never tried your hand at a do-it-yourself project, you may well be surprised as you become acquainted with your own skills and abilities—qualities you may never have dreamed you possess. There is nothing mysterious, or even particularly difficult, about doing-it-yourself. It takes some patience, attention to instructions and pride in achievement. But that is no more than is required by most things you do: your job, driving a car, creating a good meal. Unless you are all thumbs, there is no project in these pages that will be beyond your capabilities.

the key to your do-it-yourself success on these projects (other than your own prowess) is the projects themselves. Every last one of them has actually been built, as you can see by the photographs, and the step-by-step procedures were carefully noted, checked by experts, then transcribed into the language of the do-it-yourselfer. The how-to instructions are accompanied by drawings (not blueprints that you need an engineer's degree to read) that let you clearly visualize how ''things go together.'' After the instructions and drawings were completed, we tried them out on laymen who were totally unfamiliar with the projects. If they couldn't understand them, it was back to the drawing board (or desk, as the case may be). We think that you will appreciate this meticulous preparation as you are building these projects. Of course, we cannot claim infallibility. We made every effort to be accurate in design and dimensions, but there is always the possibility of error, either on our part or yours. Make sure you understand all steps involved before starting a project. If something goes wrong, we are truly sorry, and hope that it will not lessen your pleasure in doing-it-yourself.

much of that pleasure will be pride of accomplishment. But the real joy—the bottom line—for most do-it-yourselfers is in the money saved. Items that might cost $300 or more in the stores can be built for half that, or even less. Bookshelves that would cost at least $100 can be built for as little as $50. And you will be surprised at how many things you can make for less than $10—or even no cost at all, using scrap materials. We have given approximate prices for all projects (except those where it would be impractical for some reason, such as the finished off basement; the cost here will depend on your particular situation). These prices will vary from one section of the country to another; a particular project may cost you more or (happy surprise) it may cost less. But you can be certain of one thing—it will be a bargain in any case. Your do-it-yourself abilities assure it.

DO-IT-YOURSELF GLOSSARY

Here are some terms often encountered in buying materials and building home projects:

A-B

Abrasive: A material used for wearing away a surface by rubbing or friction. Some examples are sandpaper, emery cloth, steel wool and powdered pumice.

Acetate: Various alcohols combined with acetic acid, used as a solvent for nitrocellulose.

Acrylic: A plastic resin used in latex paints and in certain fast-drying enamels and lacquers. It may also be in the form of a hard, clear and easily worked plastic with many do-it-yourself applications.

Aggregate: Sand and gravel that are mixed with cement to make concrete.

Alkali: A substance that neutralizes acids. Strong alkaline solutions, commonly found in uncured concrete, plaster and similar materials, are destructive to most paint films.

Angle, angle iron: A right angle of steel used for fastening or reinforcing in woodworking and masonry.

Anhydrous: Free of moisture.

Antiquing: A furniture finishing technique that gives the appearance of age or wear; sometimes called glazing.

Apron: The molding below a window sill or cabinet.

Backfill: Replacing excavated earth in a trench or against a structure.

Back saw: A fine-toothed saw with a thin blade, usually used for mitering.

Baluster: A vertical post in a stair railing.

Balustrade: A row of balusters supporting a railing.

Baseboard: Molding to cover the floor-wall joint.

Base shoe: Molding that covers the crack between baseboard and a finished floor.

Batten: A narrow strip of wood used for a variety of purposes, such as securing thin materials to framing, covering siding joints and tying together adjoining boards.

Beading: A small, decorative molding.

Beam: A principal horizontal member of a structure, carrying a load between two supporting walls, posts or columns.

Bearing partition: A partition that supports a vertical load in addition to its own weight.

Bed: A layer of sand or mortar in which masonry units are laid.

Bevel: Slanted edge or end cut on a piece of wood.

Binder: That part of a paint or enamel that binds or cements the color pigment particles together in the dried film. Oils, resins, latex and emulsions are examples of commonly used binders.

Bird's eye: Small areas in wood with the grain forming circular or elliptical patterns remotely resembling birds' eyes. Common in sugar maple, also found in some other species.

Bleaching: Restoring wood to its original color (or making it lighter) by using oxalic acid or other compounds.

Bleeding: Discoloration caused by a stain coming through a finish coat.

Board foot: A unit for measuring lumber; one board foot is the equivalent of a piece of lumber 1″ thick, 1′ wide and 1′ long (nominal dimensions).

Bridging: Small lengths of wood or metal fastened diagonally between floor joists to stiffen the structure.

Buffing compound: A soft abrasive combined with wax.

Building code: Legal requirements governing various aspects of construction to protect the safety, health and general welfare of the community.

Building paper: Heavy paper used as a lining between materials and as a temporary protection for finished work.

Burnt sienna: Reddish-brown color made by roasting a raw pigment (sienna).

Burnt umber: Dark brown color (used for mixing browns and tans) made by roasting umber.

Butt joint: The joint formed where two pieces of wood meet squarely.

C-D

Carbon black: An intense black pigment made by burning natural gas.

Carnauba: Brazilian palm tree that exudes a waxy residue of the same name used as a base in wax products.

Casein: A product contained in milk used to make water-thinned paints and glues.

Casement window: A window that opens on hinges fastened to its vertical edges.

Casing: Trim around windows and doors.

Caulking compound: A pastelike material used to fill seams and cracks; although its surface dries and can be painted, the material remains pliable and elastic to withstand expansion and contraction.

Chamfer: Corner cut to form a bevel.

Chalk line: Spool-wound cord usually encased in a container filled with powdered chalk. The cord is pulled out and stretched taut across a surface between two end points; it is then lifted and snapped directly downward so that it leaves a straight chalk mark on the surface.

Clinch: To drive a nail through lumber and bend the point back into the wood.

Compass saw: A saw with a narrow, tapering blade used to cut curves and circles.

Coping saw: A saw with a very narrow blade that can be turned in its frame to any angle. Used to cut small-radius curves, scrolls, circles and other fine work.

Corner bead: Metal strip used to form and protect an outside corner in a gypsum board or plaster wall.

Countersink: To set the head of a screw or nail below the surface of wood.

Course: Continuous horizontal row of masonry units, such as brick or concrete block.

d: Abbreviation for "penny" used to designate nail size, originating when nails were sold by the hundred.

Dado: A flat-bottomed groove cut in wood.

Denatured alcohol: A solvent for shellac and some paints.

Dimension lumber: Lumber 2″ to 5″ thick and up to 12″ wide. Nominal size refers to untrimmed wood; true dimensions are usually ½″ to ¾″ less.

Double-hung window: A window with movable upper and lower sash.

Dowel: A round piece of wood used for joining and other purposes.

Driers: Chemical compounds used to hasten the drying of oils used in paints, enamels or varnishes.

E-F

Efflorescence: Loose white crust that forms on brick or concrete surfaces due to the presence of excessive mineral salts or moisture.

Emery cloth: An abrasive cloth or paper normally used to smooth or polish metal.

Emulsion: A thick, milky liquid formed by suspending fine particles of oil, resin or other unmixable liquid in water; used as a binder in some paints.

Enamel: A paint containing a high proportion of resin or varnish binder; normally produces a glossy finish.

Epoxy: Synthetic resin with a high resistance to most chemicals.

Expansion bolt: A bolt for fastening to masonry or plaster walls.

Extender: A pigment of low hiding capabilities, used primarily to increase paint coverage.

Fascia: Horizontal facing across the end of a structure.

Filler: A composition material used to fill pores and cracks in wood before applying finish.

Flashing: Sheet metal, copper or plastic used at joints in roof and wall construction to prevent leakage.

Flat lacquer: A lacquer that dries with a rubbed appearance.

Flat paint: Interior paint formulated to produce a flat, lusterless finish.

Flush: Surface level with an adjacent surface.

Footing: The base, usually concrete, for foundation walls, posts, chimneys and the like.

Foundation: The supporting part of a structure below first-floor level or grade level.

Framing: The rough structure or "skeleton" of a building, to be covered with finishing materials.

French polish: A combination of shellac and linseed oil rubbed on with a cloth to a high gloss finish.

Frost line: The depth to which ground freezes.

Furring: Strips of wood or metal applied to a wall or framing to form an even surface and provide a backing for paneling or other covering material.

G-H

Galvanized: Metal coated with zinc to protect against rust.

Gloss: Interior paint formulated to produce a lustrous finish.

Grain: The direction, size, arrangement and appearance of the elements of wood.

Green lumber: Unseasoned lumber.

Grout: Mortar thinned by the addition of water so that it will run freely into joints and cavities of masonry or tile work.

Hardboard: Material manufactured of reconstituted wood, utilizing the tiny fibers to make large sheets or panels.

Hardwood: Term used to specify certain types of woods, generally those from broad-leaved trees such as oak, maple, mahogany or walnut.

Header: Framing member used as a support over an opening, such as a door or window.

Heartwood: The inner core of a log composed of nonliving cells.

I-J

In-line joint: Connection made by butting two pieces of wood end-to-end and fastening them with a splice on each side of the joint.

Iron oxide: A pigment available in red, brown and yellow; also called jeweler's rouge, Venetian red, Indian red, turkey red, mineral rouge and other names.

Jamb: Casing or lining at the side of a door or window.

Japan drier: Varnish gum with a large proportion of metallic salts added for rapid drying.

Joist: One of a series of parallel framing members supporting a floor or ceiling.

K-L

Keyhole saw: Saw with a narrow tapering blade used for fine cutting.

Kiln-dried: Wood seasoned in a humidity- and temperature-controlled oven to minimize shrinkage and warping.

Lacquer: A fast-drying finish containing nitrocellulose in combination with gum resins and solvents.

Lampblack: Black pigment consisting of finely ground carbon.

Lap joint: Connection made by placing one piece of a material over another and fastening by nailing, gluing or other means.

Latex: A dispersion emulsion of natural or synthetic rubber or rubberlike resin in water.

Lath: Wood strips, expanded metal mesh or gypsum board fastened to studs as a base for plaster.

Ledger: Piece of lumber fastened to an existing structure to support the horizontal framing of an additional structure.

Linseed oil: A vegetable oil pressed from the seeds of the flax plant. Boiled linseed oil has been heated to admit the addition of a small amount of metallic drier.

Louver: An opening with a series of slats positioned to provide ventilation while excluding rain.

Lumber: Wood after it leaves the saw and planing mill without any further manufacturing.

M-N

Masking tape: Pressure-sensitive paper tape that can be applied around an area to be painted to allow sharp, even delineation.

Mastic: Cement used to fasten certain types of floor tiles.

Millwork: Generally, this refers to building materials made from finished wood, including doors, window and door frames, mantels, moldings and trim.

Mineral spirits: Thinner with a petroleum base.

Miter joint: Connection made by joining two pieces at an angle, concealing the end cuts of both.

Molding: Decorative strip of wood or other material used for trim.

Moisture content: The percentage of water in lumber when purchased (about 7 percent is right for furniture).

Mortar: A mixture of cement, sand, hydrated lime and water used for bonding brick.

Mortise: A hole cut into one piece of lumber to receive the tenon (tongue) of another, or so that hardware such as a hinge or door lock can be set flush with the surface.

Muriatic acid: Hydrochloric acid diluted with water for use in cleaning brick or concrete.

Naphtha: Hydrocarbons suitable for use as paint thinner.

Neutral oil: A low-gravity mineral oil used with pumice stone in rubbed finishes.

Nitrocellulose: Raw cotton cellulose mixed with nitric and other acids.

Nosing: The rounded projecting edge of a step or landing.

O-P

o.c.: On center, indicating the spacing of framing members as measured from the center of one member to the center of the next.

Ochre: An earth pigment of yellow iron oxide.

Oil colors: Colors ground in linseed oil to paste form.

Parging: Thin coat of coarse plaster applied over masonry for protection or decoration.

Particleboard: A composition board consisting of distinct particles of wood bonded together with a synthetic resin or other binder.

Parting strip: Strip of wood forming a runway for the sash in a double-hung window.

Partition: A wall subdividing space within a structure. A nonbearing partition supports only its own weight, and

(continued on page 18)

$10 OR UNDER HOME PROJECTS

You don't have to spend a fortune on good-looking convenience items for your home. Look at what you can build out of low-cost materials or scraps.

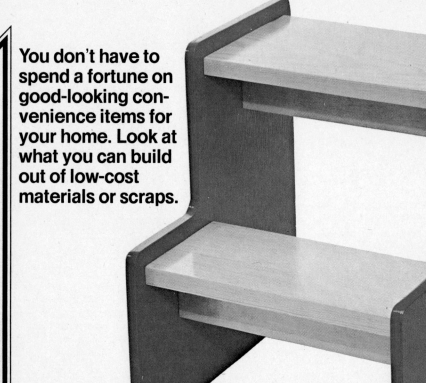

STEP STOOL
Unless your entire family is made up of pro basketball players, you can always find use for another two-step stool around the house—in the kitchen, utility room, closets and just about anywhere there are shelves. Build this sturdy unit for $8 or less.

MAGAZINE RACK
Here is a smart-looking project that you can hang on a wall to keep your favorite magazines close at hand. Make it for about $6 from a piece of vinyl, two lengths of dowel and two wood drapery brackets.

MUG RACK
This wall mug rack saves valuable space in cabinets and can be hung where most convenient. It is made from clear pine and given a hard liquid plastic finish. You can build it for approximately $5.75.

PLACEMATS
Even a child can make these no-nonsense placemats with a few dollars worth of jute upholstery webbing. Strips of the webbing are woven together and stitched.

STEP STOOL

(page 6)

MATERIALS: ½" plywood (4 sq. ft.); 1x3 clear pine (2 ft.); 1x6 clear pine (1 ft.); 1x8 clear pine (1 ft.); 4d finishing nails; white glue; wood filler; Flecto Varathane Crystal Clear #90 Gloss varnish; Flecto Varathane #100 Chinese Red; ¾" masking tape.

DIRECTIONS: Cut plywood into two pieces for ladder ends, using the dimensions in Fig. 1. Cut two 12" lengths of 1x3 for step supports; cut one 12" length of 1x6 for bottom step and one 12" length of 1x8 for top step. See directions for Shoeshine Box (page 15) for general

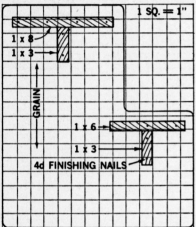

FIG. 1   TWO-STEP LADDER DIMENSIONS

1 SQ. = 1"

1 x 8
1 x 3
GRAIN
1 x 6
1 x 3
4d FINISHING NAILS

procedure. Glue and nail step supports at center of steps with two finishing nails; countersink and fill. Varnish steps (avoiding ends where fastening occurs). Then glue and nail steps in place.

MAGAZINE RACK

(page 6)

MATERIALS: 14"x54" piece vinyl fabric; needle; thread to match vinyl; two wooden drapery brackets; two ⅜"-diameter wood dowels, 17" long.

DIRECTIONS: Fold the short ends of the piece of vinyl in thirds so ends overlap 2" at back. Move overlap 1" off exact center back; sew through all thicknesses. For dowel casings, stitch ¾" from each fold. Drill holes in drapery brackets for ⅜" dowels. Place dowels in casings. Set back dowels in holes; hang front over bracket.

PLACEMATS

(page 6)

MATERIALS: For each placemat: 3½ yards jute upholstery webbing; needle and thread to match webbing.

DIRECTIONS: Cut webbing into three

19" strips and five 12" strips. Align 19" strips horizontally and weave remaining strips through them as shown in photo. Turn under every other edge ½"; whipstitch to the strip underneath. Fringe the other edges, as shown.

WALL MUG RACK

(page 6)

MATERIALS: ½x8 clear pine (2½ ft.); 1x4 clear pine (2½ ft.); twenty 1¼" brads; one ¾" nail; white glue; Flecto Varathane Crystal clear #90 Gloss varnish; Flecto Varathane #98 White Satin; spackle or wood filler; ¾" masking tape; picture frame hanger.

DIRECTIONS: Rip ½x8 pine in half to make side pieces measuring ½"x3½"x 25¾". Place 3¼" lengths of masking tape on inside of sides, starting ½" down and spacing tape 5¼" apart, leaving ¼" at front edge (Fig. 2). See directions for Shoeshine Box (page 15) to finish sides. Cut 5 pieces 1" pine, 3¼"x5". Varnish, rubbing down first coats with fine steel wool. Avoid varnishing ends where gluing occurs. Place one picture frame hanger at center of shelf. Add small nail at center. Remove tape from finished sides. Glue and nail shelves in place, adding hanger as shown in Fig. 2.

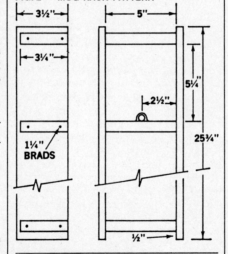

FIG. 2   MUG RACK PATTERN

3½"
3¼"
5"
5¼"
2½"
1¼" BRADS
25¾"
½"

COOKBOOK STAND

(page 10)

MATERIALS: ¼" plywood scraps (2 sq. ft.); ½x8 clear pine (3 ft.); ¼" doweling (18"); white glue; 1" and 1¼" brads; Flecto Varathane Crystal Clear #90 Gloss varnish; Krylon spray enamel #1901 Royal Blue; ½" masking tape; spackle or wood filler.

DIRECTIONS: Following directions in box on page 66, enlarge and cut out pattern in Fig. 3. Cut plywood into two pieces. Trace pattern on wood. Fasten with brads at waste. Cut out ends

simultaneously. Drill hole for page minder dowel in ends. Fill and sand ends for finishing. Trace center ½" pine book-rest section on inside of end pieces (Fig. 3). Place tape over these areas which will be glued later. Finish ends. From ½" pine cut one piece 2"x16½" and one piece 7¼"x16½". Glue and nail (four 1¼" brads) 2"x16½" piece of pine to bottom edge of 7¼"x16½" piece of pine, with edge flush at back and ends. Varnish this center section and 18" length of doweling. (Avoid varnishing ends of center section.) When dry, remove tape from ends and glue and nail pieces together. Wrap newspaper around varnished center and touch up nails with spray enamel. (Nails may be

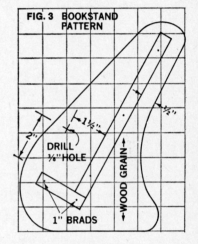

FIG. 3   BOOKSTAND PATTERN

DRILL ¾" HOLE
1½"
½"
2"
WOOD GRAIN
1" BRADS

countersunk and filled before touching up with spray enamel.)

TOWEL RACK

(page 10)

MATERIALS: Four 9" lengths of ½" square trim strip; 4 feet of nylon rope; sandpaper.

DIRECTIONS: Drill a ¼"-wide hole at each end of the four lengths of doweling. With strips 3½" apart, thread about 4 feet of rope through holes; tie knots under the holes. Loop for hanging measures about 14". Note: size of ropes and strips may be varied according to towel size.

KITCHEN MIRROR

(page 10)

MATERIALS: One standard size breadboard; dimestore mirror, 5½" diameter; white glue; 1½"-wide circular molding that is 5¾" in outside diameter (this is a stock size, available in lumber yards).

DIRECTIONS: Center mirror on breadboard and set in place with white glue. Over it, glue molding. Dry flat overnight before hanging. Needs no finish.

PIPE RACK
(page 10)

MATERIALS: One 13½" length 1x6 clear pine; ⅜" doweling; ⅛" doweling; plastic resin glue; adhesive-backed felt. As shown, the rack will hold 8 pipes. You can add to the dimensions to hold more as needed.

DIRECTIONS: From ⅜" doweling, cut two 4" lengths and nine 1½" lengths. From ⅛" doweling, cut one 9½" length. Cut 1x6 pine as shown in Fig. 4, sanding to round off corners and top. Sand ends of dowels. Drill a ⅛" hole 1" from one end of each 4" dowel, only half way into dowel, not through. Mix glue as directed on can. Glue the ⅛" dowel into the holes in the 4" dowels to connect them. While still wet, glue to the pipe rack (see Fig. 4). Glue remaining 1½" dowels to the base, where indicated. Remove excess glue. Finish underside with felt.

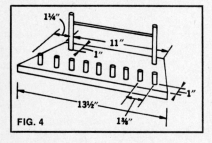

FIG. 4

BREAD-SHAPED BREAD BOARDS
(page 14)

MATERIALS: Common pine or clear pine shelving, 1x6 for the French-bread board, 1x8 for the pan-baked bread-slice board, cut to the length desired (select a consistent or unusual grain pattern); clear paste wax.

DIRECTIONS: Draw the outline of a loaf of French bread or a slice of pan-baked bread on the selected board or use our pattern in Fig. 5. Cut out with a saber

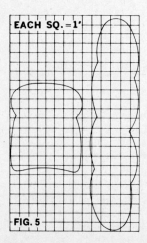

EACH SQ. = 1"

FIG. 5

saw or coping saw; sand smooth. Apply several coats of clear paste wax, following directions on container.

PLACEMAT TRAYS
(page 14)

MATERIALS (for set of two): Common pine lattice strips, two ¼"x1⅜"x6', two ¼"x2¼"x5'; 6' of backband molding; white glue; clear paste wax.

DIRECTIONS: Cut the lattice strips to 12" lengths (ten pieces of 1⅜", eight pieces of 2¼"). Use a power saw to cut several at once (or use a handsaw—preferably a backsaw along with a hardwood miter box). Make sure the ends are square; sand them smooth. Cut four 15⅞" lengths of backband molding, again being careful to keep ends square. The lattice strips are placed in alternating widths. Apply a light coat of white glue on the inside of the backband.

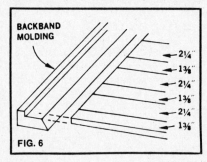

BACKBAND MOLDING

2¼"
1⅜"
2¼"
1⅜"
2¼"
1⅜"

FIG. 6

Place the first narrow strip flush with, and at exact right angles to, the end of the backband. Next place a wide strip, another narrow one, and so on until all are in place (see Fig. 6). Allow glue to dry after wiping off any excess with a damp cloth or paper towels. Make sure the other ends of the lattice strips are perfectly aligned. Sand, if necessary, then glue the second piece of backband in place. A final sanding of the tray, after glue has dried thoroughly, is all that is needed. Apply several coats of clear paste wax following manufacturer's directions on container.

PLASTIC CUBE CANISTER
(page 14)

MATERIALS: Dime-store plastic photo cube (for 3½"x3½" snapshots); 8" of ¼"x1⅞" lattice strip; 4" of ¼"x3⅝" lattice strip; white glue; clear paste wax.

DIRECTIONS: Cut the 3⅝" lattice strip to fit the inside dimension of the plastic cube. Cut the 1⅞" lattice strip into four equal squares. Apply a light coat of white glue to the large square. Glue the small squares to the larger square centering the pieces. They will overlap the large square to form the edge of the lid.

When glue has dried, sand the cover smooth. If made in quantity, the cube canisters can be used for a large variety of coffee beans or teas. Apply several coats of paste wax, following directions on container.

CLOTHESPIN TRIVETS
(page 14)

MATERIALS: Clothespins (flat on both sides—round clothespins can be substituted if flat ones are not available in your area); glue (see Buyer's Guide).

DIRECTIONS: (Snowflake design)—Lay out the design as shown in photo. Sand surfaces where clothespins will meet. On a piece of wax paper, glue together the four intermediate sections each with three alternating clothespins. Glue together these sections with the four clothespins that form the cross joining them. Allow glue to dry thoroughly,

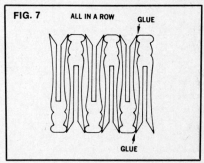

FIG. 7   ALL IN A ROW   GLUE

GLUE

then sand the surface of the trivet. (**All-in-a-row design**)—Sand edges where clothespins will meet. Apply glue sparingly and assemble pins in alternating directions (see Fig. 7). Allow glue to dry, then sand the surfaces of the trivet. The trivet may be made to any desired length. (The one partially shown in photo has 15 clothespins.)

CUBE NAPKIN HOLDERS
(page 14)

MATERIALS (for set of eight): ¼"x1⅝"x6' common pine lattice strip; white glue; clear paste wax.

DIRECTIONS: Cut the lattice strip in four 18" lengths. Apply glue to one edge of each length and assemble them, with

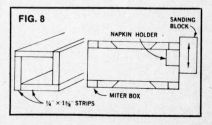

FIG. 8   SANDING BLOCK

NAPKIN HOLDER

MITER BOX

¼" × 1⅝" STRIPS

each edge overlapping the next, to create a long square tube (see Fig. 8). Wipe off excess glue, make sure the tube is perfectly square and allow to dry. Sand the outside. Cut the tube into eight 2″ lengths; this can be done on a stationary power saw or with a fine-tooth handsaw and a deep miter box. Sand the ends smooth. A good way to do this is to place the ring in the miter box and use a sanding block across the end of the box (see Fig. 8). No finish need be applied to the napkin rings, but paste wax will prevent the raw wood from soiling.

TWINE PLACEMATS

(page 20)

MATERIALS:
Stick loom; #60 polished express twine; matching heavy thread; large needle.

DIRECTIONS—General Weaving Directions: Thread the required number of sticks (wooden needles) pulling the twine through until you have two strands

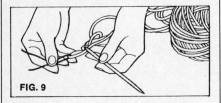

FIG. 9

(warp threads) of equal length (Fig. 9). Weave over and under the sticks, starting and ending at the center (Fig.

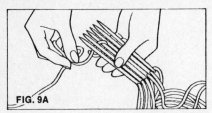

FIG. 9A

9A). As the loom fills, pull one needle at a time 2″ forward. Slip the woven rows along the warp threads (Fig. 9B).

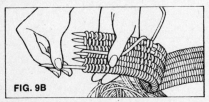

FIG. 9B

Rectangular Mat (11″x19″, including fringe): Thread six needles with 60″ lengths of twine. Weave three strips of 124 rows each. Tie each pair of warp threads into a square knot at end of the strips; cut off excess, 1″ from the knots. With heavy matching thread, sew the three strips together side by side with Knotted Blindstitch Fig. 9C, page 11, lining up the woven row at the seam. Cut thread 3″ from needle; push thread end inside woven loop.
Round Mat (about 15″ diameter): Thread two needles with strands about

GLUING PLYWOOD

TYPE OF GLUE	UREA RESIN GLUE	LIQUID RESIN (WHITE) GLUE	RESOR-CINOL (WATER-PROOF) GLUE
DESCRIPTION	Comes as powder to be mixed with water and used within 4 hours. Light colored. Very strong if joint fits well.	Comes ready to use at any temperature. Clean-working, quick-setting. Strong enough for most work, though not quite so tough as urea resin glue.	Comes as powder plus liquid, must be mixed each time used. Dark colored, very strong, completely waterproof.
RECOMMENDED USE	Good for general wood gluing. First choice for work that must stand some exposure to dampness, since it is moisture resistant.	Good for indoor furniture and cabinetwork. First choice for small jobs where tight clamping or good fit may be difficult.	This is the glue to use with Exterior type plywood for work to be exposed to extreme dampness.
PRECAUTIONS	Needs well-fitted joints, tight clamping, and room temperature 70° or warmer.	Not sufficiently resistant to moisture for outdoor furniture or outdoor storage units. (Thoroughly clean up squeeze-out in areas to receive stain finish.)	Expense, trouble to mix and dark color make it unsuited to jobs where waterproof glue is not required. Needs good fit, tight clamping.
HOW TO USE	Make sure joint fits tightly. Mix glue and apply thin coat. Allow 16 hours drying time.	Use at any temperature but preferably above 60°. Spread on both surfaces, clamp at once. Sets in 1½ hours.	Use within 8 hours after mixing. Work at temperature above 70°. Apply thin coat to both surfaces; allow 16 hours drying time.

OTHER ADHESIVES: The above glues are the most common and are generally successful. Other glues sometimes considered include: **Hot Melt Glues**—Use with relatively small parts. Remember they cool and set quickly. **Epoxy Glues**—limited use with wood (expensive; most are not ideally formulated for use with wood). Some epoxies may prove successful for some applications. **Contact Cements**—useful for applying laminates and edge stripping to plywood. Not recommended for structural joints. **Wall-Panel Adhesives**—handy for applying decorative paneling or facing. May need to use a few nails per panel, to resist any slight tendency for panels to pull away due to warping. **Casein Glues**—slow setting, permitting difficult assemblies.

You probably already have the scraps of plywood and pine needed to build this handy cookbook stand. If not, you can buy them for 50¢ or so. The only other item you'll need is some spray enamel—and a good cookbook.

HELP FOR THE CHEF

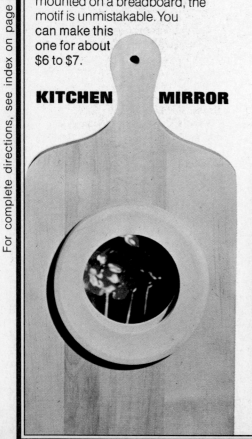

What could be more handy than a mirror placed right next to the kitchen door for a fast look-see before you leave the house? And when it's mounted on a breadboard, the motif is unmistakable. You can make this one for about $6 to $7.

KITCHEN MIRROR

For complete directions, see index on page 65.

FOR HANGING TOWELS

This towel rack of rope and wood has something of a nautical look, but

It will serve just as well in a landlocked bathroom or shower room. A simple project that you can make in about 10 minutes, for $2 or less.

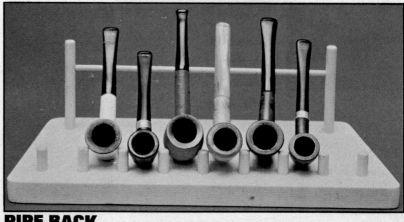

PIPE RACK

Perfect for the pipe smoker, this rack holds eight pipes of different types and sizes. Pine, dowels and glue for the rack cost less than $4.

16½" long. Weave one continuous strip the full length of the strands. Tie the warp threads into a square knot at one end of the strip. At the other end, pull up one warp thread, causing the strip to turn and coil. On a flat surface, form the strip into a circle, working from the center out; stitch coils together with heavy matching thread using Knotted Blindstitch (Fig. 9C). Cut off excess

FIG. 9C

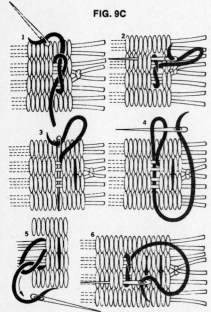

thread and warp twine, leaving 3"; push ends inside woven loop. Steam-press mat so that it lies flat.

TWINE COASTERS
(page 20)

MATERIALS: See Placemats above.

DIRECTIONS: Cut two 6½-yd. lengths of #60 polished express twine. Fold the strands in half; tape the folds to the edge of a table. Starting 2" from folds, work 4-strand round braid for their full length (see Fig. 9D). Tie an overhand knot at the end. Starting at the knot, form the braid into a coil, sewing the rows together with heavy thread. When the coil is one braid-width larger than the glass diameter, coil the braid upward to form the side of the coaster. Stitch then glue braid end firmly, flattening it as much as possible.

FIG. 9D

A B C D

B A D C

WOOD AND LEATHER PHOTO FRAME
(page 20)

MATERIALS: Plain wood plaque, 6"x8" x ¾" (available at most dime stores); wood stain; scrap leather; X-acto knife or leather-cutting tool; white glue; brass nails; one brass ring-type picture hanger.

DIRECTIONS: Sand all edges of the wood plaque and stain wood as desired. Let dry. Tape photo to wood plaque. Trim leather to size of plaque. Trace an oval onto leather that is the correct size for the photo to show through. Using X-acto knife or leather-cutting tool, cut oval out of leather. Place leather over photo; glue leather along outside edges. Add evenly spaced brass nails (we used two different sizes) around the oval. Attach a picture hanger to the top edge.

THREE-DRAWER CHEST
(page 20)

MATERIALS: ½x10 pine, 8' (or enough scrap to cut pieces in sizes given below); ¼"x3⅝" pine lattice, 2½'; ⅛" Lauan plywood, three 8"x9" pieces and one 9¼"x12" piece; ¼" manila rope, 12"; ¾" nails; 1¼" brads; eight No. 5 ½" flat head wood screws; ½"x½"x¹/₁₆" aluminum angle, 3'; white glue; wood filler; satin finish varnish; green spray enamel; felt or suede cloth, one 12½" square (optional).

DIRECTIONS—Cutting: For each drawer, cut from ½x10 pine, two 3½"x7" end pieces and two 3½"x8½" side pieces. From ⅛" plywood, cut one 8"x8½" bottom piece. Cut one 8" length of ¼"x3⅝" lattice for front face. For chest, cut from ½x10 pine, one top and one bottom piece, each 9¼" square, and two 9¼"x 11¼" side pieces. From ⅛" plywood, cut one back piece 9¼"x12¼". With hacksaw, cut four 8½" lengths of aluminum angle for drawer slides.
Assembling: With glue and brads, fasten the drawer side and end pieces together with the side pieces overlapping the ends. Glue on and nail plywood bottom piece. Glue front face piece to one short end; make an X mark 3½" from each end halfway between top and bottom edges. At each X mark, drill a ⁵/₁₆ hole only ½" deep for rope but do not attach at this time.
Chest Assembly:
With file or emery cloth, smooth the ends of the aluminum drawer slides. Using a ¼" drill, partially drill through one edge of each slide 1" from each end, to create a V-shaped crater for the screw so it will be flush with the surface. Complete drilling the hole through the angle with a ³/₃₂" bit. Mark the location of the slides on chest sides as follows: Lay a drawer on its side on a chest side piece with bottom edges even. Draw a light pencil line along the top drawer edge; draw a parallel line ¹/₁₆" above. Screw a slide in place with its bottom edge on the top line and its end flush with the back end of the side piece. Lay a

second drawer on its side with its bottom angle in the aluminum angle. Draw a pencil line and fasten second slide as for first drawer. Repeat procedure on opposite chest side piece.
With glue and brads, fasten chest top and bottom to sides. Glue on and nail plywood back piece.
Countersink brads; fill. Sand all surfaces. Varnish back; when dry, lay chest on its back. Spray sides, top, front edges and ½" inside all edges with spray enamel. On bottom, glue felt or suede cloth cut to fit. Glue 4" rope handles in drilled holes on drawers.

COVERED HANGERS
(page 20)

MATERIALS: Six pairs of old stockings for each hanger; dye remover; liquid dyes in Kelly Green, Yellow, Tangerine and Purple; wire coat hangers.

DIRECTIONS: Cut tops and feet from hose. Simmer stockings in color remover. Prepare dyes using following proportions:
Green: ½ cap Kelly Green; 1 cap Yellow; 6 pints water
Orange: 1 cap Tangerine; 1 cap Yellow; 6 pints water
Lavender: 1 cap Purple; 6 pints water
Simmer stockings in dye for 10 minutes; cool and rinse. Let dry. To cover hanger: Make two cords of six hose each, stitched together across one end. Secure to hanger neck by wrapping with thread. Using the hanger wire as an anchor cord, bring right cord to the left over hanger, leaving a little loop; cross left cord over the right, then up through the loop formed by the right cord. Pull evenly and you have the first half of the square knot. Reverse procedure for second half. Repeat until hanger is covered, tieing ends around hanger neck. Cut off excess.

WOODEN TRAY
(page 20)

MATERIALS: About 9½' of ¼"x¾" pine lattice; scrap of ¾" plywood measuring 14" square; white glue; ¾" wire brads; sandpaper; stain as desired; varnish.

DIRECTIONS: Glue strips of lattice to edges of plywood square, butting them at the corners. Then glue strips to top, flush with the outer edges of the side strips of lattice. Drive in and countersink wire brads to secure. Sand, stain and varnish all tray surfaces.

WOODEN TRIVETS
(page 20)

MATERIALS: For top trivet: ½" slices of ¼", ¾" and 1½"-diameter dowels; white glue; sandpaper. For bottom trivet, omit ¾" dowel.

DIRECTIONS: Glue slices of dowel together along rounded sides, as shown in photo; sand any rough edges.

WOODEN PHOTO FRAME

(page 20)

MATERIALS: Two pieces of ¼" plywood, 11¼" x 13¼"; 3' of ¼" x 1⅝" lattice; white glue; fine-grit sandpaper; 7½" x 10" pane of glass; varnish.

DIRECTIONS: Cut a 7¼" x 9¼" opening in the center of one of the plywood pieces. Cut two 13¼" strips of lattice and glue to the other plywood pieces, flush with the side edges. Glue a third strip of lattice between the side strips, flush with the bottom of the plywood. Glue the cut-out plywood piece to the lattice strips; allow glue to dry. Round corners with sandpaper and smooth rough edges. Finish with varnish. Slide in glass and photo.

CIGARETTE BOX

(page 20)

Note: This box is designed for regular length cigarettes. For longer types, change all of the 3½" dimensions to 4" or more.

MATERIALS: Two scrap pieces of ¾" plywood, both measuring 7¼"x9¼"; two scrap pieces of ¼" plywood, one measuring 7¼"x9¼", the other 3½"x5"; white glue; fine-grit sandpaper; varnish.

DIRECTIONS: In one of the pieces of ¾" plywood, mark a 3½"x5" opening in the center. Drill a pilot hole in one corner and make the cut with a saber saw or keyhole saw. Glue this piece to the 7¼"x9¼" piece of ¼" plywood (the box bottom). In the center of the ¾"x9¼"x 7¼" top, glue the 3½"x5" piece of ¼" plywood to fit into the box opening. Round corners, then varnish.

CHOPPING BLOCK

(page 24)

MATERIALS: 2' of 2x10 plank; ⅝" drill bit; 2' of ½" hemp; saber or keyhole saw; fine sandpaper; vegetable oil for soaking wood; wax paper.

DIRECTIONS: In the 2x10 plank, drill ⅝" holes 2" deep for hemp handle, centered in each plank edge—1" from plank end. Mark dots on the plank at same end, 1¾" from each edge. From these dots draw perpendicular lines 2½" long on board surface. Connect these lines to form a rectangle. Draw freehand curves inside rectangle corners. Cut

away wood on this line with saber or keyhole saw. Sand all edges. Pull 2' of ½" hemp through holes and knot; cut away excess. Soak block with vegetable oil; let stand overnight on wax paper.

FOLK DESIGN CUTTING BOARD

(page 24)

MATERIALS: One 1x4x24" piece of clear pine; fine and extra-fine sandpaper; vegetable oil; wax paper; coping saw or band saw; drill.

DIRECTIONS: With a pencil draw freehand cut marks, curves and hole locations on the board as shown in photo. (Folk art is characterized by its original freehand designs, rather than exact geometric shapes.) Working with the good side of the wood up, drill holes before sawing, varying hole size from ³⁄₃₂ to ⁷⁄₃₂. Cut out shapes on pencil lines. Sand in direction of wood grain. Soak with vegetable oil and let stand overnight on wax paper.

CANE OFFICE ACCESSORIES

(page 24)

CUP

MATERIALS: 3¼"x10" piece of cane (this is the woven caning used on furniture, available in hardware stores); 2½" square piece of ¼" plywood; sandpaper; white glue; carpet tacks.

DIRECTIONS: Sand the piece of plywood and round corners. Wrap the cane (along the 10" side) around the plywood base; lap and glue ends of cane. Tack cane to base to secure.

WASTE BASKET

MATERIALS: 7¾" square piece of ¼" plywood; 11¼"x31" piece of cane; four ¾"x7⅝" pieces of ⅛" plywood; sandpaper; white glue; carpet tacks.

DIRECTIONS: Wrap, tack and glue cane to sanded plywood base as for Cup. Glue the ¾" strips of plywood inside top edges of cane to provide support of waste basket sides.

PENCIL HOLDER

MATERIALS: Two 3" square pieces of ¼" plywood; sandpaper; 3¼"x12" piece of cane; white glue; carpet tacks; drill.

DIRECTIONS: Sand and round edges of both plywood pieces. Drill holes slightly wider than the diameter of a pencil in one piece. Wrap, glue and tack cane to bottom (undrilled) piece of plywood; glue other piece to inside top edges of cane for inserting pencils.

TILE BOX

(page 24)

MATERIALS: Six 6"-square tiles in desired color and design; epoxy glue; ceramic or wooden knob.

DIRECTIONS: Set up the four side tiles on bottom tile, as shown in photo, overlapping at corners. Secure with epoxy glue; let dry. Glue ceramic or wooden knob to center of remaining tile (this will be the lid).

CUTLERY CHEST

(page 24)

MATERIALS: ½x8 pine stock, 8' (or enough scrap to cut pieces in sizes given below); ¼"x2⅝" pine lattice, 2'; ¼"x 1⅞" lattice, 4'; three 7"x12" pieces of ⅛" Lauan plywood; ¾" nails; 1¼" brads; white glue; wood filler; varnish; felt, ¼ yd. 36" wide (or enough scrap to cut pieces of sizes given below).

DIRECTIONS: Cutting—For each drawer, cut from ½x8 pine, two side pieces 2½"x7", one front and one back piece each 2½"x10"; from ¼"x2⅝" pine lattice cut one 11" length for front face; from ⅛" plywood cut one bottom 7"x 11"; from ¼"x1⅞" lattice, cut two 10" lengths for drawer dividers. For chest, cut from ½x8 pine stock one top and one bottom piece, each 7¼"x12¼", two sides 6"x7¼", one center support 7¼"x11¼"; from ⅛" plywood, cut one back piece 7"x12".

Assembling—With glue and brads, fasten drawer front and back between sides. Glue and nail on bottom. Glue on front face piece; with saber saw or jigsaw make curved cutout in center of top edge. Glue lattice dividers in place, 1¾" from drawer front and back.

With glue and brads, fasten the center support piece exactly half-way between top and bottom of chest side pieces, then fasten top and bottom to sides. Nail back piece in place. Countersink brads; fill. Sand; varnish. Line the bottom of the chest and drawer sections with felt cut to size.

KEY KEEPER

(page 26)

MATERIALS: Scraps of ¼" plywood; 12" length of ⅝"-diameter wood doweling; white glue; enamel paint; hooks for keys; two ring-type picture hangers.

DIRECTIONS: From plywood, cut a ½" oval (outside measurements are 4"x2⅞") and one bit, 1¼"x2½" shaped as shown in photo. At one end of the dowel, cut a slot ¼" wide and ½" deep. Glue oval into slot. Glue bit 1" in from other end of dowel. Apply three coats of enamel paint. When paint is dry, attach key hooks and picture hangers to key rack.

TOY FERRYBOAT

(page 26)

MATERIALS: A, 1x8x19″; B, 1x4x13″ (2 needed); C, 1x6x10″ (rip to 4¼″ width); D, 2x3x2½″; E, 1¼″ dowel x 3″ (2 needed); F, 5/16″ dowel x 6¼″ (2 needed); eight 1¼″ No. 8 flat head screws; 4d finishing nails.

DIRECTIONS: Following directions in box on page 66, enlarge and trace pattern onto wood. Use a gallon paint can as a template to draw 6¾″-diameter circles on piece A, centered at each end. Connect the outer edges of the two circles with gently curving lines—use a slightly bent yardstick to guide you in drawing these curves. Cut the hull shape with a coping saw or a saber saw with the blade tilted at 10° so that hull tapers inward at the bottom (Fig. 10).

FIG. 10

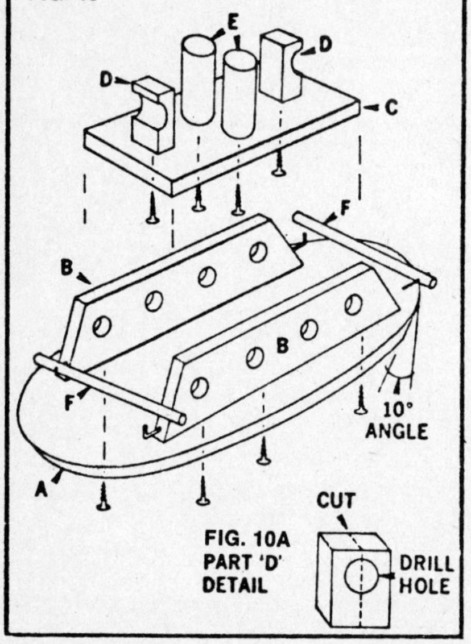
E
D
D
C
F
B
B
F
10° ANGLE
A
CUT
DRILL HOLE

FIG. 10A PART 'D' DETAIL

Cabin sides B measure 13″ at the bottom, 10″ at top. Clamp the two sides together for cutting and drilling. Draw a light line 2″ up from the bottom, then mark centers for portholes evenly spaced 2½″ apart; drill with a ¾″ wood bit.

Draw a centerline along the grain down the wide face of piece D. Make a mark 1″ down from the top of this line; drill a 1″ hole through D on this mark. Then saw down the center line to make the two wheelhouses (Fig. 10). Drill pilot holes through cabin roof C 1½″ from each end for the wheelhouses and 1″ in from each side for the smokestacks E, then assemble with glue and screws.

Attach cabin sides B to roof C with glue and nails. Center this assembly on the hull and mark around it, then drill two pilot holes within these lines on each side and drive screws up through the hull into the cabin sides.

Drill ⅛″ holes ¾″ in from one end of each guard rail (pieces F). Insert nails through the holes and drive each into one end of each cabin side piece, ¾″ up from the deck, so that the rail is separated from the side by ¼″. On the opposite side, drive a nail ⅜″ up from the deck, allowing it to protrude ¾″. Bend this nail up ¼″ from the end to make a catch when the guard rail (piece F) is lowered.

LUNCH BOX SHELF/COAT RACK

(page 26)

MATERIALS: One 20″ length 1x6 clear pine; one 20″ length 1x4 clear pine; ⅜″ doweling; finishing nails; No. 8 (2½″) round head wood screws; plastic resin glue; ring hangers.

DIRECTIONS: Drill four ⅜″ holes in the 1x4 pine at a slight angle (see Fig. 11). Sand both pieces of pine to round off corners and edges. Cut four 4¼″ lengths of doweling; sand and glue in place following can directions for mixing the glue. Dowels should be flush with back of rack. Glue shelf (1x6) flush to back of rack. Use four 1½″ or 2″ finishing nails to hold together while glue sets. Countersink nails. Add ring hangers to back, 2½″ in from each end. Fasten to wall studs by driving wood screws through ring hangers and pilot holes drilled through the wallboard.

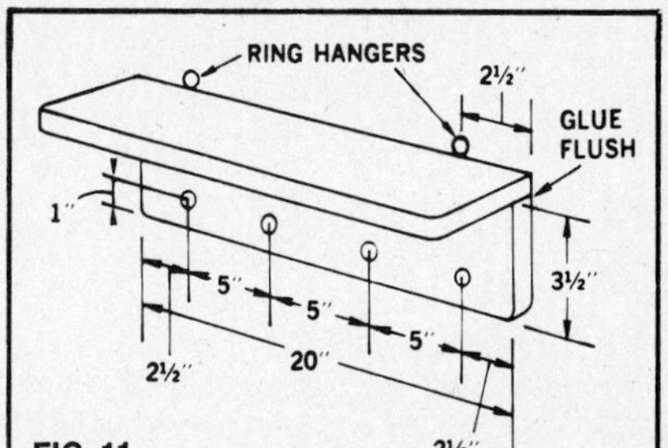
RING HANGERS
2½″
GLUE FLUSH
1″
5″
5″
5″
3½″
2½″
20″
2½″

FIG. 11

COLLAPSIBLE WINE RACK

(page 26)

MATERIALS: Two pieces ½″ APA grade-trademarked rough-sawn or sanded plywood, each 5″x27″ (check your lumber dealer's odd size bin); ¾″ wood dowel, 4½′; ¼″ wood dowel, 3′; fine sandpaper; wood filler; 4 rubber glides for bottom.

DIRECTIONS: Following the directions in the box on page 66, enlarge and cut out the pattern for the wine rack end pieces in Fig. 12. Trace pattern on plywood. Cut out with saber saw. From

CLASSIFICATION OF SPECIES IN PLYWOOD

Group 1	Group 2		Group 3	Group 4	Group 5
Apitong (a), (b)	Cedar, Port Orford	Maple, Black	Alder, Red	Aspen	Basswood
Beech,	Cypress	Mengkulang (a)	Birch, Paper	Bigtooth	Fir, Balsam
American	Douglas Fir 2 (c)	Meranti, Red	Cedar, Alaska	Quaking	Poplar, Balsam
Birch	Fir	(a), (b)	Fir, Subalpine	Cativo	
Sweet	California Red	Mersawa (a)	Hemlock, Eastern	Cedar	
Yellow	Grand	Pine	Maple, Bigleaf	Incense	
Douglas Fir 1 (c)	Noble	Pond-	Pine	Western Red	
Kapur	Pacific Silver	Red	Jack	Cottonwood	
Keruing (a), (b)	White	Virginia	Lodgepole	Eastern	
Larch, Western	Hemlock, Western	Western White	Ponderosa	Black (Western	
Maple, Sugar	Lauan	Spruce	Spruce	Poplar)	
Pine	Almon	Red	Redwood	Pine	
Carribbean	Bagtikan	Sitka	Spruce	Eastern White	
Ocote	Mayapis	Sweetgum	Black	Sugar	
Pine, Southern	Red Lauan	Tamarack	Engelmann		
Loblolly	Tangile	Yellow Poplar	White		
Longleaf	White Lauan				
Shortleaf					
Slash					
Tanoak					

(a) Each of these names represents a trade group of woods consisting of a number of closely related species.

(b) Species from the genus Dipterocarpus are marketed collectively: Apitong if originating in the Philippines; Keruing if originating in Malaysia or Indonesia.

(c) Douglas fir from trees grown in the States of Washington, Oregon, California, Idaho, Montana, Wyoming, and the Canadian Provinces of Alberta and British Columbia shall be classed as Douglas fir No. 1. Douglas fir from trees grown in the states of Nevada, Utah, Colorado, Arizona and New Mexico shall be classed as Douglas fir No. 2.

(d) Red Meranti shall be limited to species having a specific gravity of 0.41 or more based on green volume and oven dry weight.

FOR THE TABLE

Set your table with these handsome and functional accessories created from castoffs. Empty wine and beer bottles with corks cut to fit make pretty canisters for rice, beans, herbs and spices. Plastic photo cube fitted with lattice lid holds coffee beans. Bread-shaped breadboards are cut from white pine. Trays and napkin rings are glued together lattice. Even common clothespins are put to work as lacy trivets.

For complete directions, see index on page 65.

¾" dowel cut five 10½" lengths; from ¼" dowel cut twenty 1½" lengths. Drill ¾" dowel holes in end pieces, where indicated in illustration. Drill ¼" dowel holes in the ¾" dowels, as indicated. Assemble wine rack as shown (Fig. 12A). Add glides at corners.

FIG. 12 PORTABLE WINE RACK ENDS HALF PATTERNS

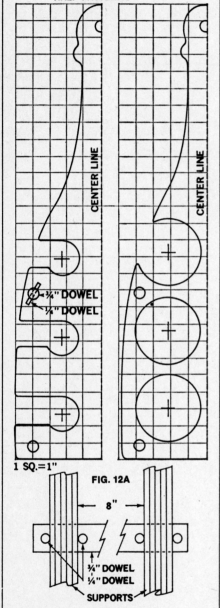

CENTER LINE

CENTER LINE

¾" DOWEL
¼" DOWEL

1 SQ.=1"

FIG. 12A

8"

¾" DOWEL
¼" DOWEL
SUPPORTS

DESK AND DRESSER ORGANIZERS
(page 28)

MATERIALS: 7"x10" cupcake pan with 6 wells; 5⅝"x9¾" loaf pan; 9½"x13¼" roasting pan; 7¾"x10" cupcake pan with 12 small wells; Flecto Varathane spray paints: #118 Bold Blue and #96 Black Satin; Krylon spray enamel (for 12 cup pan) #2401 Sunset Orange; rubber cement; scraps of felt.
For wood covers: scraps of ½" plywood; lattice in lengths and widths as needed;

white glue; ¾" wire brads; Minwax—Americolor #103, Liberty Blue; walnut stain; spackle or wood filler; Flecto Varathane Crystal Clear #90 gloss varnish; fine grade sandpaper or steel wool.

DIRECTIONS: Pans: Spray inside of 12-cup pan orange, and inside of remaining pans blue. Dry. Turn over and spray outsides black. Cut felt rectangles and circles slightly smaller than pan bottoms. Apply rubber cement to felt and pan. Allow surface to dry. Press felt in place, smoothing any wrinkles.
Wood Covers: Cut ½" plywood ⅛" larger than extreme dimensions of pan at top, with grain in crosswise direction. Stain top only with two coats of Minwax #103 for blue pans; walnut stain for orange. Then varnish with two coats of Varathane #90. Avoid varnishing edges of top. Sand lightly or steel wool both coats of varnish. Rip or score and break lattice then plane, if necessary, to appropriate widths. To determine width—measure height of pan and add ⁷⁄₁₆". Cut (2) pieces (lengths) of lattice same as top ends. Glue and nail with (3) or (4) ¾" brads ¹⁄₁₆" above top cover surface. Cut (2) lengths slightly larger than length of top plus (2) thicknesses of lattice. Similarly fasten in place, adding an additional brad at corners. Sand excess lattice to remove rough edges.

WINE BOTTLE LAMP
(page 28)

MATERIALS: One ceramic crock-type quart bottle that held wine; household putty; lamp cord and socket (these units, complete with rubber stopper and socket, are available in hardware and dimestores, or see Buyer's Guide for source); ¼" carbide-tip bit in variable-speed drill; turpentine.

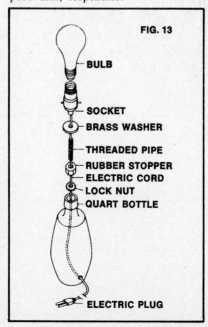

FIG. 13

BULB
SOCKET
BRASS WASHER
THREADED PIPE
RUBBER STOPPER
ELECTRIC CORD
LOCK NUT
QUART BOTTLE

ELECTRIC PLUG

DIRECTIONS: To drill a hole for a cord 1" from bottle bottom, place a wad of putty ¼" high around spot to be drilled; make a small indentation in putty; fill indentation with turpentine to lubricate bit. Run drill at medium speed. After drilling hole, remove putty and insert socket and cord, following Fig. 13. Fit lamp base with a clamp-on type shade. Note: Bottles of clear glass may be used in the same way. You may wish to use a fin-section socket kit that is adaptable to any size bottle, rather than the rubber stopper type.

SHOESHINE BOX
(page 28)

MATERIALS: ½" plywood scraps (2 sq. ft.); 1x3 clear pine (3 ft.); 1x6 clear pine (1 ft.); 4d finishing nails; white glue; spackle or wood filler; Minwax—Americolor #102, Lexington Green; clear paste wax; Krylon spray enamel #1901, Royal Blue; ¾" masking tape.

DIRECTIONS: Following the directions in the box on page 66, enlarge and cut out the pattern in Fig. 14.

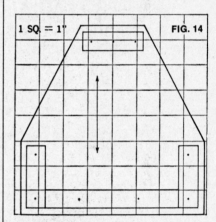

1 SQ. = 1"

FIG. 14

Cut plywood into two pieces; nail together at waste. Trace outside pattern on wood and cut out (6 sided) ends. Fill edges and sand, rounding off corners. Trace locations of center pieces on inside of ends. Tape these areas where pieces will be joined and glued. Finish ends using several thin coats of enamel (rubbing each with fine steel wool before application of final coat.).
Cut (3) pieces of 1x3 pine 12" long, and sand. Cut (1) 12" length of 1x6. Glue and nail two 12" lengths of 1x3 to sides of 1x6 keeping edge flush at bottom, using (2) nails each side; countersink and fill. Stain center pieces with one coat of green as directed. Apply two coats of clear paste wax, as directed. Remove tape from end pieces. Fasten center pieces in place with glue and nails, as shown in Fig. 14. Countersink nails and fill. Wrap newspaper around center stained pieces and touch up nails with blue spray enamel.

CHESSMEN AND BOARD

The pine lattice chessboard/box is also a handy tote for the set of wooden clothespin playing pieces—a great gift.

SPRAY— PAINT A STENCIL

Plain rockers get a classic finish with our spray-painting technique. It requires no brushes, little mess—and no time at all.

CLOTHESPIN CHESS SET
(page 16)

MATERIALS: Six feet of ¼"x⅞" lattice; four feet of ¼"x¾" lattice; 18" of ¼"x ½" lattice; 1 package round wooden clothespins; 1½"-width black cloth tape; black shoe dye; matte varnish; fine hobby saw; small triangular file.

DIRECTIONS: Cut pieces from clothespins with hobby saw. From the head end, cut Queen (1¾" tall), King (1") and Rook (⅝"). From the middle of the clothespin where wood forks, cut Bishop (1⅜"), Knight (1¼") and Pawn (⅞"). To the King, glue a crown (1¼" from head end of clothespin). To the Knight add a "nose" in the fork of the shape. Use small triangular file to notch top of Queen and King pieces to make crown effect. With a long pin, dip half the pieces in black shoe dye (1 King, 1 Queen, 2 Bishops, 2 Knights, 2 Rooks and 8 Pawns). Note: Areas and pieces not colored black can be kept clean by spraying with matte varnish. To make box: For one side cut two lengths from each width of lattice, each 7" long. Glue long sides together to form box top. Repeat for bottom. Cut ⅞" lattice into sixty-four ⅞" pieces to form chess squares for playing surface. Dye 32 squares black. Frame glued sections on three sides with ⅞" lattice (3¾" for sides, 7" for front); butt-join at corners and glue. Glue squares to top and bottom box sections alternating colors. On fourth (back) side, butt ½" lattice into frame, where it will fit snugly under the slightly extending chessboard top. Repeat for other half of box. When glue is dry, place box top on bottom; "hinge" the back with 7½" of tape.

SPRAY-STENCILED ROCKERS
(page 16)

Note: Any unfinished furniture can be decorated using these two methods, especially old pieces. We used new unpainted rockers—pricing is based on the cost of refinishing materials alone. Also, you may wish to create your own designs, rather than use those in the Dover book (see Materials).

MATERIALS: Vinyl spackle; medium, fine and extra-fine sandpaper; sealer primer; paint thinner; tack cloth; Enamelac (paint sealer); plastic coating, quart size, in various colors; screw-on sprayer unit and jars (see Buyer's Guide for last two items); pine rocking chairs (see Buyer's Guide); tracing paper; rubber cement; Dover book "Early American Design Motifs" (see Buyer's Guide) or other stencil designs; X-acto or craft knife; razor blade; yellow and green plastic coating (see Buyer's Guide); clear plastic coating (optional).

DIRECTIONS—Preparing the Surface: Fill joints and cracks with vinyl spackle. Sand surfaces with medium grade sandpaper. Brush on one coat of sealer primer thinned with paint thinner. Let dry. Resand with fine sandpaper.

With the aid of a strong light held at the edge of the piece, examine the surface for imperfections; these should be respackled and sanded. Coat knot holes with Enamelac to seal in sap and prevent bleeding. Sand with extra-fine sandpaper. Vacuum all surfaces and wipe with tack cloth to make them dust-free.

When directions call for spray painting with plastic coating, use screw-on sprayer unit with jars of colors called for. Colors can be used "as is" or custom-mixed to choice. In all cases, plastic coating must be thoroughly dry before spraying on another coat or proceeding to next step.

Keep in mind that the final finish will be only as good as the surface you prepare; the time it takes will be well-spent. It is best to experiment with the techniques on scrap pine before you work on the actual furniture.

Stenciling:
1. The finishing procedure is the same for both rockers but the plastic coating colors are used in a different order; on the small rocker, color A is green and color B is yellow—reverse the colors on the larger rocker. Both rockers will get one application of each color.
2. Spray the entire chair with color A.
3. To make the stencils, trace on tracing paper the designs of your choice or those we used from the Dover book (see Materials). Apply two coats of rubber cement to back of stencils and to chair back and seat, letting cement dry after each coat.
4. Starting from one side and slowly working toward opposite side, carefully press stencils in place on chair with cemented surfaces together. A slip-sheet of uncemented paper can be used between the surfaces. With craft or X-acto knife cut away the tracing paper except where you want the design to remain in color A.
5. Rub off excess cement from chair where stencil has been removed. Recement any loose stencil edges.
6. Spray entire chair with color B. Let dry thoroughly.
7. With point of knife or razor blade, carefully remove stencil. Spray the chair with a clear plastic protective coating (optional).

FINISHING PLYWOOD—INTERIOR APPLICATIONS

	TYPE OF FINISH*	RECOMMENDED FOR	APPLICATIONS
Paint	Oil—flat paint, semi-gloss or gloss enamel	Medium Density Overlaid, regular plywood, striated, embossed.	Apply over primer or may be self-priming.
	Latex emulsion	Regular and textured plywood, Medium Density Overlaid.	Apply with oil or stain-resistant primer.
	For textured effects	Regular plywood, Medium Density Overlaid, Texture 1-11.	Use oil base or stain-resistant primer.
Stains, Sealers		Regular plywood, textured.	Apply stains with companion sealer or over sealer separately applied. Follow with satin varnish or lacquer for increased durability. Where sealer alone is desired, use two coats.

*Use only lead-free finishes

(*continued from page 5*)

can be removed without structural considerations. (See Bearing partition.)

Paste filler: Material in paste form used to fill cracks and seams in wood, usually after being diluted with turpentine, naphtha or other thinner.

Penetrating stain: Stain color in oil or alcohol.

Pigment: Finely ground mineral material used to impart color and opacity in paints, varnishes and lacquers.

Pitch (roof): The slant of a roof from the wall to the ridge, usually expressed as a proportion of the total rise to the run.

Plank: A board, 1″ or more thick, laid with its wide dimension horizontal.

Plastic resin: A synthetic resin of very large molecular size having properties similar to plastic.

Plates: Base and top members in wall or partition framing.

Plumb: Perfectly vertical.

Plywood: A panel made of thin layers or plies of wood, or of thin plies in combination with a lumber core, particleboard core or other composition material, laminated and glued under pressure.

Polyvinyl acetate (PVA): Synthetic resin with a high degree of stability, abrasion resistance and durability, used in latex form in paints.

Post: Lumber (usually 3x3 minimum) set on end as a structural support.

Pumice: Finely ground, soft stone abrasive used to obtain a satiny rubbed effect on varnished surfaces.

Putty: A doughlike mixture of powdered whiting and linseed oil, and sometimes white lead.

R

Rabbet: A longitudinal groove cut in the edge of a board.

Rafter: One of a series of structural members designed to support a roof.

Resin: A solid or semi-solid material of vegetable or synthetic origin, usually transparent or translucent and ranging in color from yellow to amber to dark brown; soluble in alcohol but not in water.

Retarder: Slow-drying solvent added to lacquer to retard drying time.

Ridge: The junction at the top of two sloping roof surfaces.

Rise (roof): Vertical distance from the wall to the ridge.

Riser: Vertical board under a stair tread.

Rottenstone: A fine limestone abrasive used in polishing to bring out a high gloss.

Rough lumber: Lumber after original sawing, before it is dressed to dimensional size.

Rubbing compound: An abrasive mixture in paste form, commonly used for rubbing lacquer finishes.

Run (roof): The shortest horizontal distance from the center of the ridge to the outer edge of the wall.

Sapwood: The living wood near the outside of a log, generally more susceptible to decay than heartwood.

Sash: The framework that holds panes of glass in a window.

S-T

Sealer: A coat of shellac, paint or other material applied for the purpose of sealing the pores in a surface before topcoating.

Seasoning: Removing moisture from green lumber to improve its serviceability.

Semigloss: Interior paint formulated to produce a slight luster.

Sheathing: Material used to cover the exterior framing of a structure, usually as a base for the finish covering.

Shellac: Finish made by suspending in alcohol a natural resin secreted by an insect found only in the Far East. Natural shellac is orange; bleaching produces clear or white shellac.

Shim: A strip used to fill a small space between two surfaces.

Sill: The lowest framing member. The foundation sill supports the floor joists of a structure; the window sill supports the frame of a window.

Sizing: A coating of varnish or glue applied to a new wall before painting or wallpapering to prevent uneven absorption.

Soffit: A partial ceiling lower than the main one; also, the underside of a roof overhang.

Softwood: Wood derived from a coniferous tree, such as pine or fir. The term does not refer to the actual hardness of the wood.

Sole plate: The horizontal bottom member of a wall or partition.

Solvent: Any liquid capable of dissolving another substance.

Spackling compound: A finely ground mixture of powders that is combined with water to make a paste for repairing small cracks and holes in wood, plaster or gypsum board.

Span: The distance between supports of a beam, joist or other structural member.

Spar varnish: Durable varnish specially formulated to resist wear on exterior surfaces, particularly in marine applications.

Stain: Coloring matter that is completely soluble in the liquid with which it is mixed, unlike paint, which holds pigments in suspension and deposits them on the surface of the work.

Stock size: Lumber cut to standard size.

Stud: One of a series of vertical members (usually 2x4s) that make up the main framing of a wall or partition.

Subfloor: Plywood or boards laid over joists as a base for finish flooring.

Synthetic: Any finishing material made wholly or in part from artificial resins.

Tack: A slight stickiness on a freshly painted or varnished surface before it sets completely.

Tack cloth: A cloth impregnated with chemicals used to remove dust from surfaces being finished.

Tempera: Water-thinned or water-emulsion paint.

Tenon: A tongue cut on the end of a piece of wood to fit into a mortise.

Thinner: Any of a number of liquids used to regulate the consistency of paint and varnish.

Toenail: To drive nails at an angle.

Toner: Pure dye colors ground into pigment and combined with a clear lacquer.

Top plate: The uppermost horizontal member (usually doubled) in a wall or partition framing.

Tread: The horizontal part of a step or stair.

Trim: The finish materials (usually moldings) applied around doors and windows and at the floor and ceiling joints of walls.

Tuck point: Filling in old joints in brickwork with new mortar.

Turpentine: A colorless, volatile solvent used as a paint thinner.

U-V-W

Umber: An earth pigment of hydrated iron manganese ore, ranging from olive shades in the raw state to a rich dark brown when burnt.

Undercoat: Any film below a finish coat.

Underlayment: Plywood or other hardboard material laid over a subfloor to provide a smooth base for carpet, tile or sheet flooring.

Urethane (or polyurethane) resin: Synthetic resin formed by reaction of vegetable oils with certain uric acids.

Varnish: A liquid composition that is converted to a translucent or transparent solid film after being applied in a thin layer.

Varnish stain: Varnish in which a stain has been dissolved.

Vehicle: The liquid portion of a paint or varnish.

Veneer: A thin layer of wood glued to a base.

Vinyl: Synthetic resin resulting from the blending of copolymers or vinyl chloride and vinyl acetate.

Wainscot: Facing material, usually wood or paneling, applied to the lower portion of an interior wall contrasting with that on the upper part of the wall.

Wallboard: Material such as gypsum made into large rigid sheets for fastening to framing to provide interior wall and ceiling coverings.

White lead: Compounds of lead used as white pigments in many types of paint.

Whiting: Calcium carbonate, limestone or chalk used as a pigment, principally in making putty and as an extender.

DO-IT-YOURSELFER'S GUIDE TO WOOD

Wood remains the favorite medium of the do-it-yourselfer. It is easy to work, versatile, durable, beautiful and plentiful (thanks in part to improved logging and environmental practices). Your local lumberyard stocks a variety of sizes, types and grades of lumber suitable for just about any job you might want to tackle. A little knowledge will help you to buy the right lumber at the right price for your project.

Woods are properly classified as hard or soft solely by the two groups of trees they come from. Those from broadleaved deciduous trees (which shed their leaves each year) are hardwoods. Those from coniferous trees or evergreens, which have needles or scalelike leaves, are softwoods. Most of the wood in the ordinary lumberyard belongs to this class.

Rough, Surfaced and Worked

Lumber comes from the saw cut to nominal sizes such as 2x4, 2x6, 4x4, and so forth. In this form it is classified as "rough." Run through a planer, it is known as "surfaced," and decreases in size by the amount of wood removed. A nominal 2x4 surfaced on four sides (S4S) thus shrinks to 1½" x 3½" in cross section, a 1x6 board to ¾" x 5½". A "five-quarter" board, nominally 1¼" thick, comes to 1¹⁄₁₆" when dressed.

Some lumber can be bought surfaced two sides (S2S) or one side and one edge. Rough lumber, if available, can be used for some jobs, although hard on the hands. Rough rafters might be all right, for example, if care is taken to keep the top edges in line. But rough studs could cause trouble, since varying widths would make the walls irregular. Dressed or surfaced lumber, on the other hand, is uniform. Planing straightens the pieces and makes the sides and edges parallel. Uniform width or thickness is important when pieces are to form an even surface for further construction. Studs in a wall, for instance, are placed edgewise and therefore should be sided across the width on one or both edges. The same is true of floor joists. It's a waste of time to lay odd widths and then dress them to match.

A third classification, "worked" lumber, refers to stock that has been run through a molder or similar machine and made into siding, casing, bead or molding.

Surfaced, or sized, lumber is grouped in three categories: Yard lumber includes boards and dimension lumber up to 5" thick. Structural timbers are 5" or more. Both groups are graded as to quality with the use of the entire piece in mind, therefore a bad defect downgrades the piece. Factory and shop lumber, on the other hand, is meant to be cut up and permits defects between usable sections.

All but the most expensive lumber has defects. Grading regulates the size and number of these. You should know enough about grading to buy the cheapest lumber suitable for your purposes and also to recognize inferior grades if they are sent to you by mistake.

In grading framing lumber, strength is the chief criterion. For this reason not only the size of the defects and whether they're sound or loose, but also their location is taken into account. A knot near the end of a 2x4 impairs its strength less seriously than one in the middle or near the edge. Therefore larger end knots are allowed. Checks (end cracks) may be only one-fourth the thickness of a piece of No. 1 common; or, if two checks are opposite each other, their total must be no more than one-fourth of the thickness. In No. 2 common this tolerance goes up to one-third.

Money-Saving Tips

Besides using the lowest serviceable grade for the job, you can sometimes trade time for a cash saving by picking over cull lumber. Plenty of split and otherwise damaged stock is usable. But it may require extra sawing to square off the ends, and only you can decide whether it pays.

Milling defects sometimes put lumber on the bargain counter. Hit-and-miss surfacing, in which the knives missed low sections, still leaves boards suitable for sheathing and sub-floors, for instance. Some price arithmetic will show whether such lumber is worth buying.

Large beams, like those over wide doors, can be bought as timbers, but inside defects may be hidden and the pieces are hard to handle. A good alternative is to spike two pieces of 2" stock together side to side.

Clear stock comes high. A stained or natural finish can be satisfactory even if there are a considerable number of firm knots. For a painted finish you can use even rough or knotty pieces. Chisel back the knots, plug the holes with wood held in with waterproof glue, and fill rough spots with a good surfacing putty or fine sawdust mixed with waterproof glue. Sand well all over when the glue has set.

Grain appearance is a clue to how well the wood will hold paint. Flat-sawn lumber with wide slashes of hard grain may flake paint off the hard parts. If hard grain appears as threads, it should hold paint well, but the broad hard grain of summer wood makes a board a poor prospect for painting.

When You Want Boards

By boards the lumberman means stock less than 2" thick and usually over 6" wide (narrower boards may be classified as strips). Pricewise, such stock adds up fast. Therefore it's important to buy sizes that will cut with a minimum of waste, and to get the cheapest grade adequate to the job.

Grading is not an exact science, but depends upon the judgment and experience of the grader. The American Lumber Standards permit a 5% below-grade variation between graders. For this reason, and also because no two pieces of wood are identical any more than two thumbprints, even photos of typical grades can give only a rough idea of what may be expected. The better face of a board governs its grading. Within limits, the back may be poorer.

Note: The source for our guide to wood is the Family Circle DO-IT-YOURSELF ENCYCLOPEDIA, Vol. 11, copyright 1973, Rockville House Publishers, Inc.

For complete directions, see index on page 65.

TWINE MATS

Common household twine is woven on a stick loom to make the rectangular and round placemats shown below. For the coasters, it's tied in a 4-strand braid. Make several.

LEATHER FRAME

This rich-looking picture frame can be made for under $6 with scraps of leather and a few items from the dime store.

CHEST

For storing all those little things, build this three-drawer chest from about $5 worth of pine. Recycled nylons, dyed and square-knotted, make colorful, slip-proof dress hangers.

TRAY, TRIVETS

Make these kitchen accessories from scraps of plywood, lattice and dowel. And if you have some leftover varnish to finish them, they will cost you absolutely nothing.

FRAME, BOX

Two more items to make from plywood scraps. The picture frame should cost only the price of glass. The cigarette box: nothing.

Photography Credits: Clyde Baxter of Alderman Studios: furniture, page 45. **Jack Evans of Robinson Studio:** plant stand, cover; wall desk, page 35; plant stand and desk, pages 36-37. **Allan Green:** staple gun decorating, page 41. **Alan Hicks:** bookcase, page 34; Butler's table, page 38; wall shelf, page 39; stowaway furniture, pages 42-43; carts, page 49; home office, page 51; shed, pages 52-53; sewing center, pages 54-55; buffet, page 57. **Vincent Lasante:** screen, page 38. **Mort Mace:** bookcase/desk, page 39; greenhouse, page 50. **Bill McGinn:** pages 20, 24. **Earl McIntosh of Photographic House, Inc.:** kitchen, pages 58-59. **George Nordhausen:** wine rack, Tiffany lamps, slipcover, cover; table, page 2; pages 6, 10, 14; chess set, page 16; pages 26, 28; Tiffany lamps, page 34; potting table, compost bins, page 35; brick walk, page 39; slipcover, page 40; kitchen organizer, page 44; table, pages 46-47; game chest, page 52; barbecues, pages 55, 64. **Rudy Muller:** chest and quilt, cover; chest, quilt, chair, page 44. **Roy Robinson Studio:** pool table, pages 60-61. **Bob Stoller:** rockers, page 16; tables and cubes, page 33; picture frames, page 35; shelves, page 40; bar/coffee table, page 51. **Bob Strode:** planters, page 30; secretary, page 39; bed, pages 48-49; bed, pages 56-57. **Reg Von Cuylenberg:** basement, pages 62-63.

Designer Credits: Barbara Aurea-Wrenn: kitchen mirror, page 10. **Walter Brown:** barbecues, pages 55, 64. **Thomas D. Davis:** page 41. **Mary Doorley:** Tiffany lamps, cover, page 34. **Nick Fasciano:** rockers, page 16. **Gary Grosbeck, ASID:** secretary, page 39; bed, pages 48-49; bunk bed, pages 56-57. **Millie Hines:** cutting board, page 24. **Duane Hunting,** pages 46-47. **Lawrence Jacobs:** carts, page 49; barbecues, pages 55, 64. **Dale Joe:** chess set, page 16; page 33; room screen, page 38. **William J. Ketchan, CKD:** pages 58-59. **Jean Ray Laury:** quilt, page 44. **Donald MacDonald:** plant stand, cover and pages 36-37; wall desk, page 35; desk, page 36; stowaways, pages 42-43; pool table, pages 60-61. **Jeff Milstein:** planters, page 30; compost bins, potting table, page 35; bookcase/desk, brick walk, page 39; greenhouse, page 50; shed, pages 52-53. **The Mithun Associates, Bellevue, Wash.:** secretary, page 39; bed, pages 48-49; bed, pages 56-57. **Arvid Orbeck:** bookcase, page 34; Butler's table, page 38; wall shelf, page 39; bar/coffee table, page 51; sewing center, pages 54-55; buffet, page 57. **Charles S. Patrick:** kitchen, pages 58-59. **Pat Plaxico, ASID:** refinished furniture, page 45. **Bob Pfreundschuh:** step stool, mug rack, page 6; cookbook stand, towel rack, pipe rack, page 10; page 14; leather frame, chest, page 20;

ABRASIVES

There are many different types of abrasives available to the home handyman today. Most people are familiar with "sandpaper," but steelwool and mineral blocks also fall within this class. The term "sandpaper," meaning paper coated with abrasive grains, had its birth many years ago, probably when sand was actually used in that way. Today five different mineral grains are used, of various degrees of hardness and toughness, and the term "sandpaper" actually no longer describes the product.

Types of Sandpaper

Coated abrasives are almost the least expensive of the tools in your kit. The slight investment in maintaining a stock of the sizes and types you need, pays off in time saved, greater convenience and better work.

FOR REMOVING OLD PAINT—Flint paper is recommended for the job. There is little advantage in using a harder, sharper abrasive since the rapid loading of paint chips dictates the life of the paper. Use coarse grit for first rough sanding and medium grit for the second. Flint paper can be used for final sanding but other papers do a better job.

FOR WOOD—Garnet paper is the preferred choice for hand sanding and finishing wood. It comes in an assortment of grits. The following are the popular grit choices for the various stages of sanding: Very Coarse—1/2; Coarse—0; Medium—2/0; Fine—4/0 and Very Fine—6/0.

FOR HARDWOODS AND METALS—Paper and cloth such as Adalox offer the handyman a sharp, hard and enduring abrasive for finishing. It is particularly good with power sanders and can also be used for hand sanding operations. Because of its long cutting life, the sanding is seldom interrupted for renewing this type of abrasive.

FOR FLOOR FINISHING—Special grit paper is available for floor sanding machines, which are often available on a rental basis from the local hardware store. For old floors, start by sanding with Very Coarse or Coarse paper, 3½ or 4 grit. Follow this with a Fine paper, ½ and give the floors a final sanding with Very Fine floor sanding paper, 2/0. On the other hand, with new floors, either softwood or hardwood, start with Medium grit paper, 2½ and then use Fine, ½, finishing with Very Fine floor paper.

Sanding Techniques

The first step in reducing sanding effort is to select the right coated abrasive for the job. That is, the one which will cut sharpest and fastest.

The second step is to hold the work steady. This may seem like an obvious requirement, but it is too often neglected. Do not hold the work in one hand and sand with the other; it is best to avoid muscular fatigue before you start.

Always use a backing surface for the abrasive paper when sanding. Use a sanding block, even a convenient piece of wood, or a power sander; never just your hand.

Our source is Family Circle DO-IT-YOURSELF ENCYCLOPEDIA, Vol. 1, copyright 1973, Rockville House Publishers, Inc.

chopping block, cutlery chest, page 24; key keeper, lunchbox shelf, wine rack, page 26 (rack also on cover); desk and dresser organizers, shoeshine box, page 28; frames, page 35; home office, page 51; game chest, page 52; basement, pages 62-63. **Gary Porcano:** trivets, page 20; tile box, desk set, page 24. **Sherman Associates, Bethesda, Maryland:** room screens, page 38. **Peter Stevenson:** toy boat, page 26; stowaway furniture, pages 42-43. **Suzanne Stevenson:** kitchen shelves, page 40. **Rein Virkemaa:** placemats, page 6. **Carole Vizbara:** chest, cover, page 44; chair, page 1; magazine rack, page 14; placemats, wooden frame and cigarette box, dress hangers, page 20; lamp, page 28; chair and chest, page 44. **David Warren:** kitchen organizers, page 44. **William Martin Welsh, ASID:** kitchen, pages 58-59.

Acknowledgments: The editor gratefully acknowledges the help of:

American Plywood Assn.: wine rack, plant stand, cover; planters, page 30; potting table, compost bins, wall dest, page 35; desk, page 37; table, page 38; wall shelf, desk, walk, page 39; stowaways, pages 42-43; bed, carts, pages 48-49; home office, page 51; sewing center, 54-55; bed, buffet, pages 56-57; pool table, pages 60-61. **Brick Institute of America;** walk, page 39; barbecues, pages 55, 64. **California Redwood Assn.:** planters, page 30. **Masonite Corp.,** familyroom; pages 62-63. **National Assn. of Home Builders, Woman's Aux.:** kitchen, pages 58-59. **Western Wood Products Assn.:** planters, page 30; bookcase, page 34; potting table, compost bins, page 35; walk, page 39; dining table, pages 46-47; coffeetable, page 51.

BUYER'S GUIDE

Page 6: For magazine rack—"Wet Look" vinyl by Clopay, Consumer Products Div., Clopay Sq., Cincinnati, Ohio 45214.

Page 14: "Elmer's Heavy Grip" cement available at dime, stationery and variety stores; dinner plate ("Ruska") by Arabia of Finland.

Page 16: Boston rocker (#R 804-1378 A), child's rocker (#R 804-6526 A) from J.C. Penney; Early American Design Motifs by Suzanne E. Chapman, available from Dover Publications, Inc., 180 Varick St., N.Y., N.Y. 10014 ($3.50 plus 35¢ for postage and handling).

Page 28: Socket kits for lamps available at most dime stores, hardware stores, lamp stores, etc. Socket kit with rubber bottle adapter by Angelo Lamparts, Angelo Bothers Co., Philadelphia, Pa.

Page 30: All plants from McAuliffe Nursery and Landscaping, 11812 108th N.E., Kirkland, Wash.; (#6) Krylon Spray Paint by Borden Chemical, 50 W. Broad St., Columbus, Ohio 43215.

Page 33: Gift-wrap by Faroy, Inc., Houston, Tex. 77042; aluminum sheets from Reynolds Metals Co., 6601 W. Broad St., Richmond, Va. 23218 (Attn: Hardware Market Mgr.); striped calico prints, style No. 2460 and No. 2461 by Henry Glass and Co., 1071 Sixth Ave., New York, N.Y. 10018; self-adhesive vinyl ("Polished Patent") No. 2262 red and No. 2263 white by Con-Tact, Comark, 1407 Broadway, New York, N.Y. 10018; spray plastic coating ("Varathane") by the Flecto Co., Inc., Oakland, Calif. 94607; glue-glaze ("Mod-Podge") available at most dime, variety and department stores.

Page 34: Stacking bookcase—Books from Portland State Bookstore; desk accessories, lamps, uncut glass bookends and lantern from Lloyds Interiors, 1714 N.E. Broadway, Portland, Ore. 97205; stereo receiver available from The Radio Shack. Tiffany shades—Glass, copper foil, flux and antique finishing solution available from the following mail-order houses: All-Craft Tool and Supply Co., 22 W. 48th St., New York, N.Y. 10036; S.A. Bendheim, Inc., 122 Hudson St., New York, N.Y. 10013.

Page 35: Self-adhesive Con-Tact "Cushion-All" by Comark, 1407 Broadway, New York, N.Y. 10018. Compost Bins and Potting Table—

Carpentry by Al Ando, 1165 Tunnel Rd., Santa Barbara, Calif. 93105; stain by Olympic Stain, a division of Comerco, Inc., available at most paint stores.

Pages 36-37: Plant Stand and Desk—All paints by Kem-Glo (Gateway Blue Accent #565, Washington Blue Accent #1885) available at Sherwin Williams stores.

Page 39: Screen—Paint (N941 Raleigh Tavern Chinese Red, a Williamsburg color) by Martin Senour, available in paint, hardware and department stores; stain for molding (semi-transparent #906) by Olympic Stain, a division of Comerco, Inc. Location: 4620 North Park Avenue, Chevy Chase, Md. Butler's Table—Paint (Provincial Color Glaze in "Expresso") by Martin Senour available in paint, hardware and department stores; china and silverware accessories from Zell Bros., Morrison at Park Ave., Portland, Ore. 97205; flowers by Dorcas, 617 S.W. Washington St., Portland, Ore. 97205; brass hinges (#12004) available from Minnesota Woodworkers Supply Co., 925 Winnetka Ave. North, Minneapolis, Minn. 55427.

Page 39: Bookcase / Desk—Portable black-and-white television by Sony Corporation of America, 47-47 Van Dam St., Long Island City, N.Y. 11101; portable typewriter (Valentine) by Olivetti Corporation of America, 500 Park Ave., New York, N.Y. 10022; swivel chair and clamp-on desk lamp from the Children's Workbench, 470 Park Ave. South, New York, N.Y. 10016; all desk accesories scrapbooks, wastebasket and desk clock from Design Research, 53 E. 57th St., New York, N.Y. 10022. Home Office/Secretary—Ladderback chair, lamp and accessories by Ethan Allen; portable black-and-white television by Hitachi. Wall Shelf—Paint (Provincial Color Glaze in "Turkey Red") by Martin Senour, available in paint, hardware and department stores; porcelain Boehm birds from Zell Bros., Morrison at Park Ave., Portland, Ore. 97205; flowers by Dorcas, 617 S.W. Washington St., Portland, Ore. 97205. Brick Walkway — Landscaping and brickwork installed by Del Parra Landscape Construction, 612 N. Kellogg Ave., Santa Barbara, Calif. 93111.

Pages 42-43: Sling fabric, "Sunbrella" (style #1251) by Glen Raven Mills, Inc., Glen Raven, N.C. 27215; slings made by Pike Tent and Awning Co., 417 N.W. Third Ave., Portland, Ore. 97209.

Page 44: Kitchen organizers—Gloss

finish "Invisible Armor" spray polyurethane, Illinois Bronze Powder and Paint Co., Lake Zurich, Ill. 60047; cabretta leather available in most department stores, or write: House of Janice, Inc., 62 W. 36th St., New York, N.Y. 10018; teak available from Albert Constantine and Sons, 2050 Eastchester Rd., Bronx, N.Y. 10461, or send 35¢ for a catalog and order blank to Craftsman Wood Service, 2729 S. Mary St., Chicago, Ill. 60608. Ready to finish furniture from J.C. Penney catalog (armchair #R804-8969A, three-drawer chest #R804-1428A); all paints (listed by name and number) available at Sherwin Williams stores.

Page 45: Carpet, flocked wallcovering, anaglypta decals and all paint, glaze and antiquing products from Sherwin-Williams; Martha Washington reproduction chair by Hickory Chair; Chippendale accordion game table (referred to as sewing cabinet) from Antique Replicas Collection by Brandt Cabinet Works; draperies from Wedgewood Collection by Schumacher.

Pages 46-7: Covered casseroles by Dansk Designs, Ltd., Mt. Kisco, N.Y. 10549; chairs from Be Seated, 66 Greenwich Ave., New York, N.Y. 10011.

Page 48: Carpeting with Scotchgard Carpet Protector by Wunda Weve; paint and stain by Fuller O'Brien; fabric for spread, headboard and Roman shade ("Montauk"), mattress (by Sealy), toss pillows and most accessories from Ethan Allen; bed pillows of Kodel Fiberfill; fluorescent lighting over headboard by General Electric.

Page 49: Porcelainized enamel cast iron cookware from Copco, 230 5th Ave., New York, N.Y. 10001; two-burner liquid propane stove from the Coleman Company, Inc., 250 St. Francis, Wichita, Kan. 67201; Thomas PC 100 Cobalt Band China from Rosenthal Studio House, 584 5th Ave., New York, N.Y. 10036; plastic kitchen storage containers and shelf liner from Rubbermaid, Inc., Wooster, Ohio 44691 (see plans for specific listings); casters from Sears, Roebuck & Co. catalogue, Fall/Winter, No. 9H 7410.

Page 50: All plants, ground cover, gardening tools and accessories from Farm and Garden Nursery, 116 Reade St., New York, N.Y. 10013.

Page 51: Bar/Coffee Table—Glassware and ashtrays from The Pottery Barn, 231 10th Ave., New York, N.Y. Home Office—Books and office supplies from J. K. Gill Co., 408 S.W. Fifth Ave., Portland, Ore. 97204;

alarm clock from Zell Bros., Morrison at Park Ave., Portland, Ore.; manual typewriter and adding machine (Quanta-T) from Olivetti Corp. of America, 500 Park Ave., New York, N.Y. 10022; chair from Lloyds Interiors, 1714 N.E. Broadway, Portland, Ore. 97205; ceramic floor tiles ("Tides" —Flashed Walnut) by Interpace Corp., 2901 Los Feliz Blvd., Los Angeles, Calif. 90039; desk top of plastic laminate (1058LX—Coco Brown) by Parkwood Laminates Inc., 134 Water St., Wakefield, Mass. 01880; baskets from Import Plaza, 1 N.W. Couch St., Portland, Ore. 97209.

Pages 52-53: Game Chest—For catalogue to order leather, write to Tandy Leather Co., 115 W. 45th St., New York, N.Y. 10036. Storage Shed— Garden tools, tool chest, power saws, garden hoses and lawn spreader available from Sears retail stores or catalog.

Pages 54-55: Sewing machine by Singer; all sewing supplies available at Singer Sewing Centers; gingham (on wall and cutting table) from White Rose by A.E. Nathan. Barbecue—Six 12"x20" grates, Heath Metals, Munford, Ala. 36268; brick, Ante-Bellum Cherokee Brick Manufacturing Co., Macon, Ga.; stainless steel barbecue tools, Ekco Housewares Co., 9234 West Belmont Ave., Franklin Park, Ill. 60131; Armetale dinnerware, The Wilton Co., Columbia, Pa. 17512; red/white gingham napkins and potholder, Ross-Matthai Corp., 225 Fifth Ave., New York, N.Y. 10016; blueberry enameled cookware, Catherineholm Sales Corp., 299 Westport Ave., Norwalk, Conn. 06851; pine splint bucket, Artsam, 230 Fifth Ave., New York, N.Y. 10001; clay casserole, B. Altman Co., Fifth Ave. at 34 St., New York, N.Y. 10036.

Page 56: Carpeting with Scotchgard Carpet Protector by Wunda Weve; paint by Fuller O'Brien; mattresses and box springs (by Sealy); sheets ("Shaker Patch") by Cannon; stuffed toys by Possum Trot; hobby kits by Skil-Craft; games and puzzles by Whitman from Western Publishing Co., Inc.

Page 57: Paint (Provincial Color Glaze in "Colonial Blue") by Martin Senour available in paint, hardware and department stores; wallpaper by Greef Inc., 155 E. 56th St., New York, N.Y. 10022; pewterware from Zell Bros., Morrison at Park Ave., Portland, Ore. 97205; hardware available from William Hunrath Co., Inc. 153 E. 57th St., New York, N.Y. 10022.

Pages 58-59: No-wax cushioned sheet vinyl flooring ("Janiero" Shinyl Vinyl)

by Congoleum; ready-to-finish cabinets ("Bedford") by Excel; no-frost refrigerator, self-cleaning electric range, countertop microwave oven, dishwasher, food waste disposers (Disposall) and trash compactor by Hotpoint; plastic laminate for countertops and backsplash (Textolite) and fluorescent soffit and undercabinet tube and circline lamps lighting by General Electric; ventilating fan (over range) by NuTone; sheet aluminum surfacing (on custom range hood) by Reynolds Aluminum; sink ("Urbanite" in Mexican Sand) and instant hot water dispenser by KitchenAid; Vinyl-clad (Perma-Shield) wood angle bay, casement and gliding windows by Andersen Corp., Bayport, Minn. 55003, available at your local lumber dealer; interior decorative shutters of ponderosa pine by Flair-Fold, 75 Carmans Road, E. Farmingdale, N.Y. 11735; round butcher block table, rush-seated chairs and bar stool from the Door Store, 210 E. 51st St., N.Y., N.Y. 10022; shelves, brackets by Knape & Vogt; shelf lights by Edison; hand-hewn, unfinished ceiling beams of lightweight urethane by Paeco; all paint (semi-gloss "Bright-Life" in white and nutmeg and textured Interior Latex in white-sand) by Martin-Senour; blue-and-white check fabric for bench cushions and pillows by Schumacher; fabric for tablecloth, chair and stool cushions, toss pillows and shutter casements by Waverly; Toast-R-Oven, "Creative Entertainer" casserole/fondue, drip coffeemaker, stand mixer, can opener/ice-crusher, Broil-R-Grill, wall clock and FM/AM table radio by General Electric; 14-speed blender by Waring; electric bag sealer (Seal-A-Meal) by Dazey; built-in ceramic cutting surface ("Counter Saver") and cutting/warming surface ("Counter Saver Plus"), glass soufflé, spice jars and storage containers by Corning; glass cylinder and wide-mouth canisters and spice jars by Libbey; crockery, china, flatware, decorative plates, wooden salad bowl and round cutting board, pepper grinder by Denby; stainless pots and pans, colander and bakeware by Wear-Ever; drawer dividers and organizers, slide-out drawers, lid rack, wastebasket and spatula set by Rubbermaid; cutlery, pastry boards, kitchen tools and utensils, strainers, paper towel holder, meat tenderizer and measuring scoops by Ekco; dish towels and pot holders by Cannon; Trimline wall telephone, courtesy of AT&T.

Pages 60-61: Pool cues and balls from the J.C. Armor Co., Inc., P.O. Box 290, Deer Park, N.Y. 11729; Pool Table Kit FC-73 ($53.00, postpaid—New

York residents add sales tax) from J.C. Armor Co., same address as for cues and balls.

Pages 62-63: All wall and ceiling paneling, and pegboard by the Masonite Corporation, 29 No. Wacker Dr., Chicago, Ill. 60606; all flooring by Congoleum, Kearny, N.J. 07032; radiant ceiling panel heaters from Federal Pacific Corporation, 150 Avenue L, Newark, N.J. 07010; all hardware from Stanley Hardware, Division of The Stanley Works, New Britain, Conn. 06050; wood stain by Sherwin-Williams Co., 101 Prospect Ave. N.W., Cleveland, Ohio 44115. (See plans for detailed listing and catalog numbers.) "Creative Glass" serving pieces by Corning Glass Works, Corning, N.Y. 14830; "Franciscan Gourmet" dinnerware by Interpace Corp., 260 Cherry Hill Rd., Parsipanny, N.J. 07054; (middle, right) table lamp (#2225) by Electrix, Port Chester, N.Y. 10513; craft kits by Lee Wards, Elgin, Illinois 60120; fondue pots, fondue forks and coffee maker by Hoover, North Canton, Ohio 44720; hot tray by Salton Inc., 1260 Zerega Ave., Bronx, N.Y. 10462; stainless flatware by Supreme Cutlery, 1214 Broadway, New York, N.Y. 10001; napkins, Belgian Linen & Polyester by Fallani & Cohen, 14 E. 38th St., New York, N.Y. 10016; glassware by Libbey Products (Division of Owens Illinois) Toledo, Ohio 43601; wicker baskets from The Last Straw, 1115 Kings Highway, Brooklyn, N.Y. 11229; game (on table), Eccentric by Shuster & Miller, Inc., 242 E. 19th St., New York, N.Y. 10003; stereo, speakers and turntable by Magnavox, 345 Park Ave., New York, N.Y. 10022; records courtesy of Brainard's Bookstore, 44 Brink St., Crystal Lake, Ill. 60014; green chairs from Hank Lowenstein, Inc., 3105 S.W. Second Ave., Fort Lauderdale, Fla. 33315.

Page 64: Fireplace-barbecue unit, #OF-48, Majestic Co., Inc., 733 Erie St., Huntington, Ind. 46750; brick, Wood-Mold Bickerstaff Clay Products Co., Columbus, Ga.; battery operated roto spit, Rowley Co., Greenlake, Wis.; enameled cookware, teak woodenware, stainless steel carving set, glassware, "Swiss Chocolate" linens, Dansk Design Ltd., Radio Circle Rd., Mt. Kisco, N.Y. 10549; "Kitchen Chemistry" glass carafes, Pilgrim Glass Corp., 225 Fifth Ave., New York, N.Y. 10016; dinnerware (Corning-Centura Narrow Rim Tableware), Corning Glass Works, Corning, N.Y. 14830; walkway brick by Cummer, Inc. of Ocala, P.O. Box 1539, Ocala, Fla. 32670.

CHOPPING BLOCK

This sturdy portable chopping block is simple enough for even the novice craftsperson to make—and the price is right too: the short length of plank and a bit of rope should be under $3.

For complete directions, see index on page 65.

DESK SET

With a little bit of cane (available at furniture and upholstery stores and even some building supply outlets) and a few plywood scraps, you can make this set consisting of pencil holder, cup for crayons and the like, and waste basket. The look is quite distinctive, but the cost is under $4.

CUTTING BOARD

Early American folk art is the inspiration for this cutting board. Cuts and holes are made in the end of a piece of 1″ pine. The handmade look is intentional. About $2.

TILE BOX

Putting up ceramic tile in your bath or kitchen? Order a few extra and make some matching boxes. You're sure to find plenty of uses for them.

CHEST

For storing cutlery, make this small wood chest. It holds service for eight in two felt-lined drawers. $7.

PLYWOOD GRADES FOR EXTERIOR USES

GRADE (EXTERIOR)	FACE	BACK	INNER PLIES	USES
A-A	A	A	C	Outdoor, where appearance of both sides is important.
A-B	A	B	C	Alternate for A-A, where appearance of one side is less important. Face is finish grade.
A-C	A	C	C	Soffits, fences, base for coatings.
B-C	B	C	C	For utility uses such as farm buildings, some kinds of fences, etc., base for coatings.
303® Siding	C (or better)	C	C	Special surface treatment such as V-groove, channel groove, striated, brushed, rough sawn.
T1-11®	C	C	C	Sanded or unsanded, with deep parallel grooves. For siding, soffits, screens, accent panels, etc.
C-C (Plugged)	C Plugged	C	C	Excellent base for tile and linoleum, backing for wall coverings, high-performance coatings.
C-C	C	C	C	Unsanded, for backing and rough construction exposed to weather.
B-B Polyform	B	B	C	Concrete forms. Re-use until wood literally wears out.
MDO	B	B or C	C	Medium Density Overlaid. Ideal base for paint; for siding, built-ins, signs, displays.
HDO	A or B	A or B	C-Plugged or C	High Density Overlaid. Hard surface; no paint needed. For concrete forms, cabinets, counter tops, tanks.

PLYWOOD GRADES FOR INTERIOR USES

GRADE (INTERIOR)	FACE	BACK	INNER PLIES	USES
A-A	A	A	D	Cabinet doors, built-ins, furniture where both sides will show.
A-B	A	B	D	Alternate of A-A. Face is finish grade, back is solid and smooth.
A-D	A	D	D	Finish grade face for paneling, built-ins, backing.
B-D	B	D	D	Utility grade. One paintable side. For backing, cabinet sides, etc.
C-D	C	D	D	Sheathing and structural uses such as temporary enclosures, subfloor. Unsanded.
UNDER-LAYMENT	C-Plugged	D	C and D	For underlayment or combination subfloor-underlayment under tile, carpeting.

KEY KEEPER

There'll be no more wondering where you left your keys— this brightly painted giant key hanging on the wall will remind you. Make it for about $3.50.

FERRYBOAT

For bathtub and swimming pool commuters, this ferryboat can be built for a small investment in glue, nails and varnish. Wood is scrap.

This six-bottle wine rack is both portable and collapsible—when the wine cellar is bare, you can take it apart and store it flat as a pancake. Build it for under $8.

PORTABLE WINE RACK

SHELF/RACK

This lunch box shelf and coat rack is made of scrap pine lumber and wood dowels; cost, about $3.50. Hang it at kid-height on the kitchen, bedroom or entrance-hall wall.

FURNITURE FINISHING

After completing the woodworking phase of furniture making, you are ready to add the finishing touches. A good finish on the furniture will add much to its appearance. No matter how good your workmanship or the quality of the lumber used, a poor finish will result in an unsatisfactory job. Therefore, decide upon the best finish for your particular purpose and apply it carefully.

When remodeling old furniture, special attention and careful workmanship must be given to removing the old finish. This section includes information on preparation of surfaces as well as the different finishes you can apply.

Check List of Finishing Materials

1. Commercial paint and varnish remover
2. Commercial wood bleach
3. Sealers—White shellac, orange shellac, white shellac enamel (for limed effects), clear and white resin sealers, lacquer sealer
4. Stains—Penetrating oil stains, pigmented or wiping oil stains, non-grain-raising stains, colors-in-oil to tint resin sealers
5. Fillers—Paste wood filler, lacquer sanding sealer, spackling compound, wood putty, stick shellac
6. Undercoats—Flat enamel undercoat, exterior primer
7. Finishing coats—satin, semi-gloss or gloss varnish; brushing or spraying lacquer; enamel, interior or exterior; paste furniture wax
8. Thinners—Turpentine, mineral spirits, alcohol
9. Rubbing materials — Sandpaper, waterproof sandpaper, silicon-carbide paper, steel wool, rubbing compound, pumice stone, rottenstone, rubbing oil
10. Paint brushes
11. Spray equipment
12. Miscellaneous—Clean rags, cheesecloth, painter's duster, rubbing felt, sandpaper block or portable electric sander

Cleaning and Repairing Wood Surfaces

1. Before removing the old finish, repair loose joints, splits, cracks and other blemishes in the furniture. The old finish will give your furniture protection against additional scratches, mars and glue stains during the process of making repairs. Any surface scratches, gouges and abrasions should be resurfaced after the old finish is removed.

2. Apply any good commercial paint and varnish remover to the piece of furniture. Follow the manufacturer's instructions for proper application.

3. To remove the old finish from curved areas, ornamental carvings or spindles use a very fine bristled steel brush or steel wool wrapped around a pointed dowel stick or lollipop stick. Burlap, cut into strips of varying widths, can be used to remove the softened finish from turned pieces. Fine steel wool entwined with cord is effective in removing the softened finish from crevices on rounded surfaces. Steel wool on electrician's or Scotch tape is also useful for removing the finish from rounded surfaces where the see-saw motion will help you to work quickly and efficiently.

4. When the furniture is cleaned of the old finish, scrub the clean, bare surface with #2 steel wool dipped in denatured alcohol. You can also sand with fine sandpaper and wash down with a cloth dampened in gum turpentine. The washing chemical best suited for use will depend upon the type of remover you use. Be sure to follow the manufacturer's instructions to achieve best results.

5. Scars, dents, and mars must be smoothed out for a professional job and smooth surface. Shallow dents can be raised with damp cloth and a hot iron. Deeper mars should be filled with a crack filler or with stick shellac, which comes in many colors, applied hot and spread with a knife blade or palette knife. After the crack filler has hardened, sand smooth with medium fine sandpaper, rubbing with the grain of the wood.

6. Weather stains or dark woods can be bleached to the shade you desire by using a commercial wood bleach, fresh peroxide, or an oxalic acid solution. Wear rubber gloves when working with these solutions. When the surface is dry, wash well with a solution of 50% warm water and 50% white vinegar. Allow the surface to dry thoroughly and sand the entire surface with medium fine sandpaper.

Stain, Shellac and Varnish

1. If you plan to stain or bleach the furniture and finish with shellac or varnish, sandpaper the surface with fine sandpaper. (New unpainted furniture, even if it feels smooth to the touch, should be sanded with fine sandpaper before applying any finish.) Be sure that the grain of the wood is open so that it will uniformly accept the stain or bleach. Follow the manufacturer's instructions for the use of and neutralization of the bleach. If this process is not done properly, the bleach may affect the subsequent coats of finish and ruin the entire job.

2. After staining or bleaching, you may want to fill the open-grained woods such as oak, mahogany and walnut for a smoother surface. Close-grained woods such as pine, maple and birch do not need filler. Paste filler can be obtained in colors; however, if the color you want is not available, natural filler can be tinted with the stain being used or mixed with colors-in-oil.

3. An easy way to apply the paste filler is to spread the filler vigorously across and with the grain with an old stubby but clean paint brush. Rub it well into the grain. When the filler loses its gloss, rub away the excess across the grain with a pad formed of coarse burlap.

4. After the filler has dried thoroughly, the surface should be smoothed carefully with #3/0 sandpaper. Remember that you cannot obtain a professional finish unless you prepare the surface properly. Sanding the furniture surface as smoothly as possible is most important. Always dust and wipe the furniture you are working on to keep it dry and dust free.

5. The exposed end grain of wood in furniture is as absorbent as a sponge and it will soak up too much stain unless properly sealed or unless you prefer this contrast. Seal this end grain with a thin coat of clear shellac before the stain is applied. Be careful not to permit the shellac to flow onto the side grain. If it does, sand off completely before applying stain; otherwise an uneven finish will result.

6. Allow the stain to dry for 24 hours. If necessary, stain again and wipe again according to instructions until you have produced the desired shade. Let the final coat of stain dry for 24 hours. Seal the stain with a coat of white shellac. Thin your shellac 50-50 with denatured alcohol and flow on with a brush. Be sure to brush with the grain. Don't go back over the wet shellacked areas. If a spot is skipped, touch it up later when the coat is dry.

7. When the shellac is dry—allow at least three hours—smooth carefully and lightly with #3/0 steel wool.

8. Finish the furniture with two or

(continued on page 29)

DESK ORGANIZERS

Get it all together with these simple-to-make trays that hold paper, thumb tacks, paper clips and the many other small items that clutter up your desk top.

BOTTLE LAMP

After you have enjoyed the wine, enjoy the wine bottle by turning it into a lovely lamp. Many wine bottles have such graceful shapes that it's a shame to throw them away. This crockery bottle held rosé! Shade and electrical fittings: under $7.

NICE AND NEAT

Avoid dresser mess with a cupcake-pan organizer that holds cufflinks, pins and other small jewelry. Good-looking, and costs under $6.

SHINE ANYONE?

This box is a handy place to keep polish, brushes, buffing cloths and other shoe-grooming gear. Made from plywood and pine scraps, it is finished to look almost as good as the footwear it helps keep shined.

(continued from page 27)

three coats of clear satin-finish varnish.

9. Flow on the varnish carefully, brushing with the grain. Don't try to brush back over it. Watch for runs and smooth them out carefully before they have an opportunity to set.

10. Between the application of each coat and after the final coat, rub carefully and lightly with #3/0 steel wool. Dust with a rag soaked in turpentine.

11. Protect the final coat of varnish with an application of good furniture wax.

12. Do your finishing work in a dust free, well-ventilated, dry room.

Lacquer Finish

To lacquer a piece of furniture the old finish must be removed down to the bare wood. You cannot apply lacquer over paint, enamel or varnish. Follow the steps 1 through 5 described in "Cleaning and Preparing Wood Surfaces."

If you are using clear lacquer, apply stain to the wood to arrive at the desired finish. Follow steps 1 through 6 under "Stain, Shellac and Varnish." Eliminate any shellac or varnish steps.

Lacquer should be applied in a dust-free room, at a temperature of at least 70°F. Set up a fan in the room and avoid any fire or flame near the work. If you intend to apply the lacquer with a brush, be sure to get brushing lacquer. Spraying lacquer dries too quickly to spread with a brush.

1. The first coat is the primer. Both the primer and lacquer should be thinned to a milk-thick consistency. Primer as well as lacquer itself should be flowed on with a single stroke and permitted to level itself. Use the best soft varnish brush that you can buy for professional results and really fine craftsmanship.

2. When the primer is dry, smooth it with fine waterproof sandpaper dipped in water to remove the fine specks. Dry the furniture with an absorbent lint-free cloth.

3. Apply the lacquer as it comes from the can if you intend to use only one coat. For two or more coats, and a much tougher surface, thin the lacquer with one third its amount of thinner.

4. Between coats, sand carefully and lightly with fine sandpaper used wet.

5. Give the final coat a rich velvety sheen by rubbing down with a commercial rubbing compound or rottenstone.

REMOVING SCARS ON LACQUERED SURFACES—after the lacquer has hardened, a sharp blow on the surface may leave a white scar. To remove the scar:

1. Place a drop of lacquer thinner on the surface by using a toothpick, matchstick or dropper.

2. Don't touch the surface or the scar itself with the tool used to apply the lacquer thinner.

3. The thinner will soften the lacquer surface enough to remove the whitish appearance of the scar. After the lacquer thinner evaporates the lacquer will harden and the surface will be restored to its original appearance.

Enamel Finish

The durable, washable surface of enamel is due to its varnish base. However, the hardness makes it brittle and liable to chip or flake unless a careful job of preparation and application is performed. To enamel furniture surfaces:

1. Follow the step outlined for cleaning and preparing the surface described earlier in the text.

2. Seal the wood with a wash coat of shellac (50% shellac-50% denatured alcohol). The shellac will help prevent the grain from showing through the enamel.

3. After the shellac is dry, smooth lightly with #3/0 steel wool. Sandpaper doesn't work too well because shellac has a tendency to clog.

4. Tint the enamel undercoat if you plan a single finishing coat of dark enamel. Mix ¾ of the undercoat with ¼ of the enamel to be used. Enamel undercoat needs a thorough stirring. Pour off the top liquid, stir the pigment until it is smooth, return the liquid slowly as you stir it in.

5. Apply the undercoat and brush it out thoroughly. Avoid a heavy, gummy undercoat. Don't overload your brush. Start painting at a top piece on the furniture and work down. Watch carefully for sags and runs, brush them out before they harden.

6. Smooth the undercoat with #3/0 sandpaper after you have permitted the surface to dry for at least 24 hours. Use a light touch on the undercoat because it is a soft surface and easy to cut through into the wood. Dust with a turpentine-soaked rag.

7. If two or more colors are to be used, apply masking tape to stop the finishing coats on a straight line and to prevent running. Brush on the finish and strip off the tape *before* the finish hardens. Flow on enamel in small squares and smooth with a very light cross brushing. Dip in only half of the brush to avoid overloading with enamel. Work rapidly and don't overbrush.

8. One coat usually will cover; two will add durability. Roughen the first coat slightly with fine sandpaper after it dries and before you apply the second coat. A good wax can be applied if desired, for added protection.

Oil Polish Finish

To get a beautiful rich finish on hardwoods:

1. Brush boiled linseed oil on raw smoothly sanded furniture and let it soak in, then polish long and vigorously with a soft cloth.

2. Repeat each week until you have reached the desired color and sheen. Let dry for a few days.

3. Apply a thin coat of shellac and two coats of wax.

Bleached Pickled Pine Finish

1. Bleach with solution aspen concentrate decolorant or any good commercial bleach. Dry overnight and scuff with medium sandpaper.

2. Pickle with thinned solution of white shellac enamel. Dry overnight. Coat with thinned white shellac and denatured alcohol. Dry four hours. Cover again with another application of thinned shellac. Dry overnight.

3. Steel-wool with #3/0. Wax with paste wax, dry and buff.

Knotty Pine Finish

1. Sand surfaces smooth to touch with fine sandpaper. Dust.

2. Apply very light pine or oak water or alcohol stain to depth of color desired and according to manufacturer's directions. Dry overnight. Flow on thinned shellac. Do not go over wet shellacked areas. Allow the first coat to dry three hours.

3. Steel-wool lightly with #3/0 and dust surface.

4. Apply second coat thinned shellac and dry overnight.

5. Rub with fine Wet-or-Dry sandpaper and machine oil, with the grain. For a smooth luster, wax, let dry for 20 minutes and buff.

Light Modern Maple Finish

1. Bleach with aspen concentrate decolorant or wood bleach.

2. Dry 1½ hours.

3. Scuff with medium sandpaper.

4. Flow on thinned shellac with brush.

5. Dry four hours and coat again with shellac.

6. Dry overnight and lubricate as described in step 8, "Honey Color Maple Finish."

7. Sand and repeat lubricating process.

8. Wax, dry 20 minutes, buff.

Faded Mahogany Finish

1. Bleach with weak solution of Behlen Decolorant.

2. Dry overnight.

(continued on page 125)

$10 TO $60 HOME PROJECTS

1

2

3

Wood planters are a low-cost but effective way to decorate your outdoor "living room." The ones shown here are designed to hold just about every type of plant and flower to add beauty to any outdoor setting. All can be built in a short time.

4

5

6

7

8

OUTDOOR PLANTERS

(page 30)

Directions for all planters include suggestions for specific plants suitable to their sizes and shapes. Follow the cutting directions provided in each case, then assemble referring to diagrams. Drill ⅝″ drainage holes in the bottoms of all planters. All are raised on base supports to allow for proper drainage. Because of its extreme resistance to decay, redwood requires no finish—it will weather over the years to a mellow silvery gray. For longer life, lumber and plywood should be painted or finished with a preservative; the finish for each planter is given in the individual Materials list. Lumber and plywood planters must also be protected on the inside. Brush on coating of asphalt roofing paint after assembly of planter.

1. Redwood "packing crate" for evergreens (white cedar)

MATERIALS: Construction Heart Redwood: two 1x4x10″, two 1x4x8′, 2x2x4′; Ext. plywood, ⅝″x14½″x14½″; 4d, 6d galvanized finishing nails; asphalt paint (for bottom only).

CUTTING DIRECTIONS: Ten 1x4x16″ sides; ten 1x4x14½″ ends; four 1x4x 17½″ end frame verticals; four 1x4x9″ end frame horizontals; four 2x2x12″ base supports (see Fig. 15).

FIG. 15—REDWOOD "PACKING CRATE"—for evergreens

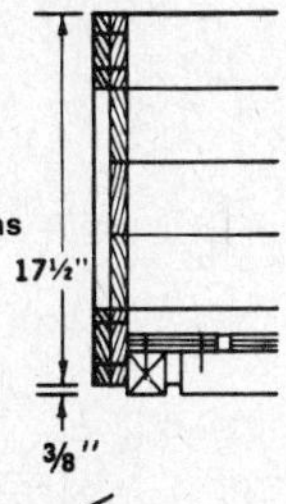

17½″
⅜″

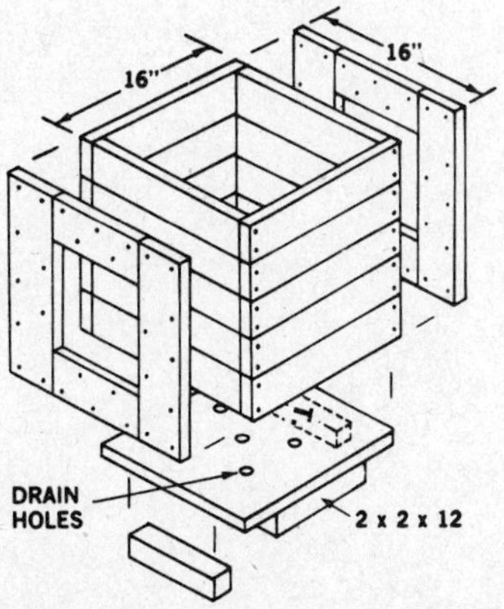

16″
16″
DRAIN HOLES
2 x 2 x 12

2. Plywood slot-together box for topiary evergreens (boxwood)

MATERIALS: Ext. or MDO plywood, ⅝″x4′x4′; 2x2x3′ lumber; 6d galvanized finishing nails; waterproof glue; asphalt paint; exterior white paint.

CUTTING DIRECTIONS: Four 17″x19½″ plywood sides (cut decorative tops and notch as shown in Fig. 16); 12⅜″x12⅜″ plywood bottom; four 2x2x9″ base supports (see Fig. 16).

FIG. 16 PLYWOOD SLOT-TOGETHER BOX — for topiary evergreens

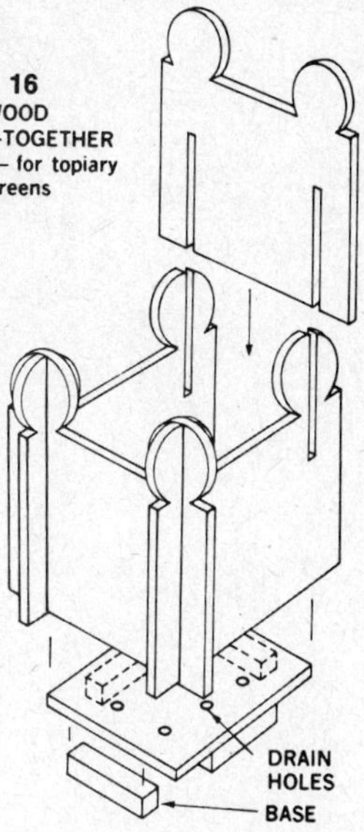

DRAIN HOLES
BASE

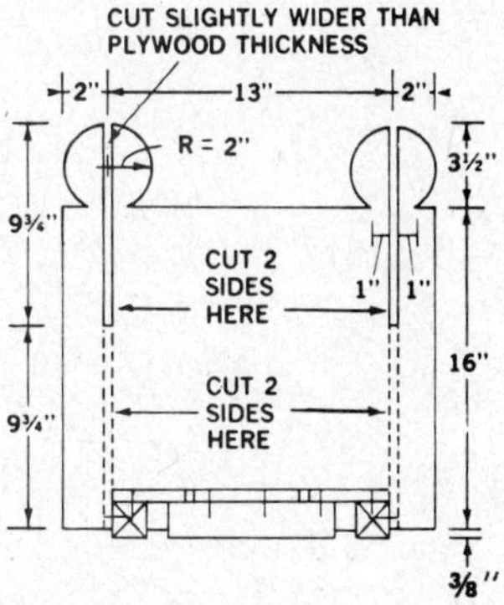

CUT SLIGHTLY WIDER THAN PLYWOOD THICKNESS
2″
13″
2″
R = 2″
3½″
9¾″
CUT 2 SIDES HERE
1″
1″
16″
9¾″
CUT 2 SIDES HERE
⅜″

3. Box and trellis for climbers or espaliers (firethorn pyracantha)

MATERIALS: (Note: We used a combination of sapwood and heartwood cedar lumber for a striped effect. You can achieve a similar effect using all fir lumber and staining alternate boards before assembly.) Heartwood cedar lumber: five 1x3x8′, one 2x2x8′, one 2x2x9′; Sapwood cedar lumber: two 1x3x7′, one 1x3x9′; ⅝″x16″x16″ Ext. plywood; 4d, 6d, 8d galvanized nails; asphalt paint; clear sealer; dark stain (if only fir is used).

CUTTING DIRECTIONS: Two 1x3x74″ heartwood cedar lumber trellis uprights; six 1x3x16″ heartwood cedar lumber trellis cross-pieces; 12 heartwood cedar lumber side pieces, 1x3x17″; 16 sapwood cedar side pieces, 1x3x17″, four to be ripped to 1¾″ for side corners as shown in Fig. 17; four 2x2x10″ base supports; four 2x2x12″ inside corners; eight 2x2x13″ horizontal framing members. See Fig. 17 for planter assembly.

FIG. 17 LUMBER BOX AND TRELLIS — for climbers or espaliers

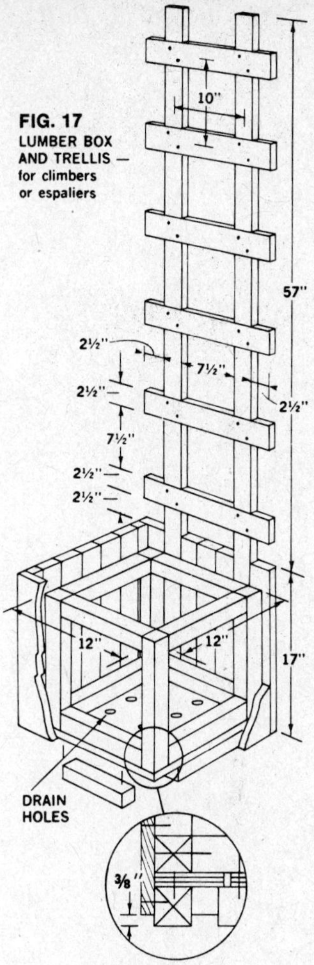

10″
57″
2½″
7½″
2½″
2½″
7½″
2½″
2½″
12″
12″
17″
DRAIN HOLES
⅜″

TOP VIEW DETAIL OF PLANTER BOX

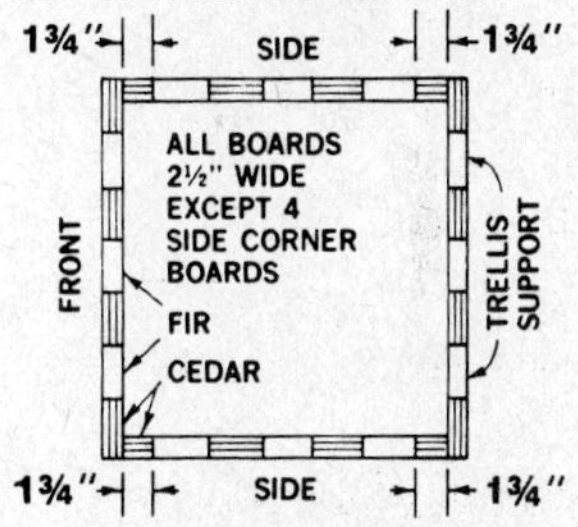

1¾″
SIDE
1¾″
ALL BOARDS 2½″ WIDE EXCEPT 4 SIDE CORNER BOARDS
FRONT
TRELLIS SUPPORT
FIR
CEDAR
1¾″
SIDE
1¾″

4. Plywood cylinders for cacti and succulents

MATERIALS (for two cylinders, 24″ and 18″): One 4′x8′ sheet of ¾″ Ext. plywood; scraps of ¼″ or ⅜″ wood or plywood; waterproof glue; wood filler; asphalt paint; marine-grade spar varnish (for waterproofing).

CUTTING DIRECTIONS: Use saber saw with circle guide to cut six large (24″) and six small (18″) rings, and one large and one small base disc. Laminate the disks with waterproof glue, add scrap pieces for feet. (See Fig. 18 on page 32.) Fill edge grain with wood filler and sand before finishing the planters. Be sure to coat both the inside and outside surfaces of planters with marine-grade spar varnish.

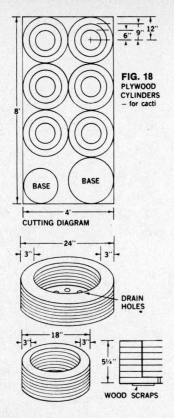

FIG. 18
PLYWOOD CYLINDERS
— for cacti

12"
6" 9"

8'

BASE   BASE

4'

CUTTING DIAGRAM

24"
3"   3"

DRAIN HOLES

18"
3"   3"

5¼"

WOOD SCRAPS

5. Redwood octagon for annuals (primroses)

MATERIALS: Clear Heart Redwood: 2x10x10', 2x2x4'; ¾"x21"x22" Ext. plywood; 6d, 8d galvanized nails; 48 2" #10 galvanized flat head wood screws; waterproof glue; asphalt paint (for plywood bottom only).

CUTTING DIRECTIONS: Eight 2x10x14" sides (set saw to bevel edges at 67½° as

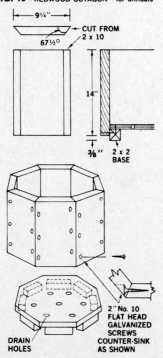

FIG. 19 — REDWOOD OCTAGON — for annuals

9¼"

CUT FROM 2 x 10

67½°

14"

⅜"   2 x 2 BASE

2" No. 10 FLAT HEAD GALVANIZED SCREWS COUNTER-SINK AS SHOWN

DRAIN HOLES

shown in Fig. 19); eight 2x2x6" base supports; assemble sides and use as pattern to cut plywood base.

6. Plywood and lumber wagon for potted houseplants (ferns and dieffenbachia)

MATERIALS: Ext. plywood, ¾"x24"x48"; Douglas fir lumber: 2x2x9', two 1x4x8', 1x4x6'; 3' of 1" hardwood dowel; 1' of ¼" dowel; eight 1" washers; 46 Phillips-head screws, 1¼" oval; eight 5/16"x3½" carriage bolts, washers, nuts; 6d galvanized finishing nails; asphalt paint (use on bottom only); clear gloss polyurethane (for body); yellow paint for wheels; orange paint for axle supports; silver paint for axles; dark blue for inside bottom.

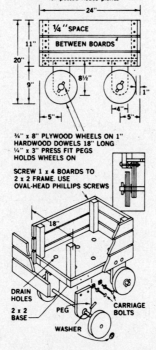

FIG. 20 — PLYWOOD AND LUMBER WAGON — for potted house plants

24"
¼" SPACE
11"   BETWEEN BOARDS
20"
9"   8½"   1"
5"   4"   5"

¾" x 8" PLYWOOD WHEELS ON 1" HARDWOOD DOWELS 18" LONG
¼" x 3" PRESS FIT PEGS HOLDS WHEELS ON

SCREW 1 x 4 BOARDS TO 2 x 2 FRAME. USE OVAL-HEAD PHILLIPS SCREWS

18"

DRAIN HOLES
2 x 2 BASE   PEG
WASHER   CARRIAGE BOLTS

CUTTING DIRECTIONS: Six 1x4x24" side pieces; six 1x4x16½" front pieces; two 2x2x22½" base sides; two 2x2x13½" base front and back; four 2x2x8⅞" inside corners; 16½"x22½" plywood bottom; four 4"x8½" plywood axle supports (cut half-round bottoms as shown in Fig. 20); four 8"-diameter plywood wheels; two 1"x18" dowel axles; four ¼"x3" axle pegs.

7. Lumber hexagon for bulbs (tulips)

MATERIALS: Douglas fir lumber, four 2x4x8', 2x2x4'; ¾"x22"x26" Ext. plywood; six 5/16"x14" threaded rods, 12 nuts, 12 washers; 6d, 8d galvanized finishing nails; asphalt paint; wood preservative (clear) for finishing and waterproofing planter.

FIG. 21 — LUMBER HEXAGON — for bulbs
1¾"
1½"
16"   67½°

5/16" CLEARANCE HOLE COUNTERBORE TOP AND BOTTOM FOR WASHERS, NUTS

14"

⅜"

2 x 2 BASE SUPPORTS NAILED TO SIDES AND BOTTOM

¾" PLYWOOD BOTTOM

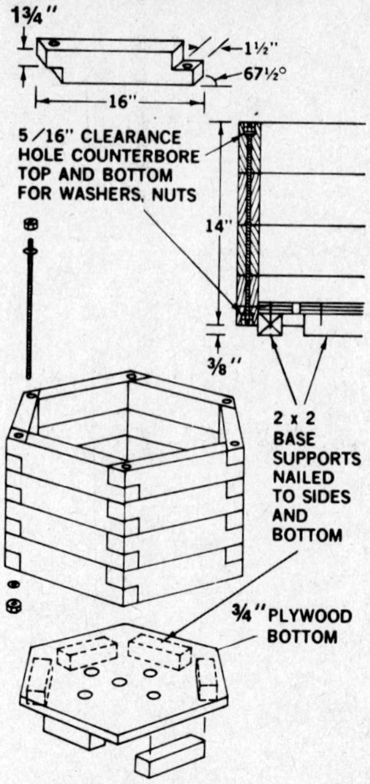

CUTTING DIRECTIONS: Twenty-four 2x4x16" side pieces, notched and angled at ends as shown in Fig. 21; six 2x2x8" base supports; assemble sides with threaded rods and use as pattern to cut plywood base.

8. Lumber box for flowering shrubs (azaleas)

MATERIALS: Douglas fir lumber: 2x8x12', 2x2x4'; ⅝"x13"x13" Ext. plywood; four 5/16"x15" threaded rods, 8 nuts, 8 washers; 6d, 8d galvanized finishing nails; asphalt paint; medium stain; preservative (clear).

CUTTING DIRECTIONS: Eight 2x8x16" side pieces, notched at ends as shown in Fig. 22; four 2x2x10" bottom supports.

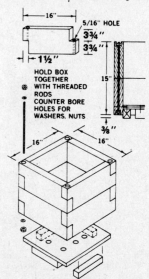

FIG. 22 — LUMBER BOX — for flowering shrubs

16"   5/16" HOLE
3¾"
3¾"
1½"
15"

HOLD BOX TOGETHER WITH THREADED RODS COUNTER BORE HOLES FOR WASHERS, NUTS

⅜"

16"   16"

BRIGHT, VERSATILE

From the top, the pieces are covered with gift wrap, self-adhesive plastic, spray plastic, sheet aluminum, aluminum foil and patchwork calico scraps.

For complete directions, see index on page 65.

You can buy these unfinished cubes and tables, then apply your own colorful touches They will brighten any room. Use them to sit on, as end tables, or group them together for a coffee table.

With amateur skills, you can produce professional-appearing results. Try one of these projects.

BOOKCASE

This stacking bookcase assembled without glue nails or screws. It is easy to take apart and reassemble if you move It is also expandable— just add on sections as needed. Ours cost $60.

TIFFANY SHADES

Authentic Tiffany stained-glass lamp-shades are expensive and hard to find. Using a simplified version of the old Tiffany copper-foil technique, you can create your own designs with the full rich colors of the famous original versions.

For complete directions, see index on page 65.

POTTING TABLE

This counter-height table is large enough for any potting job and has plenty of shelf storage. The cost: about $40.

WALL DESK

Hang this desk on the wall of your kitchen, family room or bedroom. Pigeonholes provide storage. The cost: $35.

PICTURE FRAMES

These frames do more than simply surround a picture—they actually enhance what they hold.

COMPOST BINS

Plywood sides of these compost bins slot together; backs and fronts slide up for easy removal of the compost from the bottom. Drilled holes allow aeration. Cost: about $40.

DESK/FILE

A system of interlocking slots and pegged joints makes this desk as sturdy as it is handy. The surface is at the right height for typing. Movable dividers help organize the rear file section. Cost: about $60.

PLANT STAND

Here is an elegant way to display your house plants. The stand accommodates a container up to 8" in diameter. You can build it for about $9—even less, if you rummage through your plywood dealer's odd-size bin to find some scraps.

Plywood is truly the handyperson's material-for-all-reasons. It is low in cost, readily available, easy to work with and gives a smart, professional appearance to a do-it-yourself job. Here are two plywood projects that even a beginner will enjoy building.

For complete directions, see index on page 65.

Try your hand at some of these very elegant projects, all of which are made with everyday materials that can be found at any building supply store.

DIVIDER SCREEN

Divide and conquer is one solution to spatial problems. This screen defines two room areas. It's built of standard-size flush doors, to the size that suits your needs. About $15 per panel.

TABLE TRAY

English butler's tray table stands on a 19"-high base and has a lift-off top for easy serving. Build it for $40.

BOOKCASE/DESK
Slot-together plywood bookcase/desk/ storage wall can be built in just a couple of weekends for about $50.

SECRETARY
Made from a single sheet of plywood at a cost of about $30, this home office/secretary stands against a wall.

WALL SHELF
This Early American hanging wall shelf can be built for about $18, or even less if you can find some plywood scraps.

BRICK WALK
A walkway consisting of a series of brick "stepping stones" is simple to make, and will cost about $25 per 10'.

For complete directions, see index on page 65.

Decorating doesn't have to be costly, as the projects on these pages prove.

EASY SLIPCOVER
Give new life to an old chair for less than $50 with this slipcover of three-way stretch double-knit polyester. Just ease it into place on the chair.

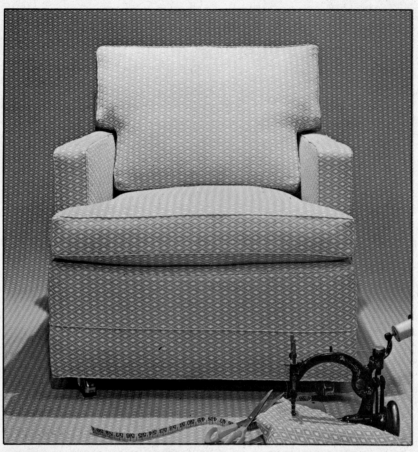

STAPLE-GUN DECORATING
The versatile staple gun is put to work applying colorful fabric to boxes, trunks, furniture, doors, woodwork and even walls, creating bright and decorative accents out of dull or dated objects.

KITCHEN SHELVES
Dress up your kitchen walls with these useful little shelf units. The one at top holds small utensils. Below it and to the left is an "herb garden" where you can grow your own. Facing them on the adjacent wall is a spice rack, accomodating nine containers behind guard rails. About $10 each.

Panel a door

Create a fabric picture

It's easy to turn these ugly
ducklings into beautiful swans.

Decorate a headboard

Re-cover a love seat

Into a planter

Dress up a trunk

For complete directions, see index on page 65.

For complete directions, see index on page 65.

A chaise, chairs and tables for comfortable warm weather living— and when the cold months come, all can be knocked down for storage.

STOWAWAYS
Weather-resistant slings and tough exterior plywood make this furniture ideal for outdoor use. The dining and coffee tables are slotted together; chair and chaise frames are assembled with dowels.

KITCHEN ORGANIZERS

Modestly priced teakwood is used for making these "Scandinavian" pieces. The indoor mailbox can even hold magazines. Others hold sandwich bags, cookbooks, recipes.

The baby quilt is machine-appliquéd with a blue tulip pattern used throughout, repeated and reversed. Blanket chest is stenciled with rows of the same blossoms.

BLANKET AND QUILT

PENNSYLVANIA DUTCH CHAIR

It looks like an authentic Pennsylvania Dutch crafted chair, but it was really just an unpainted frame that was finished with spray and brush. The seat is hooked with a punch needle on burlap or similar backing fabric. The technique uses only a single yarn strand.

NOT QUITE HEPPLEWHITE

The "Hepplewhite landscape chair" is really based on a '50s-vintage dining chair, which provided the shape (below left). After cleaning and light sanding, it was painted with an ebony enamel. For the Hepplewhite touch, it was then decorated with decals trimmed with a manicure scissors to fit the chair frame.

Before

After

Before

After

Things are not always what they seem to be. Take that Pennsylvania Dutch chair at far left, for example, or the quilt and chest next to it. Or the Scandinavian provincial wood kitchen organizers, the Hepplewhite landscape chair, the 18th-century sewing cabinet with its rich inlays.

Sewing cabinets were familiar items in 18th-century sitting rooms, for needlework was the fashionable way for fashionable ladies of the era to spend their leisure time. The sewing cabinet at left above is a more recent model from the 1920s. Its painted-on design (above right) imitates costly ebony and burl inlays.

ALMOST ANTIQUE

For complete directions, see index on page 65.

DINING TABLE

This handsome table seats six comfortably, even for the most formal meals. It is built of common lumber, and should cost less than $70. A similar store-bought table would cost five times that.

The simple lines and natural wood of this parsons-style table make it compatible with both contemporary and traditional decor and furniture styles.

For complete directions, see index on page 65.

$60 TO $100 HOME PROJECTS

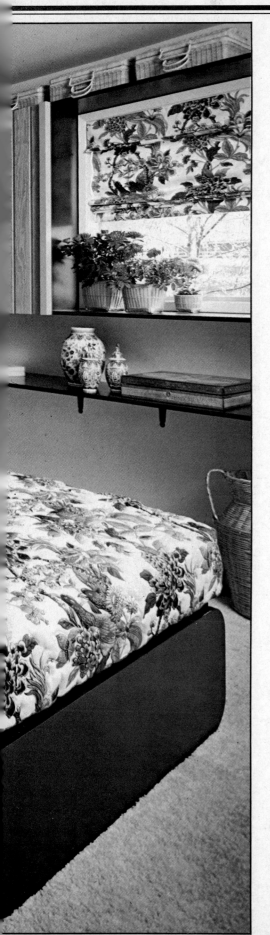

There's more than
meets the eye in
these projects—
it's storage galore.
Rollaway carts hold
most of what you need
for indoor-outdoor
entertaining. In
the bedroom, the
walls and even the
space beneath the
bed are put to work.

For complete directions, see index on page 65.

FOOD AND DRINK

In the foreground,
a complete bar cart.
Behind it is a cooking unit with two-burner liquid propane
camping stove and lots of shelves for pots, pans and dishes.

STORAGE BED

The bed has six large drawers
in its base. Quilted material
of the bedspread is also used
as a headboard. A built-in
reading light is above. Shelves
and cabinets line the walls.

Do-it-yourself projects for work (a foldaway desk), for entertaining (a table and bar) and for hobby fun (this lean-to greenhouse you can build in a weekend).

GREENHOUSE
Here's a quick and easy project for gardeners. The wood framing is permanent: vinyl glazing can be replaced every year or so when it wears. The cost is about $100.

The home-made "butcher block" top on this versatile table slides apart for access to a liquor storage bin. Open shelves at each end store glassware, and are deep enough to hold magazines and books when the bar is "closed." You can build it for about $90.

BAR/ COFFEE TABLE

HOME OFFICE

This unique desk has shelves galore to store your home office needs. The writing surface provides plenty of elbow room, and when the day's work is done it all folds neatly away. About $100.

For complete directions, see index on page 65.

Whether chessmen or lawn rakes, you need a place to store them.

GAME CHEST

This chest has compartments and drawers to store just about all your family's favorite games. This version, leather-covered, cost $68; with vinyl panels, it would be about $75.

BACKYARD SHED

This plywood and lumber storage shed looks better and costs less than the metal ones you can buy. Wide double doors will accommodate large pieces of equipment, and the wood framing allows you to attach brackets, hooks and shelving. About $100.

re are two do-it-yourself projects: one for games, the other for garden gear.

For complete directions, see index on page 65.

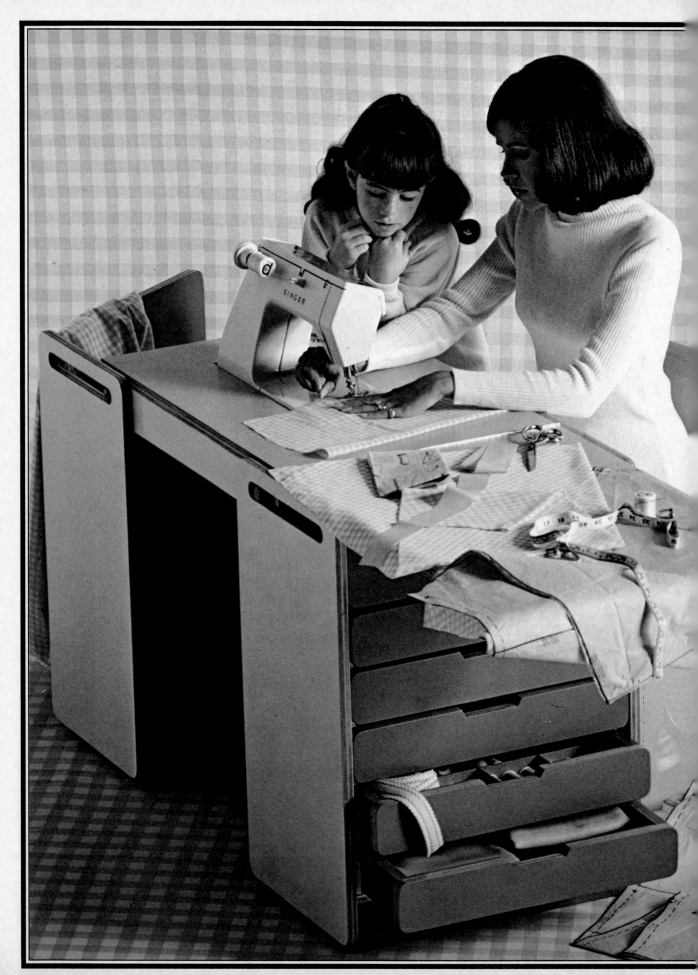

For complete directions, see index on page 65.

For people who like to *do* things—whether it's making your own clothes or cooking gourmet meals in the backyard—one of the keys to success is a convenient work unit. Try these two.

SEWING CENTER

Cramped for space? This compact but complete sewing center measures just 22″ x 30″ when closed. Open it up and it's almost 6′ wide, with a lift-up top that becomes a generous-sized cutting table. Lots of storage, too. Cost: $100.

BARBECUE

For the chef who takes outdoor cookery seriously, a sturdy, permanent barbecue is a must. This unit can be built for about $115. Although compact, it has a 20″ x 36″ cooking area, and the double-U design provides a small work surface.

$100 TO $150 HOME PROJECTS

"A place for everything," goes the hallowed household adage, and that is just what these two projects—one for the children's room and one for the dining room—are designed to provide, to keep "everything in its place."

STORAGE BUNK BED

This unique unit has one bunk on top and fits around a second, standard-size twin bed. The wardrobe section contains deep shelves and a clothes rod at children's height. Built-in cubbyholes form a ladder. You can build it for about $135.

For complete directions, see index on page 65.

COLLECTOR'S BUFFET

This stately Pennsylvania Dutch-style buffet has a removable hutch top with plate racks. Top shelf accommodates a display of large service pieces. A shelf with guard rail shows off a collection of plates. The lower shelf or cabinet top serves as a buffet.

KITCHEN EFFICIENCY

Our kitchen boasts an appliance center (on far counter in picture at right) complete with electrical outlets and storage for small portables. In the corner next to the window are pigeonhole shelves that are ideal for organizing bills, letters, stationery and other items essential to the kitchen planning and operations center.

For complete directions, see index on page 65.

A pleasant, efficient kitchen is the dream of most homemakers. Careful planning and attention to details make the dream come true. Note how all the components of this kitchen are united as a harmonious whole. Then decide which jects can be incorporated in your dream kitchen.

KITCHEN CONVENIENCE

Range island (bottom photo) has ample storage. A wine rack and stemware rack are overhead. Close-up at top left shows pull-out peg board storage. Food wrap bins (top right) keep boxes in order; knife rack stores cutlery. Photo at left shows the set-back, sit-down sink, with vegetable bins and tilt-down storage compartments.

$150 AND OVER HOME PROJECTS

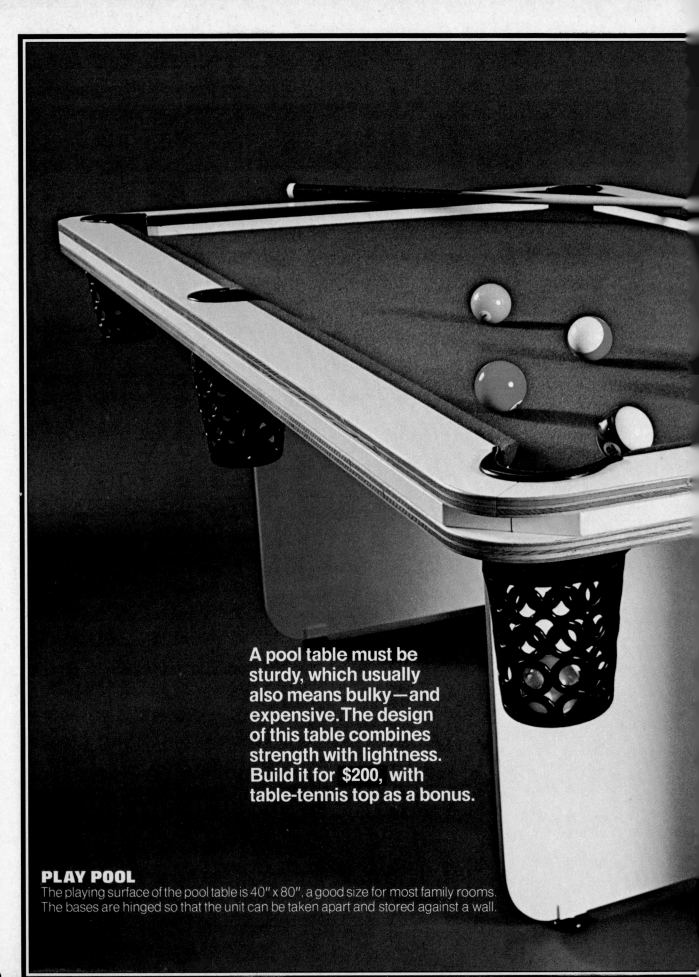

A pool table must be sturdy, which usually also means bulky—and expensive. The design of this table combines strength with lightness. Build it for $200, with table-tennis top as a bonus.

PLAY POOL
The playing surface of the pool table is 40" x 80", a good size for most family rooms. The bases are hinged so that the unit can be taken apart and stored against a wall.

For complete directions, see index on page 65.

TABLE TENNIS

The table-tennis top measures a standard 5' x 9'.
It's in sections for easy removal.

Looking for more living space? It could be right under your feet, in a finished-off basement. This one provides for activities of all members of the family, through the use of multifunctional built-ins. Materials are low-cost and easy to maintain.

BASEMENT FAMILY ROOM

Large photo shows the room set up for a party. Slide-away hobby tables are set for buffet service. Study desk at rear serves as a food counter. Detail photo at top shows how the framing hides pipes and electrical conduits. In the middle photo, cabinet behind tables is open to show hobby gear. Closet in bottom photo has movable shelves.

For complete directions, see index on page 65.

Family outdoor living
will be centered around
this large brick barbecue
with side storage and
work surfaces. When those
delicious meals are
cooked, enjoy them in
the brick "dining nook."

For complete directions, see index on page 65.

BARBECUE/TABLE/BENCH The barbecue and the table-bench unit will each cost about $175 to build.

INDEX FOR PROJECT DIRECTIONS

FINISHING PLYWOOD— EXTERIOR APPLICATIONS

TYPE OF FINISH		RECOMMENDED FOR	APPLICATION
PAINT	Acrylic Latex	Medium Density Overlaid, striated, or regular plywood panel or lap siding. Also Texture 1-11 and rough-sawn plywood.	Apply recommended non-staining primer plus two finish coats.
	Oil—Alkyd	Medium Density Overlaid.	Apply with zinc-free primer, using two or three coats (including primer). One or two coat systems as recommended by the manufacturer.
STAIN	Semi-transparent or penetrating stain	Unsanded plywood (rough-sawn and Texture 1-11).	One or two-coat systems as recommended by the manufacturer.
	Opaque or highly pigmented stain	Unsanded plywood (rough-sawn and Texture 1-11).	

Recent government restrictions on the use of lead and mercury compounds in finishes have resulted in some uncertainty regarding the performance of new paints and stains. In many cases, long-term performance information on the substitutes for lead and mercury is lacking, and results of tests in progress will not be available for some time. American Plywood Association finishing recommendations are based on experience with formulations made prior to the current restrictions. Consult supplier for interim recommendations.

GENERAL DIRECTIONS FOR WORKING WITH PLYWOOD

These general hints are designed to help you achieve the best possible results in working with plywood. They apply not only to the plans in this book, but to all projects you may undertake that include APA grade-trademarked plywood.

PLANNING: Before starting, study the plan carefully to make sure you understand all details.

MAKING LAYOUT: Following the panel layout, draw all parts on the plywood panels using a straightedge and a carpenter's square for accuracy. Use a compass to draw corner radii. Be sure to allow for saw kerf (width of cut) when plotting dimensions; if in doubt, check the width of your saw cut.

CUTTING: For hand-sawing use a 10- to 15-point tight crosscut. Support the plywood panel firmly with face up. Use a fine-toothed coping saw for curves. For inside cuts start hole with drill, then use coping or keyhole saw. For power sawing, a plywood blade gives best results, but a combination blade may be used. Place the panel face down for portable power sawing, face up for table power sawing. With first cuts, reduce panel to pieces small enough for easy handling. Use of scrap lumber underneath panel, clamped or tacked securely in place, prevents splintering on the back side. Plan to cut matching parts with same saw setting. If available, you may use a jigsaw, bandsaw or saber saw for curved cuts. In any case, be sure blade enters face of panel.

DRILLING: Support plywood firmly. For larger holes, use brace and bit. When point appears through plywood, reverse and complete hole from back. Finish slowly to avoid splintering.

PLANING: Edge grain of plywood runs in alternate directions, so plane from ends toward center. Use shallow-set blade in the plane.

SANDING: Most sanding should be confined to edges with 1-0 or finer sandpaper, before sealer or flat undercoat is applied. You may find it easier to sand cut edges smooth before assembling each unit. Plywood is sanded smooth in manufacture—one of the big time-savers in its use—so only minumum surface sanding is necessary. Use 3-0 sandpaper in direction of grain only, after sealing.

ASSEMBLY: Assemble by sections; for example, drawers, cabinet shells, compartments—any part that can be handled as an individual completed unit. Construction by section makes final assembly easier. For strongest possible joints, use a combination of glue and nails (or screws); to glue-nail, check for a good fit by holding the pieces together. Pieces should contact at all points for lasting strength. Mark nail locations along edge of piece to be nailed. In careful work where nails must be very close to an edge, you may wish to predrill using a drill bit slightly smaller than nail size. Always predrill for screws. Apply glue to clean surfaces, according to manufacturer's instructions. Press surfaces firmly together until "bead" appears, then nail, check for square, and apply clamps if possible to maintain pressure until glue sets. For exterior exposure, use resorcinol-type waterproof glue; for interior work, use liquid resin (white) or urea resin type glues. (Other glues are available for special gluing problems.)

FINISHING FOR INTERIOR USE: MDO plywood needs no preparation and is finished with conventional paints for an exceptionally smooth and durable surface. Sanded panels require very little preparation, primarily "touch sanding" (in direction of grain only) to smooth any filler or spackle applied to minor openings in the panel face or to remove blemishes. Do not paint over dust, spots of oil or glue. Any knots or pitch streaks should be touched up with sealer or shellac before painting.

Either water- or oil-base paints can be used to achieve flat, semigloss or gloss finishes. Some oil-base paints are self-priming; otherwise use recommended material for priming.

Stains may be used to obtain a natural-looking finish of plywood's grain patterns and neatly made mechanical repairs. Two methods that give pleasing results are color toning, which uses companion stains and nonpenetrating sealers, and light stain, which uses a pigmented sealer, tinting material (stain, thin enamel or undercoat) and a final finish coat (varnish or lacquer).

Whatever finishing method you use—paint or stain—always use top-quality materials, and follow manufacturer's instructions.

HOW TO BUY PLYWOOD: Plywood comes in two types: EXTERIOR for outdoor use; INTERIOR for indoor use. Within each type are grades for every job (i.e. grades with two good sides where both sides of the panel will be seen, grades with only one good side for applications where only one side will be in view in the finished job). The right grade to use for a project is given in the Materials list.

HOW TO ENLARGE PATTERNS

Draw crisscross lines, vertically and horizontally, with a ruler, on brown wrapping paper, or directly onto wood, spacing the lines as indicated. Then copy our pattern, one square at a time, using a ruler or compass. Cut out the enlarged pattern, if using paper pattern, and use as directed.

FINISHES FOR TABLES AND CUBES

(page 33)

All cubes and tables in the photo are made of unfinished wood. Cubes and small square tables measure 16″x16″x-16″; the Parsons table at center measures 16″x16″x24″. In following the directions below for various finishes, adjust all measurements to accommodate the size of your table, if different.

GIFT-WRAP CUBE

MATERIALS: One continuous roll gift-wrap paper, 36″ x 48″ (see Buyer's Guide); spray adhesive; clear plastic coating (see Buyer's Guide).

DIRECTIONS: We found that it was best to cover the top and two adjoining sides of the unfinished cube with one continuous piece of gift wrap. Cut a 16½″ strip from the full length of paper. Wrap the paper around the top and two sides of the cube, folding a ¼″ overlap around the edges. Remove paper. Cut two 16″x-16″ pieces for the remaining sides (bottom is left uncovered). Spray the cube with adhesive, following manufacturer's directions on can.

Note: When applying paper to a glued surface, use the palm of your hand to smooth out the paper, working from the center to the edges.

Glue and smooth the first long piece on the three sides (using the original creases in the paper as a guide for placement), then follow with the two end pieces which will hide the ¼″ overlap of the first piece. Stubborn air bubbles under gift-wrap may be pierced with a pin and flattened with the fingers.

For a durable finish, spray with clear plastic coating, following manufacturer's directions on the can.

LACQUER-LOOK PAINTED TABLE

MATERIALS: One can spray enamel; clear plastic spray coating (see Buyer's Guide).

DIRECTIONS: To make sure the enamel and plastic coating are compatible, ask the advice of your paint dealer. Spray the assembled table with enamel, using two coats, if necessary. Allow to dry overnight. For a glossy, lacquered look, spray with clear plastic coating.

PATCHWORK SQUARE TABLE

MATERIALS: One-half yd. each red, blue and yellow calico (see Buyer's Guide); straight pins; white glue; 1½″ paint brush; clear plastic spray coating (see Buyer's Guide).

DIRECTIONS: The calico fabric we used

is conveniently striped with a variety of prints on a single background color. By using it in three colors, we were able to cut the stripes into a large variety of 3½" patches. You can, of course, achieve the same results by using your own leftover fabric scraps. For a muted effect, consider patches in different shades of a solid color.

You will need approximately 85 patches, each 3½" square, to cover a 16"x16"x16" table. First experiment with color and pattern arrangements by pin-tacking patches on top of the assembled table, starting with the middle row. Repeat for sides and legs. Once you are satisfied with the overall placement, set the patches aside in the preferred order.

To apply patches: Mix three parts white glue with one part water. Starting with the middle row of the tabletop, apply patches, brushing table with glue as each patch is placed. Be sure they overlap slightly so that any shrinkage will not leave bare spots. For a neat finish, overlap fabric ½" at leg bottoms. Allow to dry overnight. For a durable surface, spray with a clear plastic coating.

ALUMINUM CUBE

MATERIALS: Three sheets 0.20 gauge aluminum, 24"x36" (see Buyer's Guide); 1 pint contact cement; utility knife; metal ruler or straightedge; medium grit sandpaper.

DIRECTIONS: Trace each of the sides onto the aluminum sheets and number each tracing. (Slight variations in the sides necessitate this step to make neatly joining edges). Score aluminum on the tracing lines with a utility knife and metal straightedge, making three or four passes. Bend at the cut line on worktable

edge to make a clean break.

To apply aluminum to cube: Roughen one side of each aluminum piece with sandpaper. Cover the roughened surface and the matching surface of the unfinished cube with contact cement, following directions on the container. Then, very carefully join the glued surfaces, making absolutely sure the metal is correctly positioned. Once glued, it is almost impossible to correct your mistake. Repeat for the other 4 sides. (If you do err, lacquer thinner or denatured alcohol will loosen the bond.)

CRUMPLED FOIL SQUARE TABLE

MATERIALS: One roll 18"-wide, heavy-duty aluminum foil; rolling pin; brush-on glue-glaze (see Buyer's Guide); 2" paint brush; safety-razor blade; clear plastic spray coating (see Buyer's Guide).

DIRECTIONS: Crumpling shrinks the foil, so generous excess is allowed in these measurements. To cover top and two sides, measure off 28". For remaining sides, cut two pieces each 4"x20". For legs, cut four pieces each 10"x17". In order given above, carefully crumple foil pieces individually into large, loose balls. Open carefully, but don't be alarmed if foil tears, as it is easy to mend any holes invisibly later on.

Lay the straightened larger piece on top of the unfinished table so that an equal amount overhangs at two sides. Gently press flat with a rolling pin to form interesting crinkled patterns on top and sides. (The excess at sides will be turned underneath the table later.) Remove foil, preserving contour creases.

Repeat crumpling and rolling for side pieces and legs (allowing 1" overlap at

leg bottoms). Remove foil after each piece is contoured. It is all right to overlap side, top and leg areas, as no separation shows with this kind of finish. Following label directions, brush glue-glaze on tabletop. Apply prepared foil (using the original contour creases as a guide for placement). Smooth firmly with hands or rolling pin, turning the excess underneath on two sides and letting excess overlap the other edges. Cover remaining sides and legs with glue-glaze and contoured foil, patching any torn areas with small crumpled pieces, if necessary. Trim off excess foil with a razor blade, leaving ¼" wrap-around at corners to seal the raw edges. Allow to dry overnight.

Now paint the entire table with a thin coating of glue-glaze. When dry, this provides a transparent protective finish. Optional: You may add color at this point by rubbing the table with cheesecloth dipped in any household paint. Allow to dry. For a durable finish, spray with clear plastic coating.

STRIPED SELF-ADHESIVE VINYL TABLE

MATERIALS: One yard orange self-adhesive vinyl and ½ yard white self-adhesive vinyl (see Buyer's Guide); yard-stick; safety razor blade.

DIRECTIONS: Cover the tabletop with an 18"x32" piece of white vinyl. This size allows the vinyl to extend around, then underneath the table to cover both ends (sides will be covered later). To cover the legs, cut four pieces of orange vinyl 8¼"x14½". Allow the vinyl to overlap ½" at bottom (top of vinyl should be flush with joint where leg is attached to table top). The lengthwise raw edge should be at the inside of each leg.

STACKING BOOKCASE

(page 34)

MATERIALS: Lumber: 2x6x8', two 2x6x7', three 1x12x6', 1x12x4', 13' of ¾" dowel; high-gloss brick-red enamel; ash pigmented wood stain.

DIRECTIONS for cutting:

No.	Size	Code
14	2x6x11¾"	A
8	2x6x11¼"	B
7	1x12x36"	C
38	3¾" dowels	D
4	2¼" dowels	E

Assembly: Cut and sand all pieces. In the center of each end of uprights A, drill a ¾"-dia. blind hole 1½" deep (Fig. 23). Along one side edge of each upright A, drill ¾"-dia. blind holes 1¾" deep, center 2¼" from each end (Fig. 23). Be careful to drill the holes perpendicular

to wood surface.

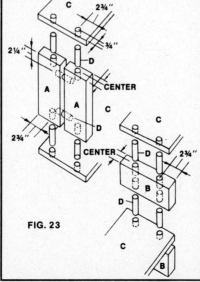

FIG. 23

In seven of the narrow uprights B, drill

¾"-dia., 1½"-deep blind holes in both long edges, centered 2¾" from each end (Fig. 23). In the remaining piece B (the end piece on the top shelf of the lower section), drill blind holes along one edge only.

Drill two ¾" holes through each end of shelves C, centered ¾" from the end and 2¾" from the long edge. Test dowel pegs in holes; they should fit snugly but easily. If too tight, taper dowel ends slightly with sandpaper.

Apply brick-red enamel to uprights A and B. Apply ash stain to shelves C and dowel pegs D and E (only a small center section of 14 of pegs D and one end of pegs E will be visible when the bookcase is assembled).

Assemble seven uprights by joining pieces A with pegs D in holes along edges of A. Assemble bookcase by stacking shelves and uprights with dowels, locking the unit together. Dowel pegs E hold top shelf in place.

TIFFANY SHADES
(page 34)

MATERIALS: Lightweight cardboard; stained glass (available from glazier or wrecking firm, or see Buyer's Guide), for large six-sided shade: 15½"x30" opaque, 15½"x2¾" opaque in contrasting color; for butterfly shade: 10"x3" clear for top wings, 12"x3" clear for bottom wings, 8½"x5" clear for bottom trim; adhesive-backed copper foil, ¼" wide (see Buyer's Guide); water-soluble flux; solid wire 64/40 solder; medium gauge copper wire (flux, solder, wire available at hardware stores); antiquing solution or patina (see Buyer's Guide).

Tools: Glass cutter (carbide-wheel preferred); pliers; household oil or kerosene; single-edged razor blades; small paintbrush; soldering iron, gun- or pencil-type; wire cutter; stiff brush (such as old toothbrush); 10" heat-proof mixing bowl (for butterfly shade only).

DIRECTIONS: As designed by Mary Doorley, the elegant Tiffany-type lampshades shown in the photo are simple enough to be made by the home craftsman. Don't let a lack of experience with glass-cutting or soldering stop you. It is easy to add these to your do-it-yourself skills.

How to cut glass: If you have never experimented with cutting glass, it is best to practice first on plain window glass. It's really quite inexpensive, and your hardware dealer may even give you some scraps on which to perfect your skill. Just remember that it's sharp stuff with which you are working, so exercise reasonable caution.

The work surface should be perfectly flat and padded with several thicknesses of newspaper. Wipe the glass clean and, if it is textured on one side (as is some stained glass), lay it smooth side up on the work surface. Measure and mark the cutting line with a grease pencil or felt-tip pen, or place a cardboard pattern on the glass (more on this later). Glass, once scored, will break in a continuing line, so when you are cutting irregular shapes, such as trapezoids or curves, first cut the glass and break into straight strips, then make the slanting or curved cuts in the straight strips.

Lightly lubricate the cutting wheel of the glass cutter with household oil or kerosene. Hold the cutter in an upright position with your thumb behind it and the handle between your index and middle fingers. If you find this awkward, hold it as you would a pencil. Firmly hold a ruler or other straightedge along the cutting line and draw the cutter toward you across the glass, starting at one edge and bearing down so that you hear a slight crunching sound. Maintain even pressure and do not make more than one pass over the same area. After scoring, place the glass so that the cut line overhangs the edge of the worktable and lightly tap the underside of the cut with the handle of the glass cutter. Now place the cut line directly over the table edge and snap off the excess glass.

If the portion to be broken off is too small to allow you to grasp it firmly, or if it is irregularly shaped, hold the larger section tightly along the cut line. Grasp the narrow section to be broken off with blunt-nosed pliers and twist downward, snapping along the scored line.

How to solder: With scissors or single-edge razor blade, cut adhesive-backed copper foil strips to fit around the rim of each glass piece, allowing a ¼" overlap where foil ends meet. Center the foil on the edges of the glass, folding it down evenly over each side, and smooth it by rubbing with the side of a pencil. Use a razor blade to trim away the excess foil at the corners.

Protect your work surface with an old cutting board or a piece of scrap lumber. You can use either a gun-type or pencil-type soldering iron, with a medium-fine tip. If the iron is new, you must first "tin" the tip. Simply let it heat up for a few minutes, then brush on some flux with the small paintbrush. Touch the iron to the solder and coat the tip until it is completely covered.

Brush flux along the full length of the foil, coating it completely. Heat the iron (this takes only a few seconds). Starting at one end, touch the tip of the iron to the foil (it should be hot enough to cause the flux to "spit"). Next touch the solder to the heated foil so that it liquefies. Move the iron slowly along the foil, with the solder following immediately so that the solder flows on smoothly, covering the foil with a neat band. When you have finished one side, allow the solder to cool, then turn the glass over and solder the other side and the edge. After the soldering is completed, gently scrub any flux residue from the glass. (Flux that is not removed can corrode the copper later on.)

To join two pieces together, simply touch the iron to the already soldered edges and fill in the joint with additional solder, using the same technique. With a little practice, you will be ready to tackle our Tiffany-type lampshades.

Making the shades: The large six-sided shade with its geometric design measures 15½" at the base, is 5½" high, and also has a built-in mounting to fit over the "harp" of a table lamp base. The 9"-wide butterfly shade fits over a globe lamp to make a hanging fixture.

Whichever shade you are making, first cut cardboard patterns for all glass pieces following the patterns (see Fig. 24). Arrange the cardboard patterns on the glass to minimize wastage, then cut all glass pieces. Apply copper foil and solder all edges.

How to assemble the large, six-sided shade: Again, the panels are individually assembled. Solder bottom pieces C and D together (Fig. 24), then add pieces E and F and piece G. Solder each seam on both sides.

Lay two of the completed panels edge to edge and lightly solder together at top and bottom. Carefully lift the two panels with the top end up and bend the joint to the approximate final form. Prop the panels upright, then add remaining panels one at a time, lightly soldering each joint at top and bottom. With all panels "tacked" together, correct where necessary to form the hexagonal shape, then

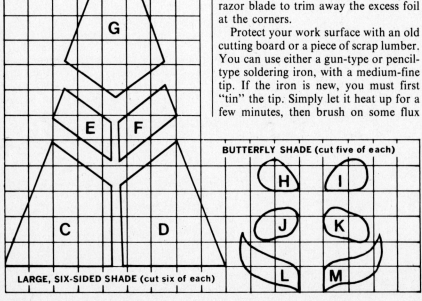

FIG. 24

G

E F

C D

BUTTERFLY SHADE (cut five of each)

H I

J K

L M

LARGE, SIX-SIDED SHADE (cut six of each)

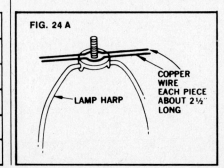

FIG. 24 A

LAMP HARP

COPPER WIRE EACH PIECE ABOUT 2½" LONG

complete soldering the outside of each seam. Cut a length of wire and shape it to fit inside the top opening; solder in place as a reinforcement. Lay the shade on its side and shape another wire to reinforce the bottom. Solder it in place, then solder all inside seams.

Cut two 2½″ lengths of copper wire; shape them (Fig. 24A), inserting a pencil between the wires to help form the center loop. Solder the wires together, then solder in place across the top opening of the shade. See Antique Finish directions below.

How to assemble the butterfly shade: Assemble each of the five butterflies by arranging wing pieces H, I, J, K as they will appear in the shade (see Fig. 24) and very lightly soldering the four pieces together. Gently curve each butterfly by pressing it against the side of the 10″ mixing bowl. With masking tape, hold one butterfly in position against the bowl, then solder a second one to it. Continue around the shade until all butterflies are soldered together.

Assemble each of the five chevrons that trim the bottom of the shade by lightly soldering pieces L and M together. Curve the chevrons by pressing them gently against the bowl, then solder to the bottom tips of the butterfly wings and to each other. Complete all outside soldering, then lift the shade off the bowl and solder inside joints.

Cut five 3″ lengths of copper wire and bend to form antennae for the butterflies. Coat with solder, then solder in place. Finish, as below.

Antique Finish:
First make sure that all flux residue is removed by scrubbing the shade gently with household cleanser. Rinse thoroughly and allow to dry. Apply patina or antiquing to the solder with a stiff brush, working it in until it becomes a rich bronze color. If it turns a filmy pink, flux is still on the surface. Scrub again and reapply patina until you are satisfied with the color. Then rinse away excess patina and dry the surface.

PICTURE FRAMES

(page 35)

DOUBLE GLASS/WOOD MOLDING PHOTO HOLDERS

MATERIALS: ¾″ ¼-round molding; 1″ ¼-round molding; ¼″ lattice; sandpaper; spray enamel; window glass; self-adhering felt paper (see Buyer's Guide); white glue.

You can purchase glass cut to size at most hardware stores. To cut it yourself, buy a cutting wheel (under $1). Hold a straightedge firmly along the cutting line and score the glass in a continuous smooth stroke. Place the scored line over a dowel or table edge and snap the glass. Remove raw edges with an oilstone dipped in water.

DIRECTIONS: To make the smaller of the frames, first cut two pieces of ¾″ ¼-round molding and two pieces of 1″ ¼-round molding slightly longer than the width of the picture to be framed. (Or you can make several of these frames at one time by cutting longer lengths, and trimming them to individual sizes after assembly.) Use a sharp knife to cut from a ¼″ lattice two strips the same length as the molding. On a piece of wax paper, glue one lattice strip between the two ¾″ (cap) moldings, the other between the two 1″ (base) moldings. Allow to dry, then cut to the width of the picture (this may be done using the 90-degree slots in the miter box). Sand and spray-paint the desired color (do not paint the underside of the larger assembly). Attach self-adhering felt to the bottom of the base frame. Place photograph between two pieces of window glass cut to the same size as the photograph. Slip the glass into the bottom frame piece; slip on the top piece.

The larger molding frame (center) is similar. Cut 2 pieces of the 1″ ¼-round molding at least 2½″ longer than the picture width, and 2 pieces of the ¾″ ¼-round at least 2″ longer. Cut two pieces of ¼″x1⅛″ lattice to the same lengths. To make a slot for the double-glass inserts, notch the centers of the lattice strips the width of the picture (plus ¹⁄₁₆″) to within ¼″ of the edges. Score across bottom of cut and break out center section (see Fig. 25). Assemble moldings and lattice with glue on wax paper, as for smaller frame.

When dry, cut off the larger (base) piece 1⅛″ outside of the slot at each end; cut the smaller (cap) piece off ⅞″ outside of the notch on each end (see Fig. 25). Use a sharp knife to trim off excess lattice.

Place each assembly in a vise and sand ends to a curve. An orbital sander will do the job quickly, but you can do as well with a sanding block and some elbow grease. When shaped, paint as above, apply felt base, insert glass and the photograph.

PLASTIC PHOTO FRAMES

MATERIALS: Reusable plastic household boxes (shown in photo are an eyelash box at top, and a razor case at bottom); cardboard.

DIRECTIONS: Cut the photo to fit snugly into the lid of the plastic box. Cut and fold a boxlike cardboard insert to fit the interior of the bottom of box, deep enough to hold the photo in the lid snugly in place.

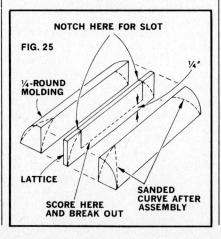

NOTCH HERE FOR SLOT
FIG. 25
¼-ROUND MOLDING
¼″
LATTICE
SCORE HERE AND BREAK OUT
SANDED CURVE AFTER ASSEMBLY

POTTING TABLE

(page 35)

MATERIALS: ⅝″ Ext. DFPA grade-trademarked roughsawn plywood siding, one 24¼″ x 72″, one 8½″ x 70¾″, two 14″ x 18″; one 2x4x12′; four 1x6x10′; thirteen 1x4x7′; one 1x1x3′; four No. 10 (1¼″) flat head wood screws; galvanized nails, as on drawing.

Note: The lumber specified above is WWP fir.

CUTTING DIRECTIONS: 2x4: Four 33¼″; 1x6; Four 72″, four 24½″; 1x4: Thirty-nine 26″; 1x1: Two 14″; cut curves in front edge of 14″ x 18″ plywood sides, as indicated in the drawing, narrowing them to 8½″ at the top.

To assemble: Nail 1x6 shelf and top supports to 2x4 legs, making sure the assembly is perfectly square. Use 5d galvanized box nails to fasten 1x4 shelving strips to lower supports, then top supports. Nail plywood sides of upper unit to top. Nail on plywood back. Predrill holes and screw 1x1 cleats ⅝″ in from back and each end of bench top. Nail top assembly to cleats.

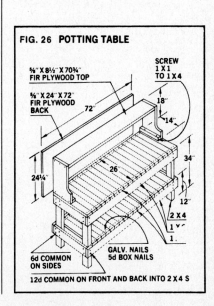

FIG. 26 POTTING TABLE
⅝″ X 8½″ X 70¾″ FIR PLYWOOD TOP
⅝″ X 24″ X 72″ FIR PLYWOOD BACK
SCREW 1 X 1 TO 1 X 4
72″
18″
14″
34″
26″
24¼″
12″
2 X 4
1″
6d COMMON ON SIDES
GALV. NAILS 5d BOX NAILS
12d COMMON ON FRONT AND BACK INTO 2 X 4 S

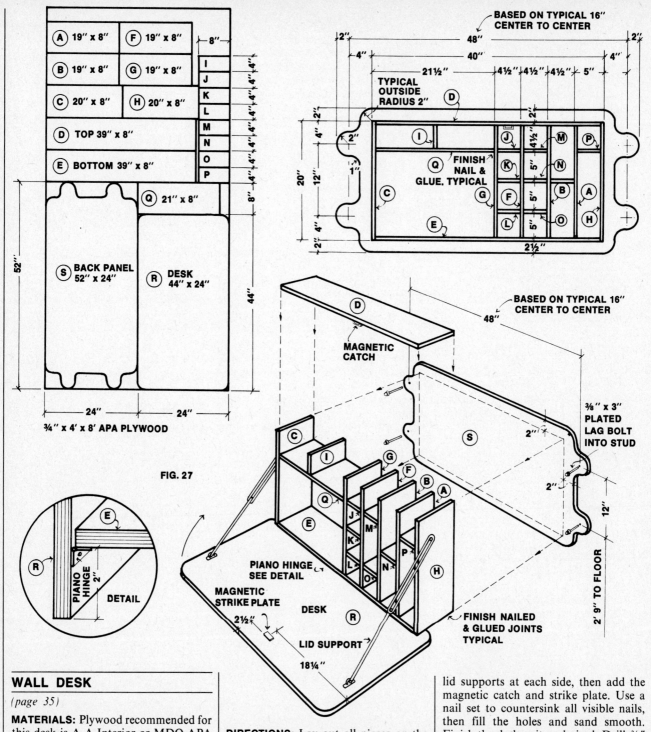

FIG. 27

WALL DESK

(page 35)

MATERIALS: Plywood recommended for this desk is A-A Interior or MDO APA grade-trademarked plywood. You will need one ½"x4'x8' panel. You will also need 1 pair 8" to 12" long chrome-plated lid supports; one 39" chrome- or cadmium-plated piano hinge; 6 No. 4 1¼" flat head wood screws; four ⅜"x3" cadmium-plated lag bolts; 1 each magnetic catch and strike plate; 8d finishing nails; glue (we used the urea resin type); filler for countersunk nail holes and for filling small gaps in cut edges; fine sandpaper; finishing material (paint, stain, etc); 16"x36" "suede finish" plastic laminate with corners rounded to 2" radius for desk surface (optional).

DIRECTIONS: Lay out all pieces on the plywood panel and mark for identification. Cut out and smooth edges, following the General Directions for working with plywood on page 66.

With glue and nails, fasten sides C and H to top D and bottom E. Make sure the frame is square, then glue to back S. Drill pilot holes through S and drive 1¼" screws through S into the frame, one each into C and H and two each into D and E. Assemble partitions and shelves inside the frame with glue and nails, being careful to keep the assembly square. With the piano hinge, fasten desk R to bottom E (see detail). Attach lid supports at each side, then add the magnetic catch and strike plate. Use a nail set to countersink all visible nails, then fill the holes and sand smooth. Finish the desk unit as desired. Drill ⅜" holes through the four tabs on back S. The 48" spacing will work on conventional 16" stud spacing or on 24" spacing. Find the positions of studs within the wall either with a magnetic stud finder, or by tapping on the wall (a hollow sound indicates a between-stud space, a solid thump means a stud), or, if all else fails, by drilling several "trial and error" holes through the wall behind where the desk will be hung until you locate a stud. Hang the desk on the wall with four lag bolts driven into the studs. Make sure it is level against the wall before tightening the lags.

COMPOST BINS

(page 35)

MATERIALS: (three bins): ⅝″ Ext. APA grade-trademarked roughsawn plywood siding, two 4′x8′ polyethylene sheets (for added life).

DIRECTIONS: Cut six 24″ x 32″ pieces from each plywood panel. In one 32″ edge of each piece, cut 12″-deep slots 2″ in from each end, slightly wider than ⅝″. Drill 1″ holes in each piece to let air enter for the decomposition process. Assemble the bins by slotting the pieces together. Make sure that the slots on the front piece are on the bottom so that it can be raised to allow access to the compost material. For added plywood life, line the bins with polyethylene sheet; punch holes in the polyethylene sides for air and in the bottom for drainage.

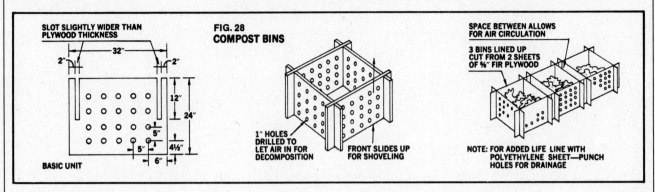

FIG. 28 COMPOST BINS

SLOT SLIGHTLY WIDER THAN PLYWOOD THICKNESS

32″ — 2″ — 2″ — 12″ — 24″ — 5″ — 5″ — 4½″ — 6″

BASIC UNIT

1″ HOLES DRILLED TO LET AIR IN FOR DECOMPOSITION

FRONT SLIDES UP FOR SHOVELING

SPACE BETWEEN ALLOWS FOR AIR CIRCULATION

3 BINS LINED UP CUT FROM 2 SHEETS OF ⅝″ FIR PLYWOOD

NOTE: FOR ADDED LIFE LINE WITH POLYETHYLENE SHEET—PUNCH HOLES FOR DRAINAGE

PLANT STAND

(page 36)

Our planter is 24″ tall, and is designed to accommodate a pot and saucer up to 8″ across the bottom; if you wish to adjust these dimensions to suit your own purposes, change the materials requirements accordingly.

MATERIALS: Plywood recommended for the stand is ¾″ A-A Interior or MDO APA grade-trademarked. You will need a piece at least 2′x2′x8½″, or four pieces 2′x8″ each, with face grain running along the 2′ dimension in either case. You should be able to find these in the "odd-lot" bin at your building supply dealer's. You will also need: 7″ length of 1x1 lumber; four ¼″x3″ cadmium-plated machine bolts with nuts and washers; four plastic furniture glides; fine sandpaper and paint or stain.

DIRECTIONS: Lay out one of the legs, following the drawing. Cut it out with a saber saw or compass saw. (See General Directions for working with plywood, page 66). Using the first leg as a pattern, cut out three more legs. Sand all edges smooth. Temporarily tack the 1x1 core to one of the legs, then drill a ¼″ hole through the leg, the 1x1 and the opposite leg. Repeat with the other two legs. Assemble the legs and core with bolts, washers and nuts. Apply desired finish. Tap on furniture glides.

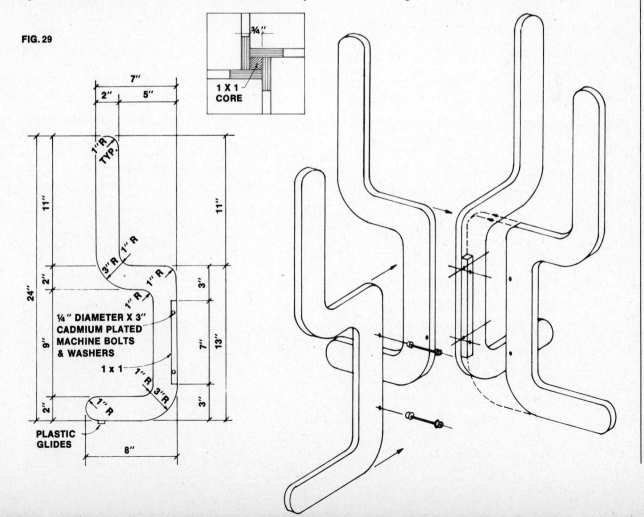

FIG. 29

¾″

1 X 1 CORE

7″ — 2″ — 5″

1″ R TYP.

11″ — 11″

3″ R — 1″ R — 1″ R

2″ — 3″

1″ R

24″ — ¼″ DIAMETER X 3″ CADMIUM PLATED MACHINE BOLTS & WASHERS — 7″ — 13″

1 x 1 — 1″ R — 3″ R

9″

2″ — 1″ R — 3″

PLASTIC GLIDES

8″

DESK AND RECORD FILE

(page 36)

MATERIALS: The plywood recommended for this project is A-A or A-B Interior or MDO APA grade-trademarked plywood. You will need two ¾"x4'x8' panels. Other materials are: 9' of ¼" diameter dowel; glue (we used a urea resin type) for installing pegs and storage spacers (these include Parts 1 through 16); wood filler for filling exposed plywood edges; fine sandpaper for smoothing cut edges; paint or stain as desired to finish desk.

DIRECTIONS: Make layout as shown on plywood panels; cut pieces following General Directions for working with plywood (see page 66). Cut slots in pieces 18, 19, 20, 28 and 29 by first drilling ¾" holes in the corners, then using a compass saw or saber saw to remove the wood. Sand insides of slots smooth.

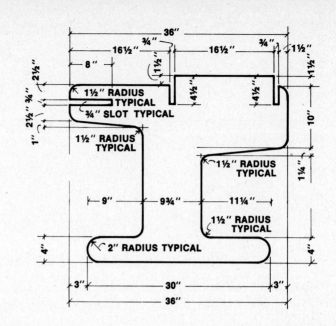

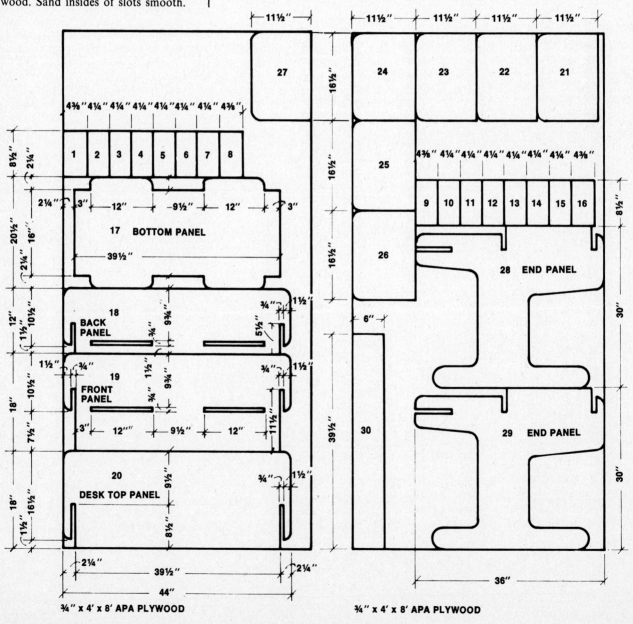

¾" x 4' x 8' APA PLYWOOD   ¾" x 4' x 8' APA PLYWOOD

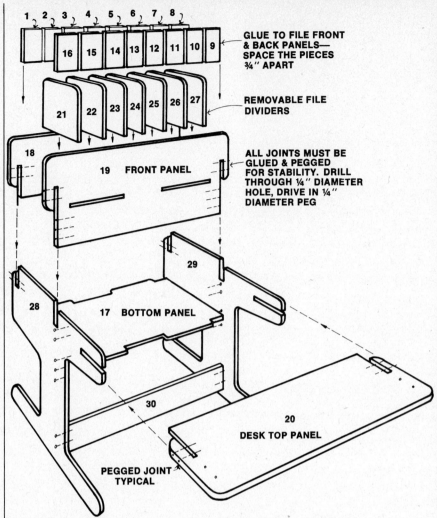

GLUE TO FILE FRONT
& BACK PANELS—
SPACE THE PIECES
¾" APART

REMOVABLE FILE
DIVIDERS

ALL JOINTS MUST BE
GLUED & PEGGED
FOR STABILITY. DRILL
THROUGH ¼" DIAMETER
HOLE, DRIVE IN ¼"
DIAMETER PEG

18

19 FRONT PANEL

29

28   17 BOTTOM PANEL

30

20
DESK TOP PANEL

PEGGED JOINT
TYPICAL

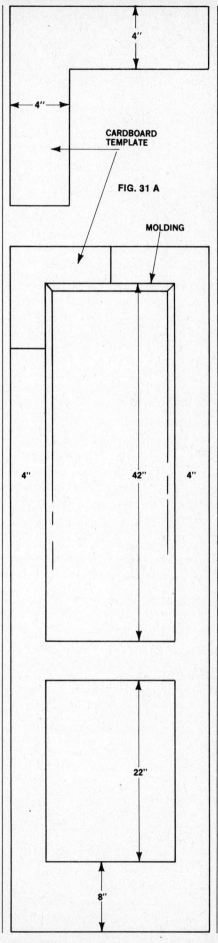

4"

4"

CARDBOARD
TEMPLATE

FIG. 31 A

MOLDING

4"   42"   4"

22"

8"

To assemble: Fit panel 19 into slots on ends 28 and 29. Place panel 17 into slots in 19, then fit back panel 18 over tabs on 17 and into slots on end panels. Secure the assembly by drilling ¼" holes 4" deep through end panels and front and back panels, placing a small amount of glue in each hole and driving ¼" dowels into them. Cut off dowels flush with the surface, using a fine-tooth saw or sharp chisel. Similarly attach lower brace (30) 2" above the bottom edges of ends 28 and 29. Fit desk top panel 20 into slots on end panels. Drill ¼"-diameter holes 4" deep through the top edges of end panels and through the desk top; glue in dowels. Drill through edges of desk top and end panels and glue in dowels. Glue pieces 1 and 8 to back panel 18, tight against the end panels. Similarly, glue pieces 9 and 16 to the front panel. Glue intermediate pieces 2 through 7 and 10 through 15 to front and back panels, spacing them ¾" apart. Insert removable file dividers 21-27 as needed. (Dividers can be shifted whenever different slot widths are needed.)
To finish: Sand the finished unit smooth and apply paint or stain as desired.

DIVIDER SCREEN

(page 38)

MATERIALS (for five panels): Five 24"x80" flush doors; ten 8' lengths 1⅛" base cap molding (attached to one side of doors only); 1" brads; fine sandpaper; two qts. red satin gloss enamel (see Buyer's Guide); one pt. semi-transparent stain (see Buyer's Guide); four 2"x2" butt hinges; four 1¼"x2" double-acting hinges; ¾" flat head wood screws for hinges; 10 furniture glides.

DIRECTIONS: Sand door surfaces and roll on two coats of enamel, sanding lightly between coats. Make all molding cuts in a miter box, angling the molding face 45° inward (see detail below) from

45° ANGLE

**MOLDING DETAIL
FIG. 31**

each 8' length, cut one 42", one 22" and two 16" pieces. Sand the molding (but not the mitered ends). Place the pieces across strips of scrap lumber and apply stain, following manufacturer's directions. Allow doors and molding to dry thoroughly.

Fastening Molding: Make a cardboard template as a guide for fastening molding (Fig. 31A). Attach top molding pieces first, using brads and a brad driver, then move down template and attach lower pieces. Connect doors with hinges screwed to door edges, 4″ from the top and 8″ from the bottom (see Fig. 31B). Use butt hinges between first

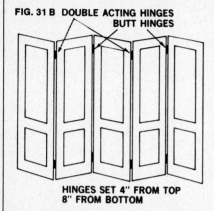

FIG. 31 B DOUBLE ACTING HINGES
BUTT HINGES

HINGES SET 4″ FROM TOP
8″ FROM BOTTOM

pair of doors on the left, double-acting hinges between the second and third doors, then butts again and double-acting between the two doors on the right. Tap glides onto door bottoms, making sure all are even.

ENGLISH BUTLER'S TABLE

(page 38)

MATERIALS: ½″x4′x8′ panel of A-A or A-B Interior or MDO APA grade-trade-marked plywood; 7′ of 2x2 lumber; 5′ of 1x2 lumber; four pair spring-lock hinges

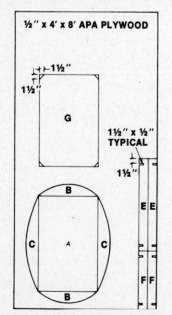

½″ x 4′ x 8′ APA PLYWOOD

1½″
1½″
G
1½″ x ½″ **TYPICAL**
1½″
B
C   A   C
B
E E
F F

(see Buyer's Guide); four furniture glides; glue (urea resin type is best); surfacing putty; fine sandpaper; stain, paint or antiquing materials.

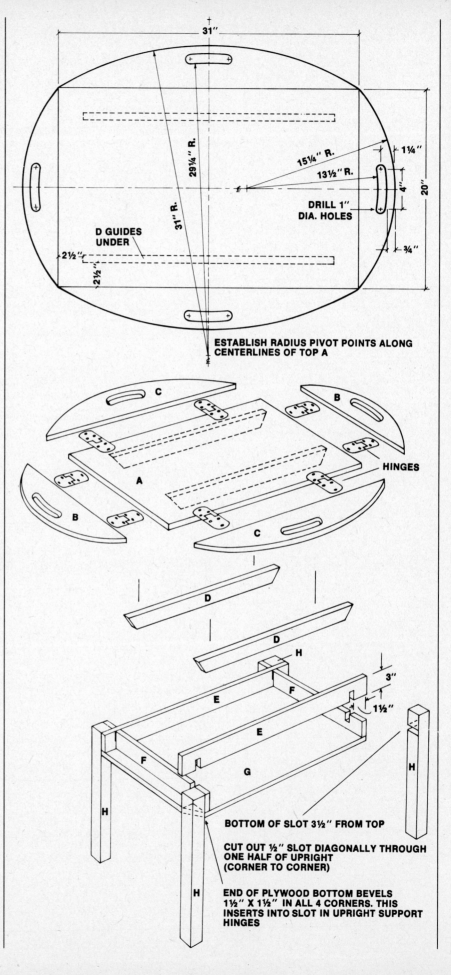

31″

29¼″ R.

15¼″ R.
13½″ R.
1¼″
4″
20″

31″ R.

DRILL 1″ DIA. HOLES

¾″

D GUIDES UNDER

2½″
2½″

ESTABLISH RADIUS PIVOT POINTS ALONG CENTERLINES OF TOP A

C
B
HINGES
A
B
C
B

D
D
H
3″
F
E
1½″
E
F
G
H
H
H

BOTTOM OF SLOT 3½″ FROM TOP

CUT OUT ½″ SLOT DIAGONALLY THROUGH ONE HALF OF UPRIGHT (CORNER TO CORNER)

END OF PLYWOOD BOTTOM BEVELS 1½″ X 1½″ IN ALL 4 CORNERS. THIS INSERTS INTO SLOT IN UPRIGHT SUPPORT HINGES

DIRECTIONS—Cutting:

Quantity	Size (inches)	Use	Code
Plywood			
1	20x31	tray	A
2	3¾x20	tray ends	B
2	4¼x31	tray sides	C
2	3x30	table sides	E
2	3x19	table ends	F
1	19x30	table bottom	G
Lumber			
2	1x2x26″	tray guides	D
4	2x2x18½″	legs	H

Cut ½″-wide x 1½″-deep notches in pieces E and F, as shown in the panel layout drawing. Use a saber saw or compass saw to curve the outer edges of pieces B and C, as shown in the top view. Cut handle openings in pieces B and C, as shown in top view, by drilling 1″ holes at each end, then removing the wood between the holes with a saber saw or keyhole saw. Cut the ends of guides D at a 30-degree angle (see the exploded drawing) so that they fit easily between the table ends. Cut ½″-wide diagonal slots halfway through legs H (see exploded drawing) with the bottoms of the slots 3½″ below the tops of legs H. Smooth and fill all rough plywood edges, following the General Directions for working with plywood on page 66. **To assemble:** Glue legs H to bottom G, then glue ends F to G and H and sides E to G, legs H and slots in F. Make sure all pieces are perfectly true and square, and wipe off any excess glue that may squeeze out. Clamp together and allow glue to dry, following manufacturer's directions. Mark locations of hinges on pieces A, B and C. With a sharp chisel, carefully cut away the plywood to mortise the hinges flush with the surface. Fasten the hinges to A with wood screws, then fasten sides C and ends B. Mark the locations of guides D on the bottom of A and glue in place. Make sure the guides clear ends F and sides E. When all glue has dried thoroughly, sand any rough spots and apply paint or stain as desired.

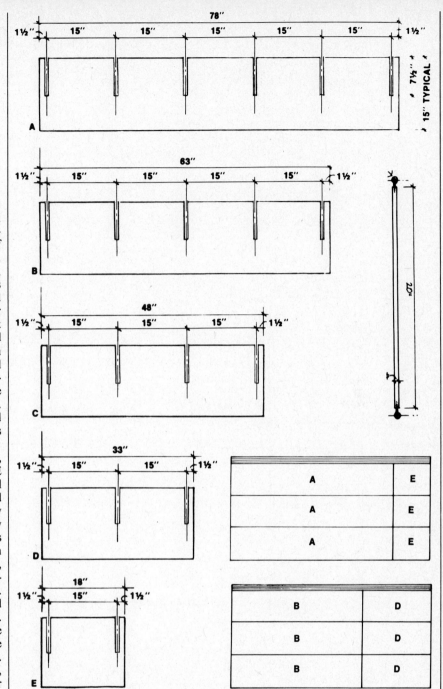

SLOT-TOGETHER BOOKCASE / DESK

(page 39)
This unique system of slot-together modules can be adapted to a number of different configurations, depending on your needs and the available space. Some possibilities are shown in the drawings, along with the number of each size module required. For the unit shown on page 39, three each of modules A, B, D and E were used.

Diagonal braces make a sturdy free-standing unit. If it is built against a wall, these braces are not required. Instead,

metal angles can be screwed to the shelves or uprights and fastened to the wall studs with 1¼″ or 1½″ wood screws.

MATERIALS (for the 78″-high x 63″-wide unit shown in photo): Two ½″x4′x 8′ panels of MDO plywood; 18′ of ⅜″ hardwood dowel; 20 screw eyes, 1″ to 1¼″ long with ⅛″ eyes; eleven ⅛″x1½″ hanger bolts, washers, wing nuts; sandpaper; wood filler; paint or stain.

DIRECTIONS: Cut pieces A,B,D and E as shown in panel layouts. Using a stationary power saw, saber saw of

finetooth hand saw, cut 7½″-deep slots in pieces as shown in the drawing, slightly wider than ½″ to allow for paint thickness. Do not cut slots where they will not be needed, as in the desk top portion of one piece B, and the flanking upright A (see drawing). Fill plywood edges and sand smooth before finishing.

Slot together the unit. To install diagonal braces, drill ³/₃₂″ holes 1″ deep at appropriate points in the plywood (see drawing). Screw hanger bolts into the holes. Cut 20″ lengths of dowel, the insert scew eyes into each end. Place screw eyes over washers on the hanger bolts, and secure with wing nuts.

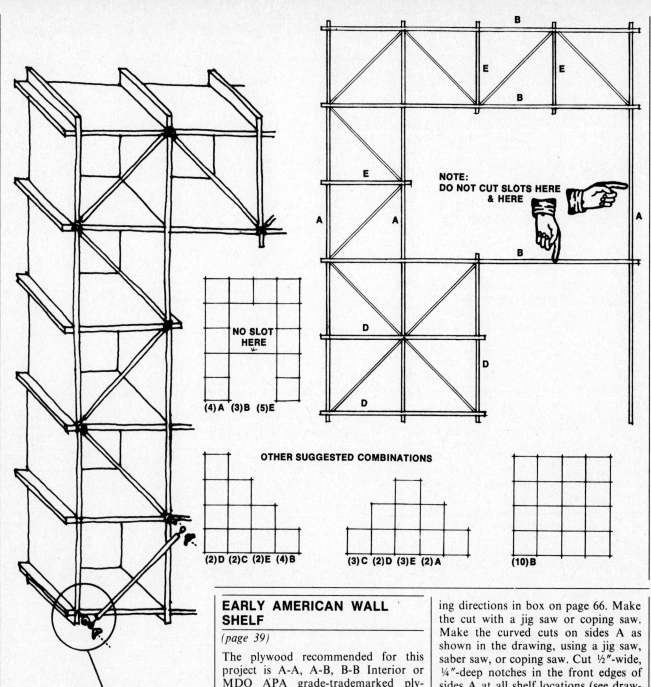

NO SLOT HERE

(4) A (3) B (5) E

NOTE: DO NOT CUT SLOTS HERE & HERE

OTHER SUGGESTED COMBINATIONS

(2) D (2) C (2) E (4) B

(3) C (2) D (3) E (2) A

(10) B

← PLYWOOD

HANGER BOLT

EARLY AMERICAN WALL SHELF

(page 39)

The plywood recommended for this project is A-A, A-B, B-B Interior or MDO APA grade-trademarked plywood.

MATERIALS: One panel ½"x4'x4' plywood; 8' of ½"x½" trim; four 1⅛"-diameter wood balls; 4d finishing nails; glue (a urea-resin type is best); surfacing putty for filling countersunk nail holes and rough edges; fine sandpaper; paint or stain for finishing.

DIRECTIONS: Cut plywood in the following sizes. See General Directions for working with plywood on page 66:
A—(ends) 2 pcs. ½"x8"x30"
B—(back) 1 pc. ½"x23"x32½"
C—(shelves) 2 pcs. ½"x7¼"x23"
D—(shelves) 2 pcs. ½"x5"x23"
Note: To cut piece B (back), enlarge and trace curved decorative pattern follow-

ing directions in box on page 66. Make the cut with a jig saw or coping saw. Make the curved cuts on sides A as shown in the drawing, using a jig saw, saber saw, or coping saw. Cut ½"-wide, ¼"-deep notches in the front edges of sides A at all shelf locations (see drawing). To assemble: Use glue and finishing nails. Fasten ends A to back B. Glue-nail lower shelves C and upper shelves D in place. Make sure the assembly is in square; clamp together until glue dries.

Countersink all visible nail heads and fill holes; sand smooth. Cut 24" lengths of ½"x½" trim strip and glue in place as shelf facing (E on drawing). Glue wood balls (F) in corners beneath the bottom shelf. Apply paint or stain as desired. We finished our shelf unit by applying a coat of red maple stain, then wiping it off with a soft cloth when we achieved the desired tone. We then applied a coat of clear shellac, let it dry and rubbed the surface with fine steel wool. This was followed by two coats of varnish, with a fine sanding between coats.

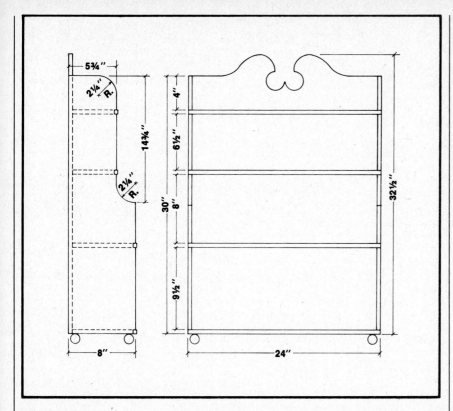

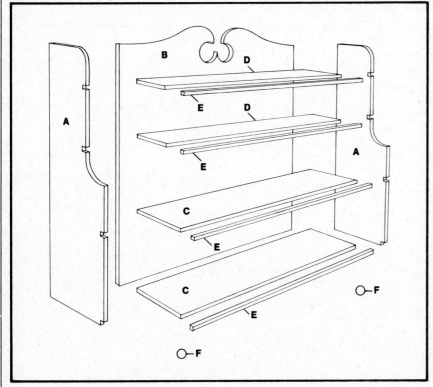

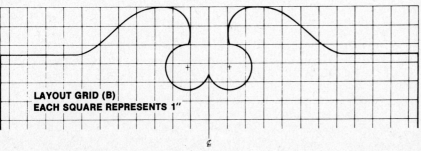

LAYOUT GRID (B)
EACH SQUARE REPRESENTS 1"

HOME OFFICE/SECRETARY
(page 39)

This unit can be built against any wall, and fastened to vertical 2x2's that are, in turn, fastened to wall studs, or it could be fastened directly to the wall by means of metal angles screwed to the inner surfaces of the sides.

MATERIALS: 4'x8' sheet of ¾" MDO plywood (see cutting diagram, Fig. 35); v.g. fir: two 1x4x46½" (F), two 1x2x16" (G); white glue; 6d finishing nails; 46½" continuous hinge with screws; wood putty to fill nail holes.

FIG. 35 CUTTING DIAGRAM

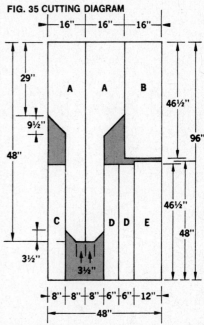

DIRECTIONS: Cut all plywood pieces as in Fig. 35. With glue and nails driven through the sides, attach shelf B to sides A, with its top 29" from the bottom edges of A. Similarly attach shelf C, with its top 9½" above B. Attach shelves D, spacing them equally between C and the top edges of sides A (Fig. 35A, p. 78).

Cut ⅞"-wide notches 1½" deep, center 9" from each end of trim and slider supports F (see Fig. 35A). Glue and nail in place between sides A and below shelf B; the front strip should be recessed ½" from the front edges of A, while the inner support strip is centered 8" from the front edges of A. Drive a nail into the edge of each desk support G, ¼" from one end, allowing the nail to protrude ½". Slide desk supports through slider support notches in pieces F, with the protruding nails behind the inner support strip (Fig. 35A).

Fasten the unit to the wall as noted above. Use a level to make sure the sides are perfectly plumb.

Fasten desk top E to shelf B with continuous hinge. Countersink all nails and fill holes. Sand before finishing.

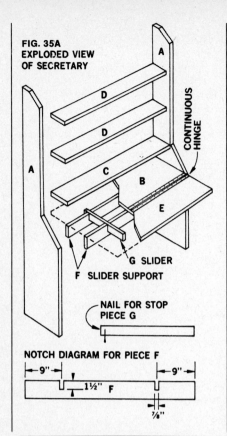

FIG. 35A EXPLODED VIEW OF SECRETARY

A

D

D

A

C

B

E

CONTINUOUS HINGE

G SLIDER

F SLIDER SUPPORT

NAIL FOR STOP PIECE G

NOTCH DIAGRAM FOR PIECE F

|← 9" →| |← 9" →|

1½" F

⅞"

BRICK WALKWAY

(page 39)

MATERIALS: (per each 16"x16" square): 8 solid, uncored bricks, 4"x8"x2¼"; one 1x4x6' piece of wood; 5d galvanized box nails; pentachlorophenol or other wood preservative; sand; cement.

DIRECTIONS: Cut four 16¾" lengths of 1x4. Soak the pieces in wood preservative before nailing them together to form a square frame, as shown in Fig. 36. Excavate the area where the "stepping stone" will be set to a depth of 3½", 16¾" square. Set the frame into the excavation, making sure it is level and flush with the surface of the ground. Spread 1" of sand in the excavation, then add ¼" of cement and mix thoroughly with the sand. Use a short straight-edge to level the mixture inside the frame; tamp the sand-cement base firmly. Lay the bricks in the pattern desired (see drawing). Add sand where necessary to raise bricks flush with the top of the frame; where bricks are above the frame, scrape away some of the sand-cement base beneath. When all bricks are in place, sweep sand over the surface to fill

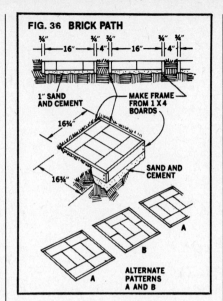

FIG. 36 BRICK PATH

¾" 16" ¾" ¾" 4" 16" ¾" ¾"

1" SAND AND CEMENT

MAKE FRAME FROM 1 X 4 BOARDS

16¾"

16¾"

SAND AND CEMENT

A

B

A

ALTERNATE PATTERNS A AND B

the joints, then sweep clean. Spray with a fine stream of water to compact the sand (but be careful not to flood the surface and force out the sand).

After the final frost of winter, check the brickwork squares for level. Scrape out or fill in beneath, as necessary, to compensate for cold-weather heaving.

CHAIR SLIPCOVER

(page 40)

Many a has-been chair or sofa has been salvaged by means of the simple slipcover. Now, you can make slipcovers that fit as you never dreamed possible—thanks to the three-way stretch of polyester double knits. The stretch factor simplifies fitting and stitching, as in the cover shown in photo, which is made without bulky openings. You simply ease it onto the chair. Once in place, the slipcover "relaxes" and hugs the contours—giving an appearance barely discernible from an upholstered piece. Though good quality double knits (they must be polyester) may seem expensive, their generous width (usually 60" or 63") means fewer yards are required. Also, welting, if used, is cut not on the bias, but on the crosswise grain (which has the greatest stretch). This saves on fabric and time, and cuts cost.

MATERIALS: Follow the directions below for measurement of chair and refer to fabric layout diagram to determine amount of fabric needed. Our slipcover fabric is polyester by Celanese.

To Measure Chair
Figs. 37A, B and C—Take measurements as shown, using the seams of the original chair covering as your guide. To allow for the stretch factor in polyester double knit, subtract ¾" from both length and width of all pieces except arm strips and

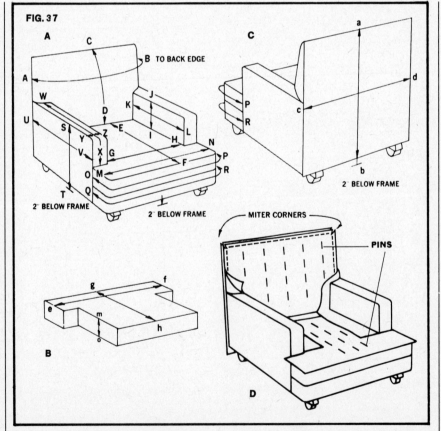

FIG. 37

2" BELOW FRAME

MITER CORNERS

PINS

cushion strips. Add 1" seam allowance on each piece. This provides for ½" seams, which are ample in this fabric. However, if you would feel more comfortable with a bigger seam allowance, by all means allow for it. For tuck-in,

add 3" at points D, E, G, H, I and K (see Fig. 37A).

Measure cushion front strip from the line at m-o (Fig. 37B) around front to same point on other side. Cushion sides will be seamed at this point (Fig. 37F).

Measure back strip from around back to same point on other side. Two back strips this length are needed, each half the width of m-o plus 1″ additional on each piece, as seam allowance for zipper. Repeat all measurements for second cushion.

Measure the length of all seams where welting is to be used.

How to Determine Yardage Requirement

Fabric width is a major consideration in yardage requirement. For this reason you will simplify your life if you shop around first and decide on, but do not buy, the fabric you want. Once you know the width of the fabric and have measured all the pieces, you can figure exactly how much fabric you need and, therefore, the most economical layout at the same time, by making a simple yardage graph and pattern diagram.

Fig. 37G—Using a ⅛″ graph paper (with each square representing 2″), draw two lines to indicate the width of the fabric selvage to selvage.

You will notice that our chair (and most likely yours) is basically a series of rectangles, making it easy to block out

FIG. 37

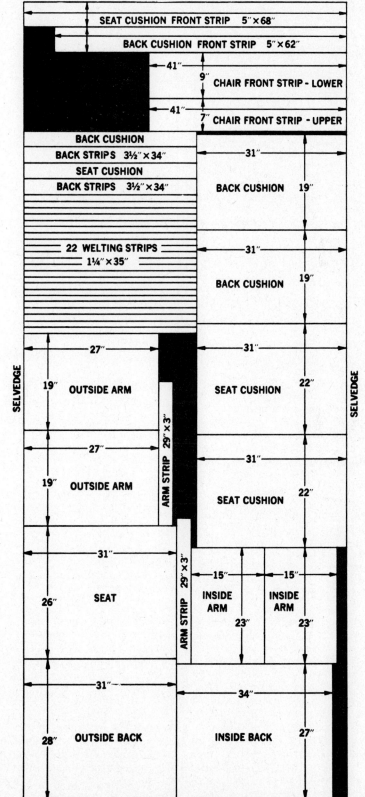

ZIPPER

the graph. For irregularly shaped pattern pieces, such as the chair's inside back and the T-cushions curved-wing back, if any, use the measurement at the widest point as the width of the rectangle on the graph. (Shaping is done when

fabric is pinned to the chair).

Block in the larger pieces on the graph first, then the smaller. Sections IJ-KL, ST-UV and WX-YZ (see Fig. A) must be cut in duplicate, so be sure to outline them twice on the diagram. Also be sure you have indicated both chair cushions, with a top and bottom, and strips for each. For welting, block out strips 1¼″

wide across the graph as many times as necessary to allow for the total length of fabric needed.

When you have blocked in all the pieces needed, count the number of squares along the length of the graph, multiply by two, divide by 36, and you will have the yardage requirement. Now you will know how much fabric to buy.

FIG. 37 G

SELVEDGE

SELVEDGE

SEAT CUSHION FRONT STRIP 5″×68″

BACK CUSHION FRONT STRIP 5″×62″

41″

9″ CHAIR FRONT STRIP - LOWER

41″

7″ CHAIR FRONT STRIP - UPPER

BACK CUSHION BACK STRIPS 3½″×34″

SEAT CUSHION BACK STRIPS 3½″×34″

22 WELTING STRIPS 1¼″×35″

31″

BACK CUSHION 19″

31″

BACK CUSHION 19″

27″

OUTSIDE ARM 19″

31″

SEAT CUSHION 22″

ARM STRIP 29″×3″

27″

OUTSIDE ARM 19″

31″

SEAT CUSHION 22″

31″

SEAT 26″

ARM STRIP 29″×3″

15″ 15″

INSIDE ARM 23″ INSIDE ARM 23″

31″

28″ OUTSIDE BACK

34″

INSIDE BACK 27″

With chalk or pins, mark cutting lines on the fabric to correspond with the layout from the graph. If the fabric's center fold does not press out, avoid it in your layout, if possible.

How to Cut And Mark Pieces

The strength and durability of polyester fibers make for difficulty in cutting. Use very sharp scissors and wipe the blades frequently to free them of lint.

Pin a label to each piece for easy identification when sewing.

Sewing

Once pieces are cut and marked, pin and sew slipcover following the instructions below. Stretch fabric like polyester double knit can be stitched on either a straight-stitch or a zigzag-stitch machine. It requires a looser tension than you generally use and, possibly, less pressure on the presser foot to ensure a smooth, unpuckered seam. Pressure, tension and balance can be checked and adjusted by means of a single test, as follows:

Figs. 37H-J—Use light ballpoint needle or a new, sharp regular machine needle, size 11. Thread machine with a cotton-covered polyester core thread which supplies the strength and "give" needed for seams in this fabric. From fabric scraps, cut two lengthwise strips about 8″ long. Place pieces together, edges even; pin at both ends; stitch, 8-10 stitches per inch.

• **If top layer ripples** (see Fig. 37H), pressure is too heavy and must be loosened. If fabric does not feed properly, pressure may be too light; tighten pressure regulator.

• **If stitch is not balanced,** loosen tension on the side where the stitching is tighter.

• **If you have made an adjustment,** cut off test-seam; repeat tests and adjustments until seam is satisfactory (see Fig. 37J).

• **If seam is puckered** (see Fig. 37I), tension is too tight, loosen top tension and bobbin screw.

Pinning, Seaming and Welting:

Fig. 37D—Pin outside back and inside back to chair—right side out (because a used chair is rarely symmetrical)—centering the pieces and keeping grain of fabric straight. Pin from center outward to edges, gently and evenly stretching the fabric to fit. (Note: Stretching is done only with double knit polyester; other fabrics must not be stretched.) Pin seams at A, B and C, mitering corners. Trim bottom of inside back, leaving a 3″ tuck-in, and tapering upward until fabric narrows to only ½″ seam allowance at top of arms. Pin seat section in place; fold back tuck-in, trimming to 3″. Cut fabric to form T-shape, leaving ½″ seam allowance at front of arms. Pin seam joining tuck-in of inside back and seat

tuck-in.

Fig. 37E—Pin outside arm, arm strip and inside arm sections to chair. Pin seam allowances where these sections join each other. Pin arm section to seat section, leaving 3″ tuck-in allowance along the sides and leaving ½″ at front of arms. Where arm joins back, pin snugly at arm top, then along tuck-in allowance to the bottom. Pin front strips to each other; now pin to seat and out-

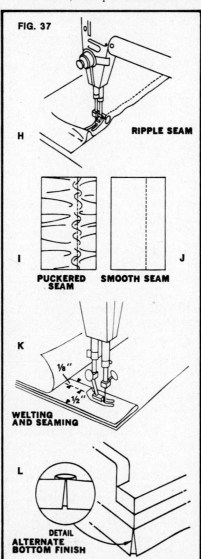

FIG. 37

H — RIPPLE SEAM

I — PUCKERED SEAM J — SMOOTH SEAM

K — ⅛″   ½″ — WELTING AND SEAMING

L — DETAIL ALTERNATE BOTTOM FINISH

side arms. Pin back of outside arms to outside back.

Tuck in allowance all around seat and check chair for fit, adjusting where necessary. Spread all the seams open with fingers, including tuck-ins, and, using chalk or pins, mark seam allowance on wrong side of every section. Before unpinning slipcover, cut notches in seam allowances at center edge of each piece to facilitate matching pieces when stitching seams. Unpin seams. Stitch welting in place (see Fig. 37K and Welting Seams). Pin slipcover sections together, right sides facing, and stitch in the same order in which pieces were fitted

(see Figs. 37D, E and F).

Constructing Cushion Covers

Fig. 37F—The cushion strips for the zipper opening are sewn first. At both ends of strips, pin 1″ seam allowance, leaving a long-enough opening in the center section for the length of the zipper. Machine-baste the opening and sew in zipper, following directions on zipper package. Join one end of zipper strip to front strip. Top-stitch seam. Sew welting to both edges of joined strips.

Pin cushion top and bottom in place; pin to strip all around. Pin remaining end of strips, cutting seam allowance to ½″, if necessary. Spread open seams and mark seam allowances with chalk or pins on wrong side. Stitch seams along stitching line that holds welting in place. Top-stitch seam in strip. Repeat for second cushion.

Welting Seams

If welting is to be used (see below), stitch it to the smaller section first, then stitch the construction seams. Do not attempt to pin and stitch welting and seams all in one operation. Stitch seams in same order in which they were pinned. Keep a light touch—do not stretch as you stitch. Change your needle if it becomes blunted or burred (polyester fibers are hard on needles as well as scissors).

Fig. 37K—To accent the seams with welting, use uncorded welting cut 1¼″ wide on the crosswise grain. (Or, seams may be opened flat and top-stitched for an effective accent.)

Fold strips down the center (Fig. 37K) with right side out. Pin strips to right side of slipcover section, the smaller of the two to be joined, with edges even. Stitch ⅛ from folded edge. Pin other section in place, right side to right side and edges even. Reverse fabric and stitch along the line of stitching that holds the welting in place. The regular presser foot can be used for this, unlike corded welting which requires a zipper foot.

Finishing the Bottom

The chair pictured is finished at the bottom by turning the 2″ allowed to underside of chair. Pin-miter the four corners. Cut away fabric that forms the miter. Stitch a strip of Velcro fastener to the fabric underfold. Tack the matching Velcro strip to the wooden frame. (Note: It is not necessary to hem the raw edge, as polyester double knit does not ravel.)

Fig. 37L—Alternate bottom finish. If you prefer, finish the bottom with a tailored skirt, making allowance for additional fabric for all four corners and adjusting layout diagram accordingly. The skirt is constructed first, welting sewed on, and then the skirt stitched on, as shown in Fig. 37L.

KITCHEN SHELF UNITS

(page 40)

HERB PLANTER

MATERIALS: One 7' length of clear 1x6 white pine (actual dimensions: ¾"x-5½"); two 1¾" lengths of ½" doweling; white glue; 6d finishing nails; wood putty for filling nail holes.

DIRECTIONS: Cutting: Mark all cutting lines accurately with a square and a sharp pencil. You will need three 14½" lengths of 1x6 (one shelf and two vertical pieces), one 15¼" length (the bottom) and two 7½" lengths (top and one side). On two of the 14½" lengths, use the square to mark ¾"-wide notches 6" in from one end (Fig. 38A). The depth of

the notches should be half the width of the boards, or 2¾". Use the crosscut saw to cut along the lines on both sides of each notch. With the board on a firm base, place the chisel on the end of the notch and tap with a hammer to break out the piece. On the upright notched piece, mark and drill ½"-diameter holes for dowel pegs, center 1½" in from each

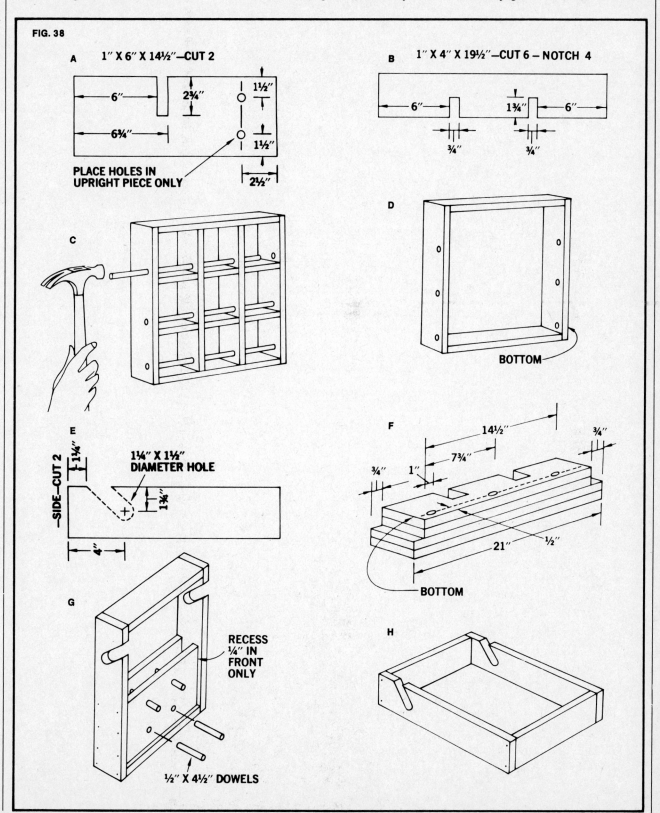

FIG. 38

A   1" X 6" X 14½"—CUT 2

6"

2¾"

6¾"

1½"

1½"

2½"

PLACE HOLES IN UPRIGHT PIECE ONLY

B   1" X 4" X 19½"—CUT 6 – NOTCH 4

6"

1¾"

6"

¾"

¾"

C

D

BOTTOM

E

1¼"

—SIDE—CUT 2

1¼" X 1½" DIAMETER HOLE

1¾"

4"

F

14½"

7¾"

¾"

¾"

1"

21"

½"

BOTTOM

G

RECESS ¼" IN FRONT ONLY

½" X 4½" DOWELS

H

edge and 2½" down from the top (Fig. 38A). Drill over a scrap piece of wood to avoid splintering.

Assembling: With glue and nails, fasten the 15½" bottom piece to the unnotched 14½" end piece. Assemble the two notched pieces with glue, then glue and nail them to the top and side, using the square and a rule to make sure the assembly is in square. Glue and nail the 7½" top piece in place, then set the unit on end and fasten the remaining end piece. Apply a small amount of glue inside dowel holes and tap in dowels.

Finishing: Use a nail set to sink all nail heads below the surface. Fill holes with wood putty. Sand all surfaces, then apply satin-finish varnish or paste wax.

SPICE SHELF
MATERIALS: Two 5' lengths and one 4' length of 1x4 clear white pine (actual dimensions: ¾"x3½"), plus three 21" lengths of ½" doweling; 6d finishing nails; wood putty.

DIRECTIONS: Cutting: Mark all cuts with a square and sharp pencil, for accuracy. From the 5' lengths of the 1x4, cut six 19½" pieces (for top, bottom and grid). From 4' length, cut two 21" sides.

Clamp or tape together four of the 19½" pieces. With the square, mark ¾"-wide notches 6" in from each end (Fig. 38B); the depth of the notches should be half the width of the board, or 1¾". Saw along these notch lines.

Unclamp the boards. With the board on a solid surface, place a ¾" chisel at the end of each notch and tap it out with a hammer.

Drilling: Clamp or tape two of the notched pieces to the two 21" end pieces so that they are centered on the end pieces, ¾" in from both top and bottom (Fig. 38F). Clamp a scrap piece of wood to the bottom of the assembled boards to prevent splintering when drilling. On the top board, draw a light pencil line ½" in from the unnotched edge the full length of the board. Next, make cross marks 1", 7¾" and 14½", measuring from the bottom of the board. Carefully drill ½" holes at these marks through all the clamped-together boards.

Assembling: Nail top and bottom pieces flush between side pieces, with dowel holes toward the front. Assemble the notched pieces to form a grid, with the dowel holes aligned toward the front. Fit the grid inside the outer frame. Drive dowels through one end piece, through the holes in the grid, and into the other end, to hold the entire assembly together (Fig. 38C).

Drive one nail through the frame into the end of each grid piece to hold them flush with the frame.

Finishing: With a nail set, drive each nail head ⅛" below the surface. Fill holes with wood putty. Sand the unit smooth, then paint with satin-finish varnish, or rub with paste wax.

UTENSIL ORGANIZER
MATERIALS: One 5' length of 1x4 (actual dimensions: ¾"x3½") and one 2' length of 1x6 (¾"x5½") clear white pine; 20" of ½"-diameter wood dowel; white glue; 6d finishing nails; wood putty. Note: You will also need a hole-saw attachment for the drill, of 1¼", 1⅜" or 1½" diameter, depending on the size of your rolling-pin handles.

DIRECTIONS: Cutting: Mark all cutting lines with the square and a sharp pencil for accuracy. From the 1x4, cut two 15" side pieces and two 12" pieces, one each for the top and bottom. From the 1x6, cut two 12" pieces for front and back. Cut four 4½" dowel lengths.

Drilling: Clamp or tape the two 15" side pieces together. On one piece, make a mark 4" from one end and midway between the board edges (1¾"). With this as a center point, use the proper size hole saw (see Note above) to cut through both pieces; place a scrap of wood below the lower piece to prevent splintering.

With the pieces still clamped together, measure 1¼" down the front edge of the top board and mark a line from this point to the top of the hole. Draw a parallel line to the bottom of the hole. Cut along these lines to complete the notches for the rolling-pin handles.

Clamp or tape the 1x6 front and back pieces together and mark the positions of the four dowels. These are centered 4" in from each end, 1" from top and bottom (Fig. 38G). Drill ½" holes at these points, using a scrap of wood beneath to prevent splintering.

Assembling: Nail top and bottom pieces flush between the two side pieces. Nail front and back pieces within the frame, tight against the bottom and flush both at front and back. Apply a small amount of glue inside the dowel holes and insert dowels, flush with the back piece and protruding from the front as peg hangers.

Finishing: With a nail set, drive all nail heads ⅛" below the surface. Fill holes with wood putty. Sand the unit smooth; apply satin-finish varnish or paste wax.

STAPLE GUN DECORATING
(page 41)

GENERAL MATERIALS: Staple gun, plus staples and white glue (we used the new Swingline Staple Gun Sewing Kit); newspaper, yardstick, pencil, cardboard, screwdriver, small pliers, new unpainted or old furniture, plus enough fabric to cover the item.

To determine yardage needed for a project: Measure each section of the piece of furniture to be covered. Mark these measurements on a piece of paper. Add two extra inches on each side to allow

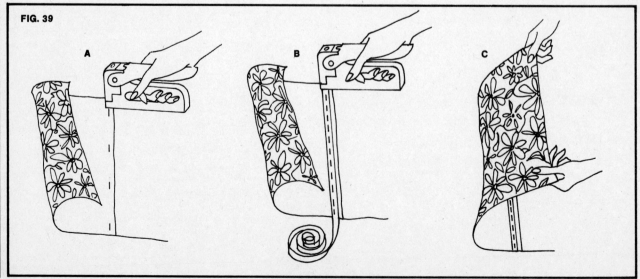

FIG. 39

A   B   C

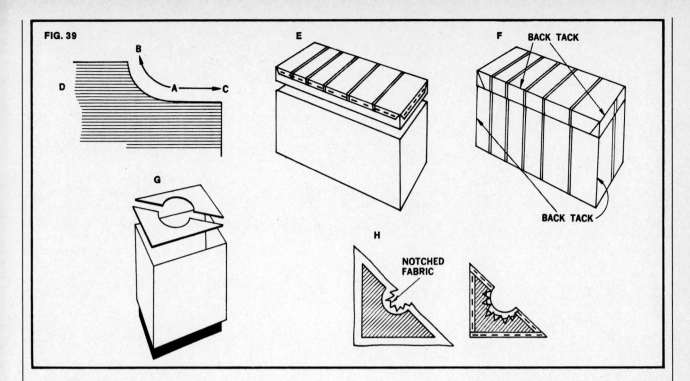

FIG. 39

for wrapping fabric around edges and corners. Cut out. To figure yardage, lay paper pattern pieces out to fit within the width of the fabric you plan to buy. Measure length of layout and allow an extra ¼ to ½ yard for matching, if fabric pattern requires it.

GENERAL DIRECTIONS: Remove any hinges, knobs or other hardware before you begin. Next, cut fabric to coincide with pattern pieces, taking care to match fabric design where necessary. Always staple fabric over one edge completely first, opposite edge next, pulling fabric taut but taking care not to stretch or distort it. Miter corners by folding fabric neatly around them; trim excess.
Specific instructions are given for each project pictured.
Two techniques used in the projects that follow are Back-tacking and Gluing. Back-tacking is the professional method of hiding staples while joining fabric sections smoothly. It also helps to achieve a straight, sharp edge.
Back-tacking: Place a fabric edge along the edge of the item to be covered (Fig. 39A). Staple fabric edge at several points, then place upholsterer's tape (from upholstery supply outlets) or a ½"-wide strip of cardboard along the stapled edge. Staple through tape, or cardboard, and fabric (Fig. 39B). Bring fabric over tape, right-side out (Fig. 39C). Smooth fabric; staple the opposite edge. Repeat the back-tacking with the edge of the next fabric piece, overlapping the stapled edge of the first.

FABRIC PICTURE
You'll need a canvas stretcher (from an

artist's supply store) and a piece of fabric 4" longer and 4" wider than the stretcher. Center the stretcher on the wrong side of the fabric and staple the edges, following General Directions.

BED HEADBOARD
The simpler the shape, the easier the project. To cover the rectangular shape shown, follow General Directions for cutting fabric and stapling, centering the fabric on the front of the headboard. If you wish to cover the back also, use fabric 1" longer and wider; press edges under ½" all around and staple. On a curved area, as in the headboard shown in photo, staple the fabric in the center of the curve first (letter A, Fig. 39D). Work out from A to B and A to C, pulling the fabric extremely tight to eliminate wrinkles.

WOODEN TRUNK
First, unhinge the lid; treat lid and bottom as two separate pieces. Following General Directions, cut fabric for both pieces. Center fabric on the lid top and fold over all edges. Staple to the side of the lid (Fig. 39E). Back-tack strips along the top edge of each lid side (Fig. 39F). Miter and staple corners. Staple lower edge of each side strip to the inside of the lid. Back-tack fabric to the sides of the trunk bottom, gluing the final edge. Staple fabric top edge to the inside, and bottom edge to underside of the trunk.

DOORS
Doors with molding take well to fabric trim. Cut artist's foamboard (from an

artist's supply store) to fit each panel. Following General Directions, cut and staple fabric to the foamboard. Attach foamboard to door with brads or staples. Glue braid or soutache trim on stapled edges.
To cover a flat door: Remove the door from its hinges. Following General Directions, cut two pieces of fabric and cover the front of the door with one, stapling it to hinged edge and opposite edge. Back-tack the second piece over the first on the door front edge; glue final edge over staples on hinged edge. Fold fabric over top and bottom door-edges; staple. Miter and staple corners.

CUBE PLANTER
This is a simple plywood cube on a 3"-high wood base. The top consists of two triangular pieces with cut-away for plants (Fig. 39G). Cut fabric for top 1" larger all around than the triangular pieces. Notch the curved edge (Fig. 39H). Wrap fabric around edges and staple on the underside. Cover cube sides and base, following directions for trunk bottom above. Glue top pieces to cube, or tack with small brads.

LOVE SEAT
This method is suitable only for furniture that has an exposed wood frame all around. Remove the old fabric and use it as a pattern to cut the new covering. Paint the wood frame and let dry thoroughly. Staple fabric to the wood all around, keeping fabric taut for a smooth finish. Glue braid or soutache trim over the stapled edge overlapping trim ends and folding raw edge under.

STOWAWAY FURNITURE

(pages 42-43)

MATERIALS (For chaise, four chairs, patio table and coffee table):

Quantity	Description	Use
4 panels	¾"x4'x8' A-A EXT-DFPA (or MDO) plywood	basic parts
16 pcs.	1⅜"x28½" dowels	chaise, chairs
6'	½" dowel	chaise, chairs
16'	⅜" dowel	chaise, chairs
7 sets	glides	all pieces
as needed	canvas	chaise, chairs
12	1" metal angles with 24¾" screws	tables

You will also need: surfacing putty for filling exposed plywood edges; #120-grit sandpaper, as needed; non-lead base undercoat and finish coat of high grade exterior type enamel for plywood; clear sealer for plywood edges and dowels (optional).

DIRECTIONS: Parts for all furniture pieces are combined on panel layouts for most economical use of plywood. It is best to lay out all plywood parts on the panels before cutting them out. Dimensions for these parts are shown in the drawings. To obtain curved shapes, see instructions in box on page 66 for enlarging and transferring patterns. Mark each piece for later identification, then cut out and true edges, following General Directions for working with plywood on page 66. Drill 1⅜" holes in chaise and chair sides where shown. Drill ½" holes in all stretchers (see drawing). Cut notches and slots to the widths shown in chair and chaise sides and table legs, first drilling pilot holes in the corners of the slots, then removing the wood with a saber saw or compass saw. Drill four ⅜"-diameter holes through each 1⅜" dowel length, centered 1¼" and 2½" in from each end.

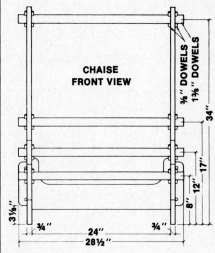

CHAISE FRONT VIEW

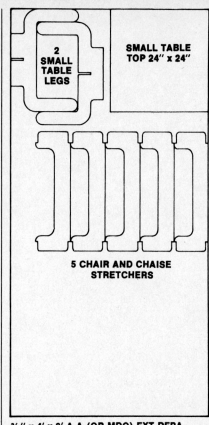

5 CHAIR AND CHAISE STRETCHERS

¾" x 4' x 8' A-A (OR MDO) EXT-DFPA

CHAISE

The chaise is held together with dowels for easy assembly and disassembly. Cut four ½" dowels 3" long to hold the stretcher to the sides. Cut sixteen ⅜" dowels 2½" long to hold the 1⅜" dowels

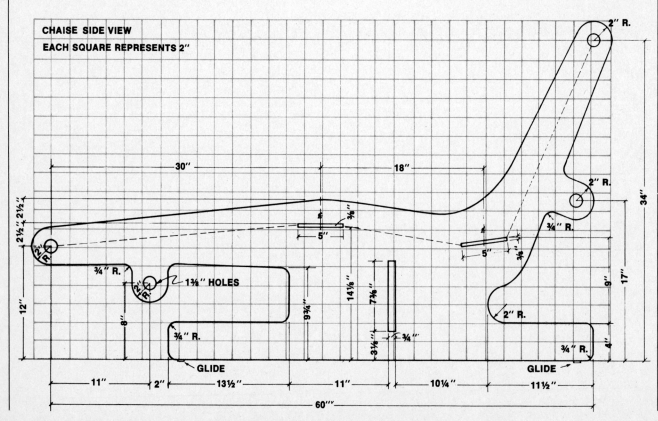

CHAISE SIDE VIEW

EACH SQUARE REPRESENTS 2"

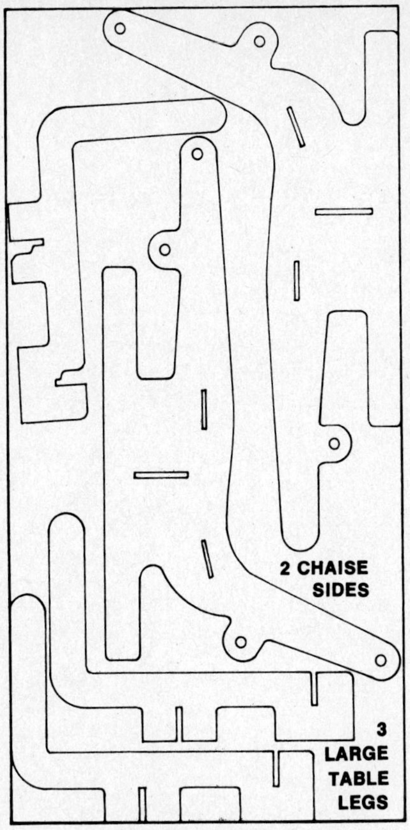
2 CHAISE
SIDES
3
LARGE
TABLE
LEGS

¾" x 4' x 8' A-A (OR MDO) EXT-DFPA

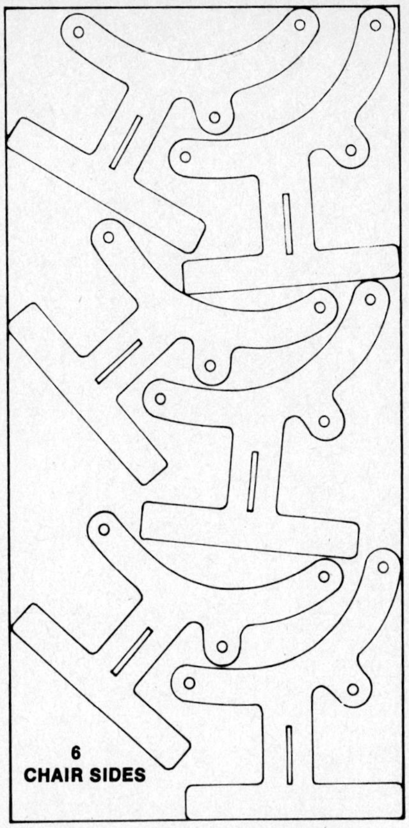
6
CHAIR SIDES

¾" x 4' x 8' A-A (OR MDO) EXT-DFPA

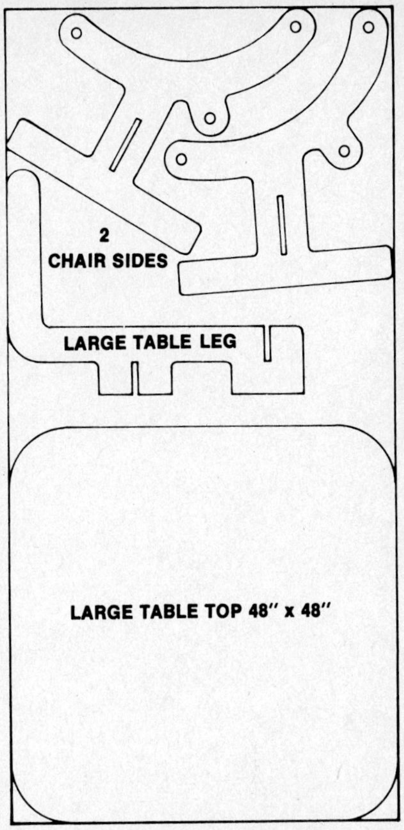
2
CHAIR SIDES
LARGE TABLE LEG
LARGE TABLE TOP 48" x 48"

¾" x 4' x 8' A-A (OR MDO) EXT-DFPA

between the sides. Cut four ½" dowels 7" long to hold the canvas cover in the side slots. Assemble the unit to make sure that all parts fit properly. If they do, disasemble and paint. Make the canvas cover as described on page 86. Reassemble the unit, with the cover in place. Attach glides to the bottoms of the sides. Dowels should fit snugly in their holes. If they become loose after frequent disassembly, replace them with new dowels.

CHAIRS

The chairs are made much the same as the chaise; the plywood stretchers are

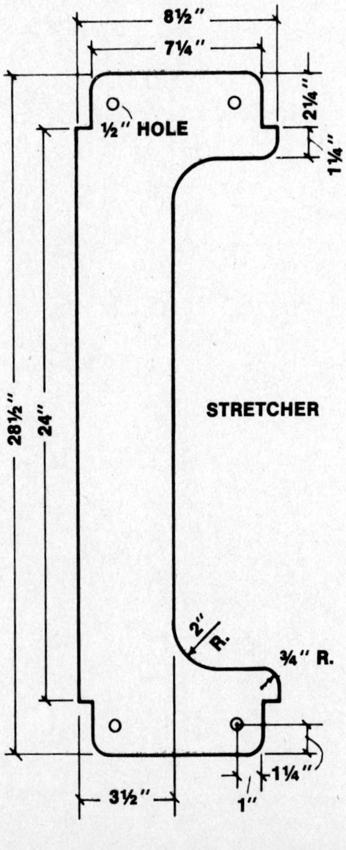
8½"
7¼"
½" HOLE
2¼"
1¼"
STRETCHER
28½"
24"
2"
R.
¾" R.
1¼"
3½"
1"

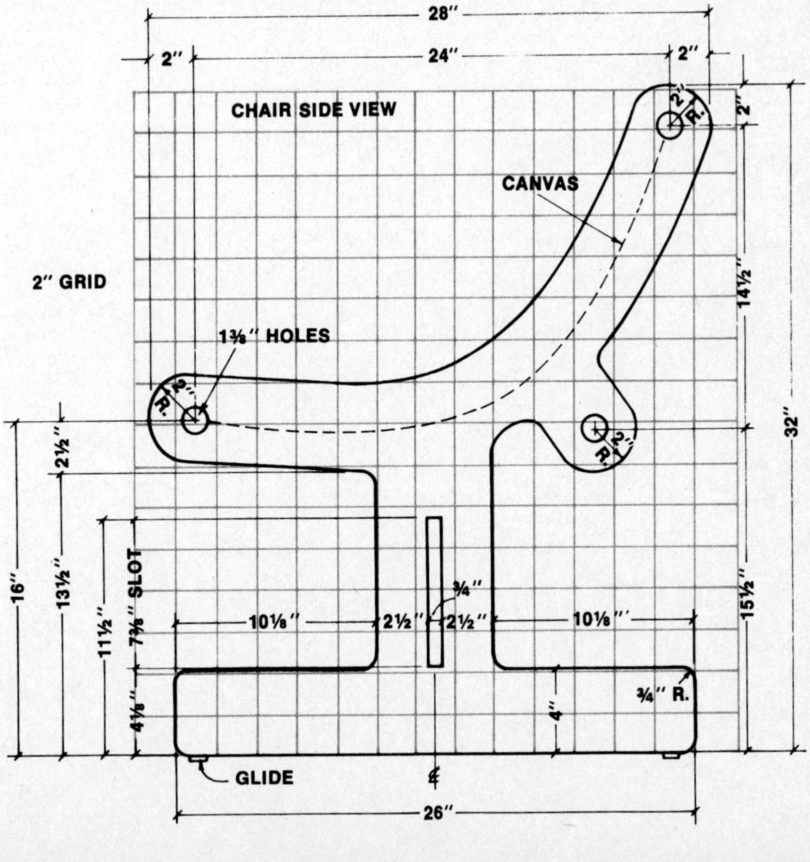
28"
2"
24"
2"
CHAIR SIDE VIEW
2"
R.
2"
CANVAS
2" GRID
14½"
1⅜" HOLES
R.
2"
2½"
32"
16"
13½"
11½"
7⅜" SLOT
¾"
10⅛"
2½"
2½"
10⅛"
15½"
4⅛"
4"
¾" R.
GLIDE
26"

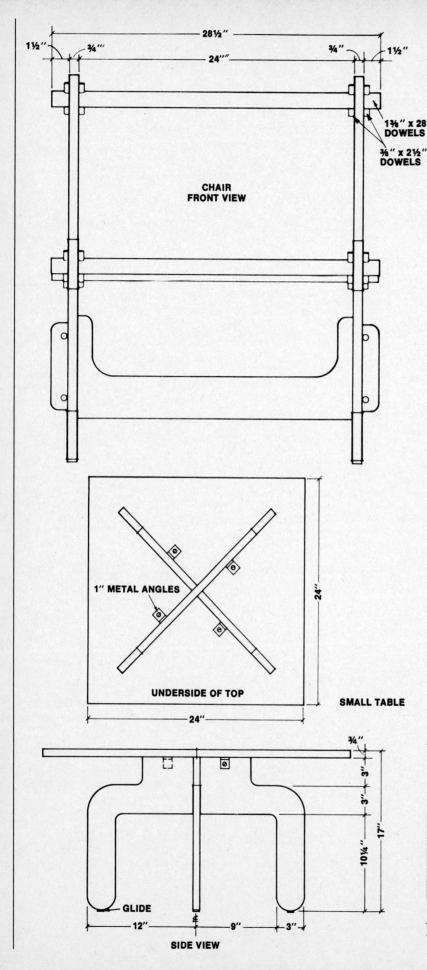

**CHAIR
FRONT VIEW**

1⅜" x 28½
DOWELS

⅜" x 2½"
DOWELS

1" METAL ANGLES

UNDERSIDE OF TOP

SMALL TABLE

GLIDE

SIDE VIEW

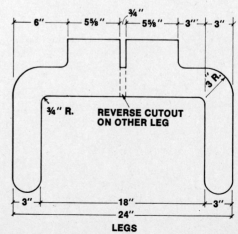

¾" R.

**REVERSE CUTOUT
ON OTHER LEG**

LEGS

identical. For the four chairs, cut 16 ½"
dowels 3" long and 48 ⅜" dowels 2½"
long. Make a trial assembly, then disassemble and paint. Make the canvas
cover (see below), then reassemble.

COFFEE TABLE

The coffee table is 2' square by 17" high.
It consists of only three plywood parts,
plus four metal angles with eight screws.
Note that one leg has a cutout notched
from the top, while the other is notched
from the bottom. The two legs interlock
at the notches. Place the top upside
down on a flat surface and draw
diagonal lines on the bottom to indicate
the positions of the legs. Set the leg assembly in place, predrill screw holes and
fasten legs to the top with metal angles.
If all fits properly, disassemble and
paint. Note that there is enough excess
plywood to make another coffee table.

PATIO TABLE

This table is 4' square and 28" high.
Metal angles hold the top to the interlocking legs. (Note that one leg must
have wider notches. This is the last leg to
be placed in the assembly, and will not
fit without the wider notches). Place the
table top upside down on a flat surface.
Assemble the four legs, set them in place
on the top and attach with eight metal
angles and screws driven through
predrilled pilot holes. If all parts fit
properly, disassemble the table before
painting.

CANVAS

Choose the canvas colors you want for
the chaise and four chairs. Finished
dimensions of the canvas and tie straps
for the chaise and chair covers are
shown in the drawing. When you order,
include enough canvas length for the 5"
overlap at each cover end, and a 4"
overlap at each side. Sew the canvas
covers as shown, and attach the tie
straps. Or, if you prefer, have an awning,
tent or upholstery firm make the canvas
covers for you.

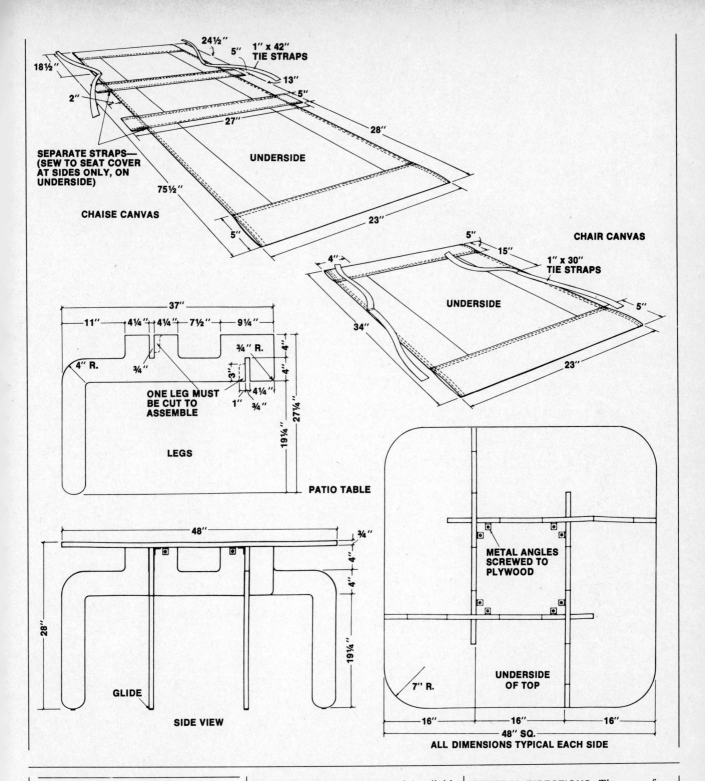

18½" **24½"** **5"** **1" x 42"
TIE STRAPS**

13"

2" **5"**

27" **28"**

UNDERSIDE

**SEPARATE STRAPS—
(SEW TO SEAT COVER
AT SIDES ONLY, ON
UNDERSIDE)**

75½"

CHAISE CANVAS

5" **23"**

5" **CHAIR CANVAS**

15"

4" **1" x 30"
TIE STRAPS**

34" **UNDERSIDE** **5"**

23"

37"

11" **4¼"** **4¼"** **7½"** **9¼"**

¾" R. **4"**

4" R. **¾"** **3"** **4"**

**ONE LEG MUST
BE CUT TO
ASSEMBLE** **4¼"** **27¼"**

1" **¾"** **19¼"**

LEGS

PATIO TABLE

48" **¾"**

4"

**METAL ANGLES
SCREWED TO
PLYWOOD**

28" **4"**

19¼"

GLIDE **7" R.** **UNDERSIDE
OF TOP**

SIDE VIEW

16" **16"** **16"**

48" SQ.

ALL DIMENSIONS TYPICAL EACH SIDE

STENCILED DRESSER

(page 44)

Follow the procedures outlined in the General Directions below for the stenciled dresser shown in photo, or make your own stencil design. Specific materials for the dresser tulip design are listed at the end of this section.

GENERAL MATERIALS: For making stencils and stencil guide: tracing paper; cutting board; X-acto knife with No. 10 curved blade; masking tape; 8-gauge clear plastic sheet by the yard (available in dime stores); ruler. For painting stencils: Artist's oil paints in small-size or medium-size tubes; linseed oil for thinning; acrylic paints in medium-size tubes; round brushes, #5 or #6 (bristle for oil, nylon for acrylic); palette knife (optional); palette; paper punch. For making and applying glaze (see Directions for quantities): artist's oil paint in small-size tubes: boiled linseed oil; Varathane satin finish; turpentine (for mixing furniture glaze); cheesecloth; varnishing brush.

GENERAL DIRECTIONS: There are four steps involved in these projects:
1. Preparing the surface to be stenciled.
2. Making the clear plastic stencils and stencil guides.
3. Stenciling (painting) the designs.
4. Making and applying the glaze.
Preparing the Surface to Be Stenciled: If you are using an old, painted piece, the surface should be smooth and clean with no chipped or peeling paint. If the piece needs repainting or you are using a new unfinished piece, buy good quality paint and follow the manufacturer's directions

for use. When paint is thoroughly dry, make this test in an inconspicuous spot: Dab on a bit of the stenciling paint you are going to use; rub off while still wet. If the base paint did not come off, all is well; if it did come off, paint the surface with Glaze (see Glaze Directions). Let dry, then proceed. This test is important because there may be times when you make a mistake and want to wipe off the stenciling paint.

GENERAL INFORMATION ABOUT PAINTS

Stenciling can be done with either artist's oils or acrylic paints. The oil paints work best on alkyd enamel surfaces, go a long way, are slower to dry and can be bought in small tubes. The acrylics work best on flat latex surfaces or on alkyd enamel surfaces which are first coated with glaze. They are quick-drying and because of this do not go as far as oils and should be bought in larger tubes. When stenciling, squeeze a small amount of paint onto a palette. The paint should be dry, rather than runny. If too thick, thin out with a small amount of linseed oil for artist's oils or water for acrylics. Keep acrylics covered when not in use to prevent drying. Take a small amount of paint on the brush and dab it onto the area exposed by the cut-out stencil. If a darker color is desired, more paint can be added when the first coat of acrylic has dried; oils can be worked over any time.

Note: In our projects we used Rogers brand paint for base coats (see Buyer's Guide). In the materials for the dresser, the color numbers listed are Rogers' numbers. For stenciling, we used Liquitex acrylic and Windsor oil paints. Any paint comparable in quality and color can be substituted in all cases.

Making the Stencils and Stenciling Guides:
The designs for the dresser are given full size. Trace the designs on tracing paper. Tape the tracings to a cutting board. Cut pieces of plastic each about 2″ larger than the design all around; tape over the tracings, one at a time. Bearing down firmly on the X-acto knife, carefully cut through plastic on the design lines showing through the plastic. Work slowly and start over again if you make a mistake; the cut edges should be smooth and sharp without jags that will mar the clarity when the stencil is used.
To make a stencil for the dot required in some designs, simply use a paper punch. Cut all the stencils you will need for your design and set them aside while you make a stenciling guide.
Stenciling Guide: If you try to stencil, using only your eye as a guide to placement, you may end up with unevenly spaced and poorly lined-up motifs. A

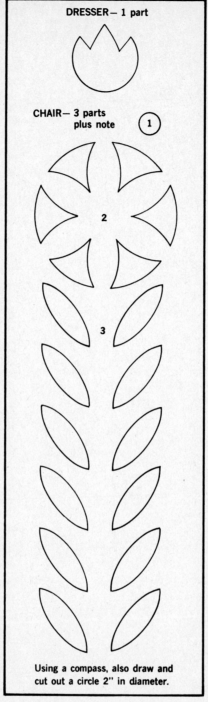

DRESSER— 1 part

CHAIR— 3 parts plus note ①

2

3

Using a compass, also draw and cut out a circle 2″ in diameter.

HEX SIGN

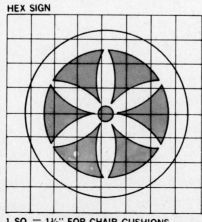

1 SQ. = 1¾″ FOR CHAIR CUSHIONS

stenciling guide will prevent this. To make a guide, cut a piece of tracing paper slightly larger than the area to be stenciled—for example, a chair slat. (This applies to our stenciled chair shown on page 44.) Lay the chair on its back, on the paper, and trace the shape of the slat. In the center of the outline and at both ends, trace the 2″ circle and the flower in the circle from the original patterns. Using a ruler, measure off the space in between and trace the leaf shapes at regular intervals, and the same distance from the top and bottom edges. If you make a mistake it is easy to erase the pencil lines and try again until the spacing is absolutely accurate. In this same way, make a guide for the dresser drawer, etc.

Stenciling the Design: (Note: You may want to test your stenciling technique on a spare piece of painted wood before starting on the furniture.)
• See materials for dresser for paints and stencils to use.
• Place or lay the piece of furniture in such a way that the area to be stenciled is horizontal rather than upright; for example, lay the chair on its back as you did to trace the slat. It is easier to stencil this way.
• Tape the top edge of the stenciling guide to the surface. Slip the plastic stencil under the guide, exactly lining up the cutout design with the traced design; tape stencil in place. Apply paint.
• To avoid smudges and smears, let the paint dry in one area before laying the stencil over it to paint the next area or before adding another color. Clean stencil often, wiping off oils with a rag. To clean acrylic stencils, lay on a flat surface under running water and scrub with a nail brush.

How to Make and Apply Glaze: Mix together 1 to 2 teaspoons of oil paint and 1 tablespoon boiled linseed oil. Add ¼ cup of turpentine, then ½ cup of Varathane.
After stenciling paint is thoroughly dry, apply glaze generously with a varnish- or soft-bristle brush. After a few minutes, brush off with a dry brush or wipe with cheesecloth. For a darker effect, apply a second coat after first coat has dried thoroughly. Test on a small area before glazing the entire surface.

MATERIALS FOR DRESSER: You will need items listed in General Materials, plus the following paints: Latex Flat Alhambra White #4381 for base paint, 3 coats on drawers; Latex Flat Lake Blue #4672 for base paint, 2 coats on dresser; oil tube yellow ochre mixed with Windsor Blue to glaze entire dresser before stenciling; acrylic tube colors as follows: phthalocyanine blue (⅔) mixed with white (⅓) for tulip; phthalocyanine green (⅔) mixed with cadmium yellow medium (⅓) for rim around drawers and tulip design.

DIRECTIONS FOR DRESSER: Prepare surface of dresser following procedure outlined in General Directions and using glaze and base paints. Trace tulip design and make stencil; apply stencil designs using photo of dresser as a guide for design placement.

STENCILED CHAIR WITH HOOKED CUSHION

(page 44)

To paint the chair, follow the procedures outlined in the General Directions for Stenciled Dresser on page 87, using patterns on opposite page. Specific materials for the chair are below.

MATERIALS: Latex Flat Firecracker #4106 for base paint, 2 coats on arms, slats and rungs; Latex Flat Alhambra White #4381 for base paint, 2 coats on legs; acrylic tube colors as follows: white for 2″ circle and dots; phthalocyanine blue mixed with white and yellow orange, azo for flower in circle and leaves plus stripes around legs and knobs; cadmium red light for dots; oil tube color yellow ochre as glaze for entire chair (wipe off on white).

HOOKED CUSHION

Hooking with a punch needle is fast work once you get the hang of using the needle, as you work with one continuous strand of yarn. Draw sample designs on softly woven fabric like burlap or monk's cloth, place on frame and prac-

tice with the needle, spacing the stitches about ⅛″ apart. Fill the areas by following the design lines. For example, circles would be filled with concentric rows of stitches worked closely together to completely cover the fabric. Rectangular areas would be covered with straight rows. The bold motif on our hooked seat cushion was designed for those inexperienced with punch-needle hooking.
Note: The design of your choice can be transferred to the back of the burlap with felt markers before attaching the fabric to the hooking frame. If you use monk's cloth, however, it is better to transfer the design after the cloth is attached to the frame, as this cloth is very soft and slides easily.

MATERIALS: Burlap, 1 yd.; craft and rug yarn, 1 skein each—eggshell, village blue and mid-orange (you should have enough left to hook another cushion with the color scheme reversed); punch needle; hooked rug adhesive backing (see Buyer's Guide for all items above); cardboard; adjustable hooking frame or canvas stretchers (available at crafts and hobby shops); cord or twine; waterproof felt tip markers.

DIRECTIONS: Enlarging the Pattern: Using the directions in the box on page 66, enlarge the 12″ diameter hex motif for chair on paper or cardboard, spacing the lines 1¾″ apart. Cut out pattern, then cut out inner shaded areas.
Transferring the Design: Measure seat of chair. Cut the burlap backing to the dimensions of the chair seat, adding 6″ all around. Draw the outline of the chair dimensions on the back of the burlap backing, centering it on the fabric. Center the motif inside the outline and trace. Now machine-stitch a 2″ hem all

around the backing to reinforce the edges. This leaves a 2″ area between hem and marked outline.
Putting the Backing on the Frame: Following manufacturer's directions, attach the backing wrong side up inside frame through reinforced hem.
Note: It is important that the grain of the fabric be straight after all the sides have been tightened. For smaller projects you may find it adequate to thumbtack the fabric to stretcher bars.
Hooking: One strand of yarn is used throughout; set needle adjustor to make ¾″ loops, following the directions that come with your punch needle. Begin hooking at the center of the backing wrong side. Work the small areas first, outlining with a row of loops and then filling in the areas. When you come to the end of a skein of yarn or change colors, push all yarn ends through to the front side and cut off even with the loops. In large areas (like the background) all hookings should be done in the same direction (that is, either up and down or sideways). Keep the rows close to insure a thick and solid pile on the right side. Do not hook the 2″ area between the outline and the hem.
Adding Latex Backing: Before the fabric is removed from the frame, the back should be coated with latex rug backing. This serves two purposes: It anchors the stitches and prevents sliding and skidding. Apply the latex with a piece of cardboard, thoroughly saturating the lines of stitching. Let dry overnight.
Finishing the Edges: Remove fabric from frame and cut off the hem. Turn under the raw edge of the unhooked area ½″ and machine-stitch all around. Now turn the entire unhooked area to the back and whipstitch with heavy-duty thread to backing (not to yarn stitches).

RECIPE FILE AND COOKBOOK RACK

(page 44)

MATERIALS: One-quarter inch teak, five pieces 5″x48″, one 6″x48″; ¾″ teak, 6″x-12″ (see Buyer's Guide); 3′ of ⅛″ dowel; epoxy glue; 2 ceramic drawer pulls; linseed oil; turpentine.

DIRECTIONS: First make the drawer (see detail). Edge-glue the two base pieces, allow to dry, then cut to finished size. Cut the four inner-base pieces and the three dividers and glue them in place. Cut two sides and the three front pieces. Mark the chamfers (beveled edges) on the two front faces and cut these with a sharp plane. Glue the face pieces to the front piece. When dry, bore holes for the drawer pull screws, then glue the front and the sides to the rest of the drawer assembly. Each of the two base pieces is

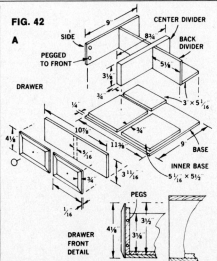

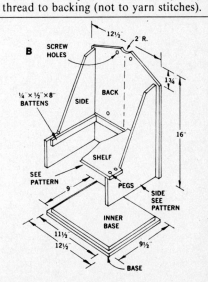

FIG. 42

glued up from two pieces of stock (Fig. 42B). Edge-glue these, allow to dry, then laminate the base pieces. Sides, shelf and back piece are also glued up from two pieces of teak. Allow to dry,

then cut to finished size and shape. Bore hanger holes in the back. The curve at the top of the back was cut with a 2″ drum sander; if you do not have such a tool, you can cut it with a scroll saw and sand smooth. Cut three battens; glue on back and sides.

Glue back and sides to the base, then glue the cookbook shelf in place. When dry, drill holes for dowel pegs at joints.

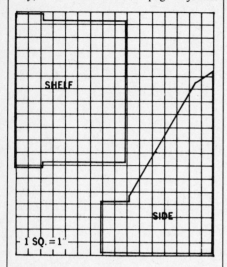

Apply oil finish before attaching drawer pulls. Sliding partitions in each drawer compartment support recipe file cards. Partitions are two pieces of ¼" teak glued in "L" shape.

SANDWICH BAG CHEST

(page 44)

MATERIALS: One-quarter inch teak, 5"x36", 5"x24"; ¾" teak, 6"x12" (see

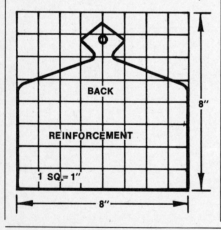

TULIP BABY QUILT

(page 44)

Finished size without optional scalloped border is 36"x48". Machine appliqué is ideal for workers who want to see results in a hurry. A satin stitch is machine-sewn around the edge of each pattern piece, finishing the raw edge while appliquéing the piece to the backing fabric. For machine-appliquéd projects a firmly-woven, slightly stiff cotton-blend fabric with good body is essential. Kettlecloth, skillet cloth, lightweight sailcloth and sports cotton work well. (If ever you have trouble with a fabric that

Buyer's Guide); 3' of ⅛" dowel; epoxy glue; cabinet hinges and screws; linseed oil; turpentine.

DIRECTIONS: Cut all pieces to size (see Fig. 43). To facilitate cutting the shape on the back piece, begin by boring ³⁄₁₆" holes in the teak on either side of the curves at the neck, then cutting to shape with a saber saw, jigsaw or keyhole saw. Bore the hole for the wood-peg hanger in the back. Glue the ¾" teak reinforcing plate to the back and allow to dry, then bore ¹¹⁄₆₄" holes for the hangers. Glue the two base pieces together and allow to dry. Glue back, side and front to the base. When dry, use a block plane

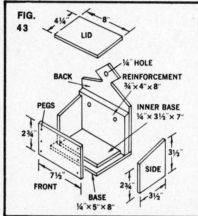

to bevel the top edge of the front to match the angle of the sides. Also, bevel the rear edge of the lid so that it meets the rear reinforcing plate, then fasten the lid with hinges. The hinge screws will penetrate the teak lid; use a wire cutter to nip them off, then file flush with the surface of the wood. Remove hinges when applying oil finish, then reinstall with a drop of epoxy glue beneath each leaf. After glue dries, drill holes, tap in ⅛" dowels to strengthen joints.

INDOOR MAILBOX

(page 44)

MATERIALS: One-quarter inch teak, 6"x48" (see Buyer's Guide); 3' of ⅛"

is too light to machine appliqué, try spray-starching it to achieve temporary body and that will ease the sewing.) The Tulip Quilt is made with machine-appliquéd tulip motifs, and for anyone who has never quilted before, this is a good size on which to learn. Once the blocks are appliquéd, the quilting is done with a simple series of running stitches in straight lines. Experiment with fabric scraps, and make a few sample appliqués before starting on the quilting itself. The time you take to practice satin stitching curved edges beforehand on scrap fabric by machine will be well spent.

dowel; epoxy glue; linseed oil; turpentine.

DIRECTIONS: Cut the teak piece to size (see below). Glue together the two base pieces. Plane the upper edge of the front

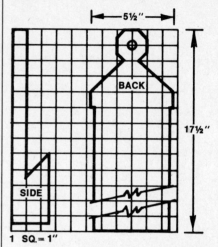

piece to the angle of the sides (be careful not to plane away too much). Bore the holes in the back. Lay the back down, glue the bottom to it, then glue on sides, top and front piece. When the assembly has dried, drill holes and insert dowels at joints (see Fig. 44). Apply oil finish.

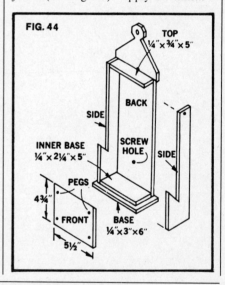

MATERIALS: Washable cotton or cotton-blend fabric. Choose a firmly-woven fabric (not a stretch material); broadcloth, lightweight sailcloth or sports cotton are all practical and come 44"-45" wide. You will need 3 yds. light blue (1½ yds. for quilt, 1½ yds. for scalloped edge), 3 yds. dark blue (1½ yds. for quilt, 1½ yds. for scalloped edge), 2⅓ yds. dark green and ½ yd. white; 4 yds. 44"-45" neutral color thin cotton-blend fabric for lining the quilt and scalloped border (2 yds. for quilt and 2 yds. for scalloped edge); Dacron polyester quilt batting; seven 5-yard packages of blue bias binding (for scalloped edge); heavy-duty thread in blue, white and dark green for machine appliquéing; quilting thread in blue; cardboard; ruler; pins or pinless pattern holder spray (see Buyer's Guide).

DIRECTIONS—Enlarging the Pattern: Following the directions in the box on page 66, enlarge the tulip with stem motif (see Fig. 45A) on paper or cardboard, spacing the lines 1″ apart, including the shaded stem portion and a pair of leaves. For optional scalloped border, enlarge the basic scallop/flap pattern (Fig. 45B), as well as a heart shape (Fig. 45C) which will be used at each of the four corners. Cut out patterns and use as directed.

Cutting: Cut all required pieces from the straight grain of the fabric. Our quilt top is made of 36 blocks; 18 light blue and 18 dark blue (finished size of each block is 6″x8″; cut size of each is 7″x9″). Each block is machine-appliquéd with the tulip and leaf design, then joined together in horizontal rows, lined, backed and quilted.

• BLOCKS
Light Blue: Cut 18, each 7″x9″
Dark Blue: Cut 18, each 7″x9″

• APPLIQUÉS
Tulip Heads: Cut 18 white; cut 18 light blue
Tulip Stems: Cut 36 dark green
Tulip Leaves: Cut 72 dark green

• LINING—Cut one piece, 2″ larger all around than finished size of joined blocks for quilt top (see Sewing, Step 7).

• BORDER—Dark Green
Quilt Front: Cut two strips 3½″ by 42″.
Cut two strips 3½″ wide by 54″.
Quilt Back: Cut two strips 4½″ by 42″.
Cut two strips 4½″ wide by 54″.

* SCALLOPED EDGE (optional, Fig. 45B)
The flap pieces are cut into rectangles first, then cut into oval shapes after stitching. For the layered scalloped edge, our quilt required 11 light blue flaps for each short side and 13 for each long side. We used 10 dark blue flaps for each short side and 12 for each long side, plus a dark blue heart at each corner of the dark blue layer.
Light Blue: Cut 48 rectangles, 5″x6″.
Dark Blue: Cut 44 rectangles, 5″x6″.
Cut four hearts (one for each corner of scalloped edge).

• LINING FOR SCALLOPED EDGE—Cut same amount as needed for flaps and hearts.

Sewing
1. For a two-piece look, make a row of zigzag stitching on the tulip head as indicated by dotted line, using matching thread.
2. Pin appliqués to blocks, or hold pieces in place with a spray of pinless pattern holder, following manufacturer's

directions.
3. Using heavy-duty matching thread and a narrow and open zigzag stitch, machine-baste (or hand baste) pieces in position. All thread should lie on top of the appliqué pieces, with the outer edge of the stitch on the cut edge of the appliqué. Baste all 36 blocks.
4. Adjust zigzag indicator to obtain a wide closed zigzag (also called satin stitch). Stitch over all the previously stitched lines.

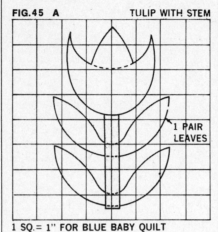

FIG. 45 A   TULIP WITH STEM

1 PAIR LEAVES

1 SQ.= 1″ FOR BLUE BABY QUILT

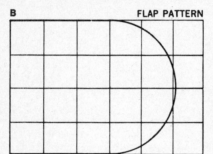

B   FLAP PATTERN

1 SQ. = 1″

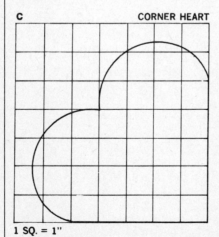

C   CORNER HEART

1 SQ. = 1″

Joining the Blocks—When all blocks have been appliquéd, you are ready to join them.
5. Place all blocks on table to determine arrangement. Ours is done in rows of alternating pairs (see photo). Taking ½″ seams, join blocks on long edges to make six horizontal bands of six appliquéd blocks each.

6. Stitch bands together with ½″ seams, making sure to match all vertical seams. This is now called the quilt top.
7. Measure top. Cut lining fabric 2″ larger than quilt top all around.
8. Cut a thin layer of batting the same size as the lining (separating layers if they seem too thick).
9. Place batting over lining, edges even.
10. Center quilt top over batting and pin through all three thicknesses (the batting and lining will extend 2″ all around top).
11. Baste diagonal lines from corner to corner, then at center across length and width, making sure the lining side is not puckered or wrinkled; redo, if necessary. Remove pins.

Quilting the Layers—Start quilting stitches at one edge and continue stitching across all six blocks to the opposite edge, instead of outlining individual blocks one at a time.
12. Using a single strand of quilting thread, take small running stitches straight up and down through all layers, working ¼″ inside the seams.
13. At this point the quilt can be finished by covering the edges with green strips (Figs. 45E and F, p. 92) and simply eliminating the scallops. A scalloped edge made with lined flaps and hearts (96 pieces in all) may be added as follows.

Scalloped Edge
14. Place each flap piece on top of a lining piece, edges even. Pin together.
15. Trace the flap pattern piece on the top fabric; do not cut out yet (Fig. 45D).
16. Open bias tape and place on flap with right sides together, so that the raw edge of the tape is flush with the pencil line (the bias tape lies on the inside of pencil line). Stitch tape on first fold.
17. Cut away excess fabric on the pencil line. Pull the bias tape over the raw edges and slip-stitch on the lining side. When all flaps are completed you are ready to attach them to the quilt with the green border.
18. The scalloped edge is made up of four layers: The 3½″-wide front green border, the two layers of flaps and the 4½″-wide back green border. All pieces are stitched to the quilt edges in one stitching operation, as in Fig. 45E. Take the time to study the position of the layers, as described in Step 19. It's easier than it looks.
19. The lining extends 2″ beyond the quilt all around. Layering of the following pieces is done from the bottom up.
• Place 4½″-wide green strip over backing so it butts the quilt top edge.
• Place bottom layer of flaps 1″ out on green border with their side edges flush (placing hearts at corners so curved edges extend beyond dark blue border.)
• Place top layer of flaps ½″ inside quilt

FIG. 45 D CUTTING AND STITCHING FLAP

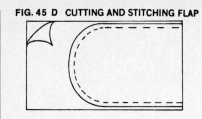

top edge, as shown.
• Place 3½" wide green strip as shown, even with the curved ends of the top row of flaps.
• Stitch as shown in Fig. 45E.
20. Place some scraps of batting on the green borders before pulling them over

E LAYERING SCALLOPED EDGE FOR STITCHING

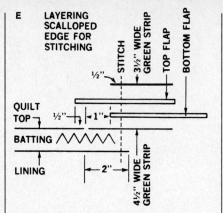

F FINISHING GREEN BORDER

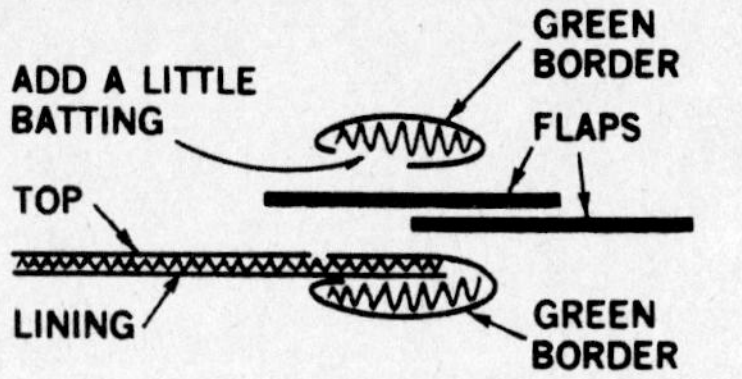

the quilt edges. Turn green edges under ½" and slip stitch to quilt on front, then on back (Fig. 45F), trimming and mitering corners.
21. Finish quilting the perimeter of the quilt. Remove lines of basting.

USED FURNITURE INTO 'ANTIQUES'

(page 45)

• In the directions that follow, the paint colors specified are the ones that we used. All are by Sherwin-Williams. You may want to substitute colors of your choice, but substitutions in the type of paint should not be made. For example, if flat latex is called for, enamel will not give the desired results.
• Follow manufacturer's directions.
• Consult your paint-store dealer for help in estimating the quantity of paint needed for large areas.
• For small projects, buy the product called for in the smallest quantity available (or use leftovers from other projects, if you have them).

LANDSCAPE CHAIR

MATERIALS: Kem-Glo Enamel, Ebony Black; Rub 'n Buff, one tube each of Gold Leaf and Copper; Classic Antiquing Glaze, Glitter Gold; Meyercord Decals, #619A Buildings and #X545C Gold Roses; cheesecloth; 2" paintbrush; small artist's brush; transparent tape; manicure scissors; shield-back chair; striped upholstery fabric.

DIRECTIONS: While following the techniques described, use the close-up photo of the chair as a guide.
1. Paint chair with Ebony Black Enamel; let dry 24 to 28 hours.
2. Decals: #619A—With manicure scissors, cut building motif to fit the center of the chair back (see photo). Glue building decal in place.
   #X545C—Cut individual roses from decal sheet. With small pieces of tape, temporarily stick decals to the chair, arranging them as shown. When both sides are the same, glue decals in place. With a tiny brush and Copper Rub 'n Buff, shade the bottom and left side of each for a hand-painted look.
3. Chair Legs: Alternating Gold Leaf and Copper Rub 'n Buff, paint three ¼"-wide vertical lines on the front surface of the front legs. Let dry. Paint diagonal bands, as shown, with Glitter Gold Glaze which is transparent—the vertical lines will show through.
4. To give a hand-rubbed finish, wipe entire chair with crumpled cheesecloth dipped in Glitter Gold Glaze.
5. Upholster chair seat in striped fabric.

SEWING CABINET

MATERIALS: Flo-Lac Varnish Stain, Ground Coat and Mahogany; Flaxoap,

Oil Soap; Kem-Glo Enamel, Ebony Black Accent; Classic Antiquing Glaze, Olive; white glue; seashell prints (cut from book or magazine); grease pencil or chalk; 1" paint brush; small artist's brush; sewing cabinet.

DIRECTIONS: While following the techniques described, use the close-up photo of the sewing cabinet as a guide.
1. With Flaxoap, remove grime, grease, old wax, etc. from cabinet.
2. Using a grease pencil or chalk, draw an oval shape in the center of the table-top and of each drawer. On the ends of the table-top, draw a fan design, scalloping three of the fan edges as shown.
3. Paint the center top oval, center of fan, and scallops Ebony Black. Let paint dry thoroughly.
4. With Ground Coat, paint the scalloped wedges of the fan; paint ½"-wide oval bands on the drawers.
5. With 1" paint brush and Ground Coat, stipple the top of the cabinet in a random pattern as shown.
6. When dry, paint entire cabinet with Mahogany varnish stain. Ground-coated areas will look like wood inlay.
7. Paste the seashell photo in center oval; brush a thin coat of Olive Glaze on the picture.

PARSONS TABLE

(page 46)

MATERIALS: Fir—four 3x3x29" legs (A), two 2x3x35" end aprons (B), two 2x3x-55" side aprons (C), three 2x2x37" cross members (D), four 1x2x18" cleats (E), two 1x2x35" cleats (F), twelve ¾"x-3¼"x57" flooring (G); fourteen ⁵/₁₆"x5" hex-head lag bolts (J) and washers (H), four ³/₁₆"x3" lag bolts (K) and washers (L); white glue; 6d finishing nails; polyurethane finish.
Note: The exposed face of the flooring should measure 3⅛"; if that which you purchase is wider, trim edge pieces to fit.

DIRECTIONS: Drill ⁵/₁₆" pilot holes in the top ends of the legs, centered ¾" in from

the outside edges and 1¾" down from the top for the bolts going into the end aprons, ¾" from the top for bolts going into the side aprons. Counterbore the holes so that the washers and bolt heads will be slightly below the surface. Drill and counterbore holes ¾" from the bottom of side aprons C, ¾" in from each end and in the exact middle of the apron. Drill but do not counterbore ³/₁₆" pilot holes in two of the cross members D, ½" in from each end.

Apply glue to all joining surfaces before assembling with nails or lag bolts. Assemble the cross members D with the lag bolts and the intermediate cleats E with nails to one side apron C. Top edges of D and E should be exactly the thickness of the flooring below the top

edge of C; check by laying a piece of the flooring in place before fastening D and E. Countersink bolt heads by using a socket wrench. Fasten cleats E to the remaining side apron C, and drive lag bolts partially into cross members D, but do not tighten.

With a saber saw or back saw, cut a 1" x 1" notch at each end of the grooved edge of the first piece of flooring. Set the flooring in place on pieces D and E with the grooved edge tight against the assembled apron C. Toenail to center piece D, placing the nail on the front edge immediately above the tongue, and driving it the last ¼" or so with a nail set so as not to damage the wood surface. Then toenail to each end piece D, making sure that the board is tight against apron C.

Slide the groove of the second piece of flooring over the tongue of the first, hiding the nails in the first, and nail as above. Install all but final board.

Using a straightedge or fence with a saber saw, or a fine-tooth crosscut saw, trim the tongue from the last piece of flooring. Notch the two ends on this

edge 1″x1″, as you did the first piece of flooring. Check for fit, then loosen lag bolts and remove apron C to allow

toenailing through edge of final board. Tighten lag bolts holding apron C to cross members D.

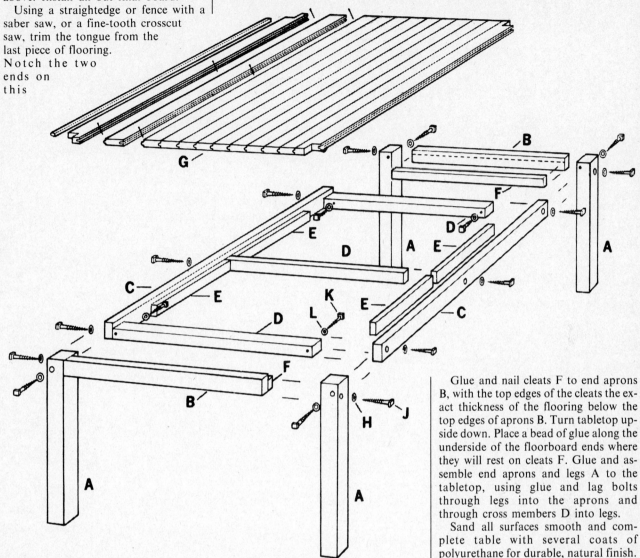

Glue and nail cleats F to end aprons B, with the top edges of the cleats the exact thickness of the flooring below the top edges of aprons B. Turn tabletop upside down. Place a bead of glue along the underside of the floorboard ends where they will rest on cleats F. Glue and assemble end aprons and legs A to the tabletop, using glue and lag bolts through legs into the aprons and through cross members D into legs.

Sand all surfaces smooth and complete table with several coats of polyurethane for durable, natural finish.

PLYWOOD VENEER GRADES

A   Smooth and paintable. Neatly made repairs permissible. Also used for natural finish in less demanding applications.

B   Solid surface veneer. Circular repair plugs and tight knots permitted.

C   Knotholes to 1″. Occasional knotholes ½″ larger permitted providing total width of all knots and knotholes within a specified section does not exceed certain limits.

C   Improved C veneer with splits
Plgd limited to ⅛″ in width and knotholes and borer holes limited to ¼″ by ½″.

D   Permits knots and knotholes to 2½″ in width and ½″ larger under certain specified limits. Limited splits permitted.

STORAGE BED

(page 48)

The bed shown is queen size, and can be fitted with a standard foam mattress.

MATERIALS: ¾″ MDO plywood: two 13″x60″ (A), two 12¼″x60″ (B—notch as in Fig. 22), 10¾″x78½″ (C—notch as in Fig. 22), two 30″x78½″ (D), six 25½″x28¼″ (E), six 25½″x11″ (F), six 9½″x9½″ (cut in half diagonally for pieces G—see Fig. 00); fir lumber: 2x6x78½″ (H), twelve 2x4x25⅝″ (J), for 2x2x20¾″ (K), twelve 2x2x23⅛″ (L), twelve 2x2x26⅝″ (M); 1¼″ No. 10 flathead wood screws; white glue.

DIRECTIONS: Round all corners of pieces A and B, and the outer corners of pieces D to a 3″ radius. Round corners of pieces F to a 1″ radius.

Use glue to assemble "eggcrate" center board C and intermediate panels B. Add end panels A and center support H, securing with glue and screws driven through predrilled holes. Glue and screw intermediate supports J at top and bottom, 3″ in from the outer edges of panels A and B (see drawing, page 94).

Glue and screw drawer supports L to the insides of end panels A and to both sides of intermediate panels B, flush with bottom edges of the panels. Glue and screw drawer guides M, 3″ in from the front edges of the panels, allowing a ⅞″ gap between pieces M and L. Fasten top supports K to the insides of end panels A, flush with top edges.

The bed has six spacious drawers. Assemble each by gluing and screwing a front F to bottom E, allowing a ¾″ overlap at the bottom as shown. Add gussets G, 2″ in from each edge, gluing

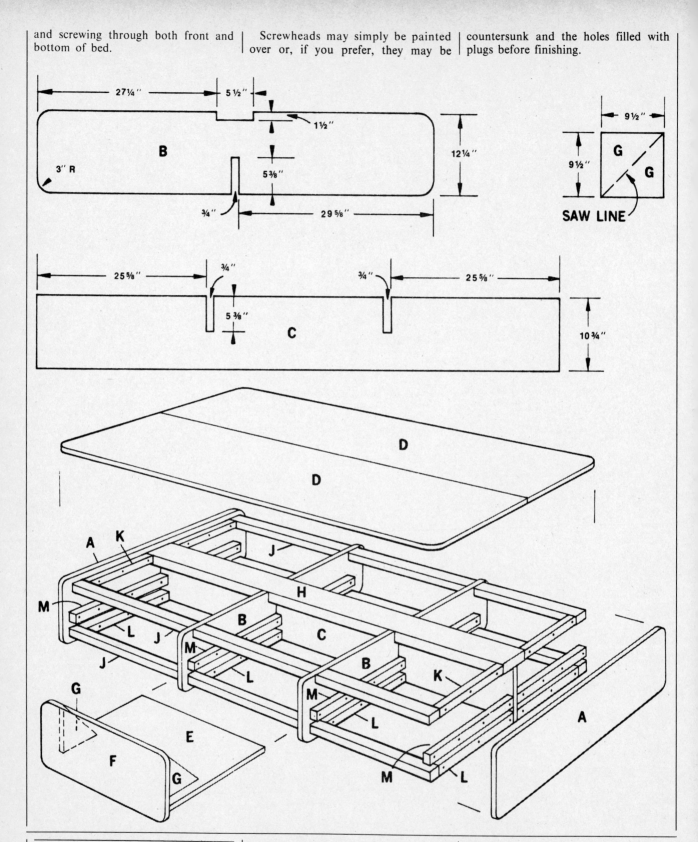

QUILTED BEDSPREAD, HEADBOARD PANEL AND QUILTED PILLOW COVERS

(page 48)

QUILTED BEDSPREAD

Note: We give directions for a double-size bed as it affords the most efficient use of 54″ wide fabric; adjust measurements and fabric requirements for beds in other sizes.

MATERIALS: Print fabric, 54″-wide, 5½ yds. (we used "Montauk" from Ethan Allen in blue, see Buyer's Guide); cotton lining fabric, 54″-wide, 5½ yds.; bonded polyester quilt batt, one piece 54″ x 75″ for top and two pieces 9″ x 75″ for side

panels; neutral-color thread; 1″-wide twill tape, 2 packages.

DIRECTIONS: Cutting: From the full width of printed fabric (54″) cut a length of fabric equalling your mattress length, plus two times the thickness of your mattress, plus 4″ hem allowance. (Our bed measured 75″ long, plus two times 9″

for mattress thickness, plus 2" extra at each end for hem, totaling 97".) This piece of fabric will cover the mattress top and the depth at the foot and head in one continuous strip. Making sure you are matching the pattern repeat on the top piece, cut two side panels from remaining fabric, the width measuring the thickness of mattress, plus ½" for top seam and 2" for hem (ours measured 11½" wide). For the length of the panels, measure the length of the mattress, plus 2" at each end for hem allowance (our length measured 79"). Cut same size pieces of lining fabric.

Assembling the bedspread top piece: Spread the bedspread top lining piece on the floor. Center the batt on top of the lining. Place the print fabric right side up, over the batt so that the edges of the print piece are flush with the edges of the lining. Pin the pieces together through all layers, making sure the lining fabric on the bottom is smooth and un-puckered. Baste by hand with large stitches from corner to corner, top to bottom, side to side, to temporarily hold layers together.

Quilting: Set machine straight stitch at medium-to-long length. For outline-quilting, machine stitch around the edges of the design motifs. Remove all basting.

Assembling side panels: Spread lining pieces on floor. Place batt on top of lining, ½" from long top edge and 2" from each end. Place print fabric, right side up, over batt, edges flush with lining. Stitch outline quilting, as you did top piece. Remove basting.

Assembling bedspread: Find and mark

the middle of the spread-top side edges, and the side panel top edges. With right sides together, pin side panels to bedspread top, matching middle marks and pinning toward each end from those points; stitch, taking ½" seams.

Fitting and stitching the corners: Place the bedspread on the bed, wrong (lining) side up—the corner angles of the spread aligned with the corners of the mattress. Pin a snug seam at each corner. Take spread off the bed, turn right side out and put back on the bed. If any of the seams need readjusting, repin and fit again. Starting at point ¼" above the pins, stitch the seams as you would a dart, tieing thread ends. Trim seams to ⅜"; press open. Cover the entire seam with 1"-wide twill tape, catch-stitching both tape seams to lining layer only.

Hemming: Place spread on bed again and turn under excess fabric to form a hem. Stand away from the bed to make sure none of the mattress shows; if it does, lengthen the hem. Mark the fold all around with tailor's chalk or a line of basting. Trim hem to 1". Machine stitch 1"-wide twill tape around entire spread edge. Turn up hem on marked foldline, catch-stitching other tape edge to lining layer only. Press hem on lining side.

HEADBOARD WALL PANEL

To estimate the yardage needed, measure the width of the bed and the length of the wall from ceiling (or soffit) to bed height (or baseboard). Cut fabric batting and lining this size. Outline-quilt the fabric as you did for the bedspread. Turn raw edges under ¼"; topstitch. Along wrong side of top and bottom

edges, attach long strips of Velcro double-face self fasteners, with the mating strip glued to the wall.

QUILTED PILLOW COVERS

MATERIALS (for two 16" x 26" pillows): Print fabric, 54"-wide, 1 yd. for pillow tops and covered welting (Montauk from Ethan Allen); lining fabric, 54"-wide, 1 yd.; bonded polyester quilt batts, two pieces each 16" x 26"; jumbo welting cord, 5½ yds. (or purchased covered welting in contrasting color); two pillow forms or polyester fiberfill.

DIRECTIONS – Cutting: From print fabric cut 17" long piece from the full width of the fabric; cut in half lengthwise to make two 17" x 27" pieces for pillow tops. From remaining print fabric cut 4"-wide bias strips to cover welting cord. From lining fabric cut two 17" x 27" pieces for the pillow top lining and two more the same size for pillow backs.

Quilting: Layer the lining, batting and print fabric as you did for the bedspread; baste and quilt tops for both pillows.

Sewing: Stitch bias strips to make one continuous strip and cover welting cord. Trim welting seam allowance to ½". Pin welting around right side of quilted fabric, edges flush; stitch on welting seamline (using zipper foot); overlap welting at ends. Baste pillow back fabric on top of welted fabric, edges flush; stitch ½" seams, leaving 18" opening in one long side. Trim corners into curves. Remove basting. Turn pillow cover right side out. Stuff with pillow form or fiberfill. Turn raw edge under ½" and whipstitch opening closed.

HANGING STORAGE UNITS AND READING LIGHT

(page 48)

These are strictly "space-available" projects, with shelf and cabinet lengths and widths depending on such factors as room layout, door and window locations and furniture placement. Shelves in our bedroom range from 8" to 12" deep.

MATERIALS: ½" and ¾" plywood; ½" channel-groove plywood; 2x2 fir; ½"x ¾" trim; shelf brackets; concealed cabinet hinges; door pulls; magnetic catches; 4d, 8d finishing nails; ¾", 1½" flat head wood screws; white glue; fluorescent fixture(s); translucent pan-

el(s); small cup hooks.

DIRECTIONS: Shelves are cut to desired size from ¾" plywood. Fasten brackets to wall by driving 1½" screws through wallboard into studs (these are normally spaced on 16" centers—find one by tapping on the wall or using a magnetic stud finder, then measure to find the rest).

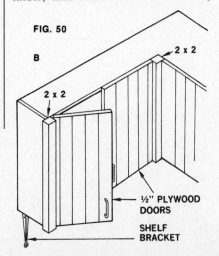

FIG. 50

Make sure brackets are all level and aligned. Fasten shelves to brackets with ¾" screws. Make shelf ends of ¾" plywood, with top and bottom corners rounded to a 2" radius (Fig. 50A).

To convert shelves to cabinets, close off the ends of the shelves with ½" plywood, then add 2x2 corners with glue and 8d nails (Fig. 50B). Hang doors of channel-groove plywood; add pulls and catches. Screw hooks inside doors. If you decide to stain or leave door fronts natural, coat with a varnish or clear plastic coating.

For the reading light (above the bed headboard in photo), attach a 6"-wide valance board of ½" plywood below the top shelf, gluing and nailing it through

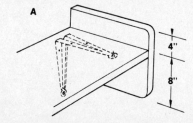

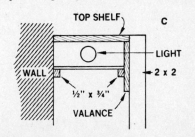

the shelf and to the 2x2 cabinet corners at each end (Fig. 50B). Install fluorescent fixture to shelf behind valance. Glue ½"x ¾" trim strip behind valance, flush with the bottom, and nail a matching strip to the wall (Fig. 23B). Set translucent panel on trim strips.

ROLLAWAY BAR CART

(page 49)

MATERIALS:

Quantity	Description	Use
2 panels	¾"x4'x8' EXT plywood (MDO both sides)	sides, bottom, doors, shelves, partition handles (2)
4½" linear feet	1⅝"-dia. dowel (wood to match butcher block)	
9 linear feet	1x1 standard grade	shelf, door framing
16 linear feet	2x2 standard grade	bottom, butcher block framing top
1 laminated butcher block	1½"x25"x30" (cut to two 25"x15" pcs.)	
4	swivel plate steel casters and screws	moving unit
4	18" shelf standards, brackets, screws	adjustable shelf
4	pivot hinges and screws	door hinges
2	touch latches and screws	door catches
6	chrome screw hooks	utensil rack
1	1½"x24" continuous hinge (and screws)	to hinge butcher block assembly
1 box	6d finishing nails	assembly
1 box	3d finishing nails	assembly
1 doz.	No. 8 (2½") flat head wood screws	butcher block framing
2	vinyl basins (to fit)	removable ice bins

You will also need: surfacing putty for filling nail holes and holes at exposed edges; #120 grit sandpaper and wood glue, as needed; clear sealer for exposed panel edges and dowels, if desired; nonlead base undercoat and finish coat of high grade interior type (exterior type for outdoor use) enamel for exposed plywood surfaces, as needed.

DIRECTIONS: Lay out plywood panels

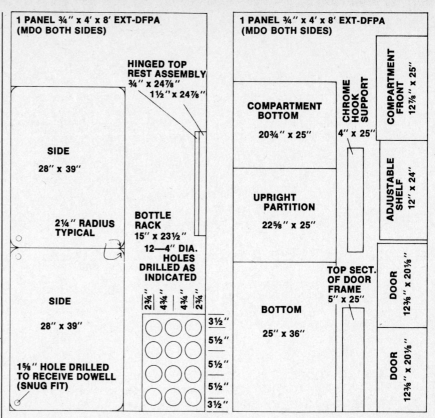

1 PANEL ¾" x 4' x 8' EXT-DFPA (MDO BOTH SIDES)

HINGED TOP REST ASSEMBLY
¾" x 24⅞"
1½" x 24⅞"

SIDE
28" x 39"

2¼" RADIUS TYPICAL

BOTTLE RACK
15" x 23½"
12—4" DIA. HOLES DRILLED AS INDICATED

SIDE
28" x 39"

1⅝" HOLE DRILLED TO RECEIVE DOWEL (SNUG FIT)

2¾" 4¾" 4¾" 2¾"

3½"
5½"
5½"
5½"
3½"

1 PANEL ¾" x 4' x 8' EXT-DFPA (MDO BOTH SIDES)

COMPARTMENT BOTTOM
20¾" x 25"

CHROME HOOK SUPPORT
4" x 25"

COMPARTMENT FRONT
12⅞" x 25"

UPRIGHT PARTITION
22⅝" x 25"

ADJUSTABLE SHELF
12" x 24"

TOP SECT. OF DOOR FRAME
5" x 25"

BOTTOM
25" x 36"

DOOR
12⅜" x 20⅛"

DOOR
12⅜" x 20⅛"

for cutting as shown in the cutting diagram. Cut out pieces and true edges, following General Directions for working with plywood, page 66. Drill 1⅝"-diameter holes through side panels to accept dowels. Doors may be painted at this point. Cut lumber framing, blocking, bottle rack legs and dowels to dimensions shown in drawing. Plane edges of the opening half of the butcher

block to avoid rubbing. Fasten both pieces of butcher block together with continuous hinge. Position 2x2 framing on bottom of butcher block, as shown, and glue. Predrill holes through framing and into butcher block. Fasten with flat head screws. Then nail and glue plywood top section of door frame to 2x2 framing. For support at opposite end of hinged butcher block, cut

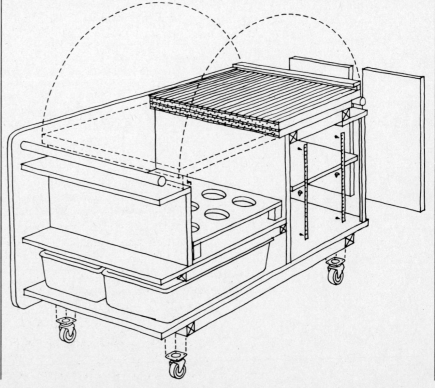

plywood strips 24⅞" long by widths shown; tack them together, then glue. Predrill, countersink and screw them to butcher block. Glue and nail bottom panel to 2x2 framing. Glue and nail 1x1 compartment bottom framing to upright partition, and nail bottom panel (from underneath) to upright partition. Next, glue and nail two remaining lengths of compartment bottom framing to side panel. Glue and nail 1x1 door framing to each side panel, and install shelf standards. Glue and nail plywood bottle rack to legs, as shown in detail A. Glue and nail plywood chrome hook support to compartment front (see drawing). Glue and nail compartment bottom to com-

partment front (see drawing). Now glue and nail one side panel to 2x2 bottom framing, and tack upright partition in place (near the top). Place one end of dowel handles in the side panel, then fasten the other side panel. Place compartment assembly in place and glue-nail compartment bottom to framing. Nail side panels to ends of compartment front and plywood chrome hook support. For added strength, at top of door frame, nail through side panels into plywood top section ends. Set butcher block in place and nail side panels to butcher block framing. Screw pivot hinges to doors and install doors to framing on unit. Install touch latches for

doors. Next, turn unit bottom-side up and install casters. (Additional framing around casters may be required). Countersink all visible nails; fill holes; allow to dry and sand smooth. Sand sharp edges off plywood corners and wipe all plywood clean. (be sure all edges are filled.) Edges and wood dowels may then be finished natural with several coats of a clear sealer. If painted edges are desired, apply several paint undercoats before applying finish coat. Also apply undercoat to MDO plywood surfaces before painting finish coat. Complete by placing adjustable shelf, bottle rack and ice basins in the appropriate storage spaces.

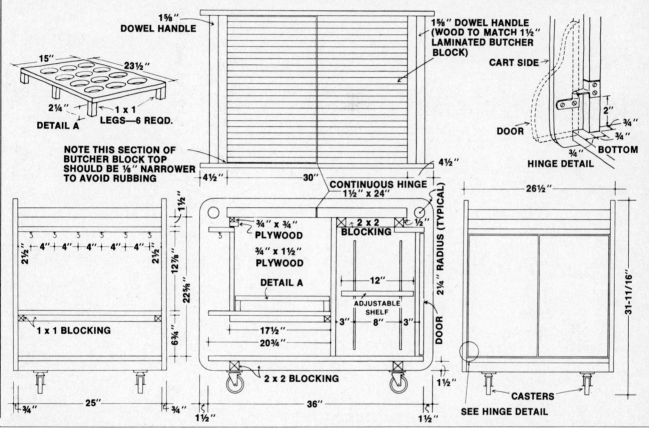

COOKING UNIT

(page 49)

MATERIALS:

Quantity	Description	Use
2 panels	¾"x4'x8' plywood (MDO both sides)	sides, bottom, doors, shelves partition
4½ lin. ft.	1⅝"-dia. dowel (wood to match butcher block)	handles (2)
2 lin. ft.	3x4 standard grade	blocking door stove
16 lin. ft.	1x1 standard grade	shelf, door framing
18 lin. ft.	2x2 standard grade	bottom and butcher block framing
1 laminated butcher block	1½"x25"x30"	top
1	18"x10½"x5½" Coleman liquid propane stove #5409-731	cooking
4	swivel plate casters and screws	moving unit
4	18" shelf standards, brackets, screws	adjustable shelf
4	14½"x5½"x5" vinyl food containers	storage bins
4	pivot hinges and screws	door hinges
2	touch latches and screws	door latches
1 box	6d finishing nails	assembly
1 box	3d finishing nails	assembly
2 doz.	No. 8 2" flat head screws	butcher block framing

You will also need: Surfacing putty; #120 grit sandpaper; wood glue; clear sealer for exposed panel edges and dowels, if desired; non-lead base undercoat and finish coat of high grade interior type (exterior type for outdoor use) enamel for exposed plywood surfaces in colors desired.

DIRECTIONS: Lay out plywood panels for cutting as shown in the cutting diagram. Cut pieces following General Directions for working with plywood on page 66. Drill 1⅝"-diameter holes through side panels to accept dowels. Doors may be painted at this point.

Cut lumber framing, blocking and dowels to dimensions shown in drawings. Measure Coleman stove width and length, and determine dimensions required for stove lip to fit over butcher block. Mark dimensions on butcher block and cut out for stove.

Position 2x2 framing on bottom of butcher block (opposite stove end) and glue. Predrill holes through framing into butcher block. Fasten with flat head screws. Then nail and glue plywood top section of door frame to 2x2 framing, as shown. Glue and nail bottom panel to 2x2 framing. Then glue and nail 1x1 fixed shelf framing to upright partition. Nail bottom panel (from underneath) to upright partition. Glue and nail 1x1 shelf framing to side panels. Also glue and nail 1x1 door framing to each side panel, and install shelf standards.

To assemble: Glue and nail one side panel to 2x2 bottom framing. Tack upright partition in place (near the top). Insert ends of dowel handles in holes in side panel, then set second side panel in place and fasten. Glue and nail bottom shelf to framing. (Countersink nails after you nail each shelf.) From bottom of middle shelf, glue and nail shelf dividers in place and glue-nail middle shelf and top shelf to framing. Nail dividers in position through top shelf. For added strength at top of door frame, nail through side panels into plywood top section ends. Glue and toenail 3x4 blocking to top shelf for butcher block support. Set butcher block in place and nail side panels to butcher block fram-

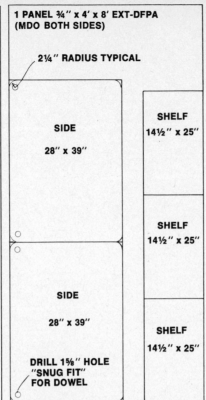

1 PANEL ¾" x 4' x 8' EXT-DFPA (MDO BOTH SIDES)

2¼" RADIUS TYPICAL

SIDE 28" x 39"

SIDE 28" x 39"

DRILL 1⅝" HOLE "SNUG FIT" FOR DOWEL

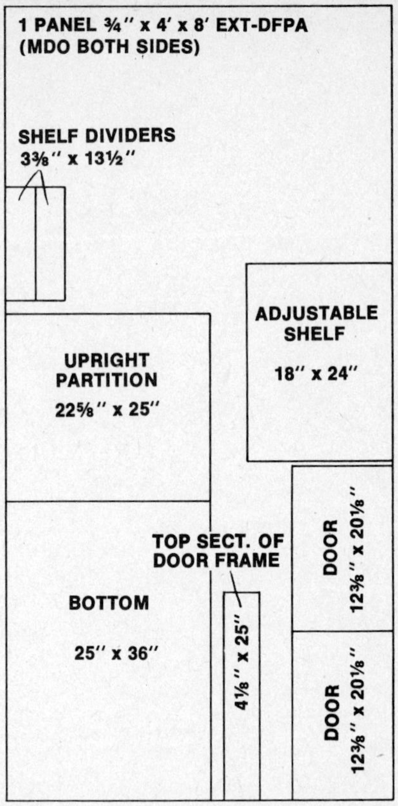

SHELF 14½" x 25"

SHELF 14½" x 25"

SHELF 14½" x 25"

1 PANEL ¾" x 4' x 8' EXT-DFPA (MDO BOTH SIDES)

SHELF DIVIDERS 3⅜" x 13½"

UPRIGHT PARTITION 22⅝" x 25"

ADJUSTABLE SHELF 18" x 24"

TOP SECT. OF DOOR FRAME 4⅛" x 25"

BOTTOM 25" x 36"

DOOR 12⅜" x 20⅛"

DOOR 12⅜" x 20⅛"

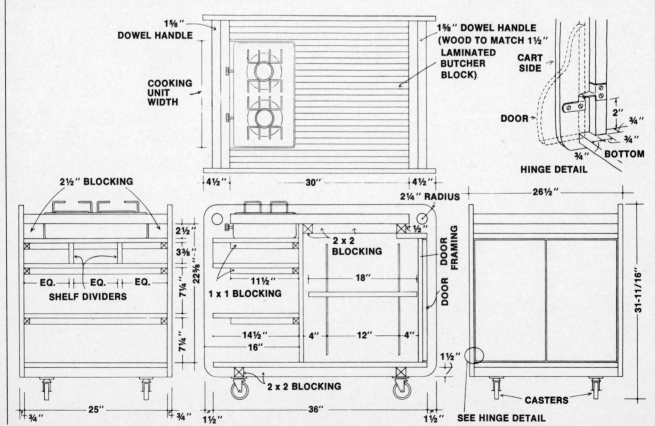

1⅝" DOWEL HANDLE

COOKING UNIT WIDTH

1⅝" DOWEL HANDLE (WOOD TO MATCH 1½" LAMINATED BUTCHER BLOCK)

CART SIDE

DOOR

HINGE DETAIL

2½" BLOCKING

SHELF DIVIDERS

EQ. EQ. EQ.

4½" — 30" — 4½"

2¼" RADIUS

2 x 2 BLOCKING

1 x 1 BLOCKING

2 x 2 BLOCKING

11½"

18"

14½"

16"

4" 12" 4"

DOOR FRAMING

2½" 3⅜" 7¼" 22⅝" 7¼"

25"

36"

¾" ¾"

1½"

1½"

26½"

31-11/16"

CASTERS

SEE HINGE DETAIL

2"

¾"

¾"

¾"

BOTTOM

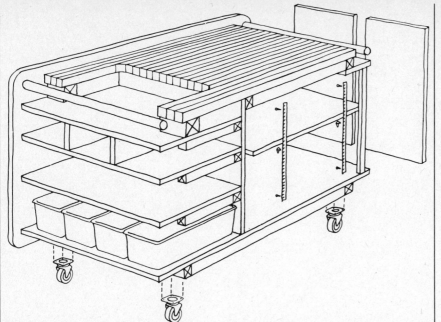

<table>
<thead>
<tr><th colspan="2">MATERIALS:</th></tr>
<tr><th>Quantity</th><th>Description</th></tr>
</thead>
<tbody>
<tr><td>12</td><td>2x2x8'</td></tr>
<tr><td>12</td><td>2x2x10'</td></tr>
<tr><td>2</td><td>2x4x8'</td></tr>
<tr><td>2 bundles</td><td>1½"x ⅜"x4' lath (50 pc.)</td></tr>
<tr><td>2</td><td>pressure treated 2x4x8'</td></tr>
<tr><td>28</td><td>¼"x4' galvanized carriage bolts</td></tr>
<tr><td>40</td><td>¼" galvanized washers and wingnuts</td></tr>
<tr><td>12</td><td>¼"x3' galvanized hanger bolts</td></tr>
<tr><td>1</td><td>4'x1½" plastic "polyhinge" (see Buyer's Guide)</td></tr>
<tr><td>2</td><td>galvanized 2" butt hinges (door)</td></tr>
<tr><td>1</td><td>drawer pull</td></tr>
<tr><td>1</td><td>2" hook and eye</td></tr>
<tr><td>4'x35'</td><td>plastic glazing material**</td></tr>
<tr><td>30'</td><td>⅜" foam weatherstrip tape</td></tr>
<tr><td>24'</td><td>¾" foam weatherstrip tape</td></tr>
<tr><td>6 cu. ft.</td><td>gravel or crushed stone</td></tr>
</tbody>
</table>

You will also need: waterproof glue (resorcinol resin recommended); 8d galvanized finishing nails; 4d galvanized

ing. Drill into butcher block for two screws on each side and drive in screws. Screw pivot hinges to doors and install doors to framing on unit. Install touch latches for doors. Next, turn unit bottom-side up and install casters. (Additional framing around casters may be required.)

Countersink all visible nails; fill holes; allow to dry; sand smooth. Sand sharp edges off plywood corners and wipe all plywood clean. (Be sure all edges are filled.) Finish to match Bar Unit. Complete by installing stove, adjustable shelf and food containers.

GREENHOUSE

(page 50)

Designed for cool, moderate or warm weather gardening, this lean-to greenhouse is built against a house, garage or other structure. For a freestanding greenhouse, two of the lean-tos can be bolted together back-to-back, with a 2x6 roof ridge to provide the necessary structural strength (see Double Unit drawing). Ground stakes will secure the unit. Assembly of the greenhouse is with carriage bolts and wing nuts, making disassembly easy if you wish to move it or store it in areas where the winters are exceptionally harsh. Redwood or cedar are the best woods to use because of their high degree of decay-resistance, but they are also the most expensive. Any other wood species will do, but it should be painted or stained to protect it from the elements. The 2x4 sills that are in contact with the ground should be pressure-treated with preservative to guard against rot. If you are unable to find pressure-treated lumber, you can treat it yourself by soaking it in pentachlorophenol or other wood preservative (not as effective as pressure-treating, but it will do the job), or by brushing the preservative onto the wood (less effective still, but it will help, especially if you soak the thirsty end grain of the wood).

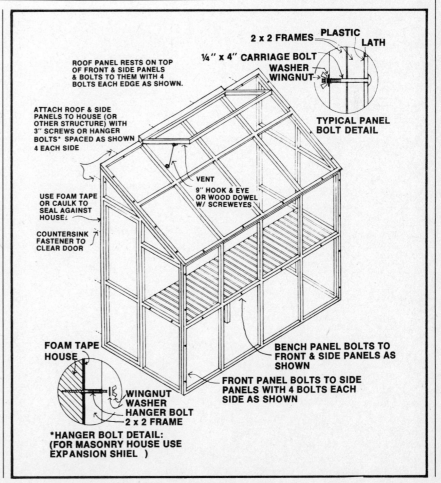

ROOF PANEL RESTS ON TOP OF FRONT & SIDE PANELS & BOLTS TO THEM WITH 4 BOLTS EACH EDGE AS SHOWN.

ATTACH ROOF & SIDE PANELS TO HOUSE (OR OTHER STRUCTURE) WITH 3" SCREWS OR HANGER BOLTS* SPACED AS SHOWN 4 EACH SIDE

USE FOAM TAPE OR CAULK TO SEAL AGAINST HOUSE.

COUNTERSINK FASTENER TO CLEAR DOOR

2 x 2 FRAMES
PLASTIC
LATH
¼" x 4" CARRIAGE BOLT
WASHER
WINGNUT
TYPICAL PANEL BOLT DETAIL

VENT
9" HOOK & EYE OR WOOD DOWEL W/ SCREWEYES

BENCH PANEL BOLTS TO FRONT & SIDE PANELS AS SHOWN

FRONT PANEL BOLTS TO SIDE PANELS WITH 4 BOLTS EACH SIDE AS SHOWN

FOAM TAPE
HOUSE
WINGNUT
WASHER
HANGER BOLT
2 x 2 FRAME
*HANGER BOLT DETAIL: (FOR MASONRY HOUSE USE EXPANSION SHIEL)

finishing nails; 2½″ galvanized wood screws. **Plastic glazing material is available in two varieties: 6 mil. vinyl should last 3 years in the sun; 10 mil. mylar should last for 5 years in the sun, and is exceptionally strong. Both vinyl and mylar are available through Sears Suburban Farm and Ranch catalogue.

DIRECTIONS: Front, side, roof, door and vent framing are assembled as individual panels. Rip a 2x4 as shown in the detail to provide the top plate of the front and the half-ridge of the roof. Half-lap joints (see details) are used for the front, sides and door; assemble them with glue and 4d nails. Cut tops of side studs to follow angle of roof. On the roof, use half-lap joints only where the rafters meet the top and bottom pieces. Intermediate bracing should be cut to fit between the rafters and toenailed with 8d nails.

Excavate the area where the greenhouse is to be located to a depth of 2″. Spread a level bed of gravel or crushed stone in the excavation, flush with grade level. Set front and side 2x4 sills on the gravel, making sure that they are level and even. Place side panels on sills and nail. Place foam tape or beads of caulk to seal the house-side panel joints. Make sure the sides are perfectly plumb (vertical), then fasten the side panels to the structure with hanger bolts (use expansion shields on a masonry structure). Countersink the fasteners on the door side.

Hold front panel in place and drill bolt holes through corner framing pieces of front and sides. Seal front-side joints with foam tape and bolt together. Similarly fasten roof panel to house, sides and front.

Assemble the bench by nailing lath strips to a 2x2 frame (see drawing). Bolt the bench to the front and side framing, with a 2x2 support in the middle resting on the stone floor or a brick.

Staple the plastic to the frames in 4′-wide sections. Begin at the mid-point of each section and work toward the corners, stapling several inches along one side, then moving to the opposite side.

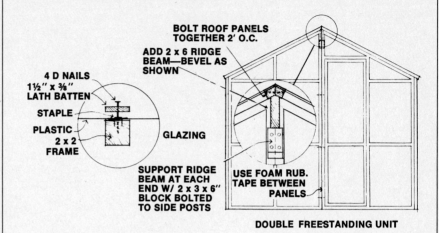

DOUBLE FREESTANDING UNIT

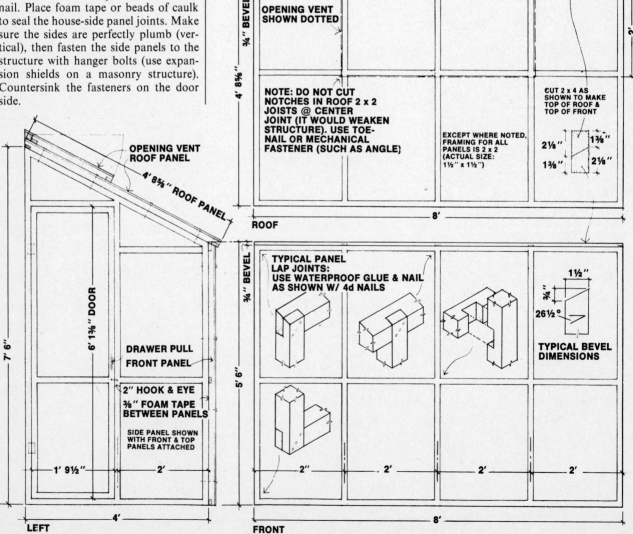

When stapling is finished, nail lath battens over the plastic into the framing.

Rip the vent mount from 2x4 (see detail) and fasten it to the upper roof framing. Fasten the vent to the mount with a continuous plastic hinge. To hold the vent open, use a long hook and screw eye, or a wood dowel with screw eyes in

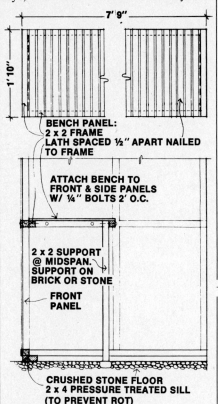

BENCH PANEL: 2 x 2 FRAME LATH SPACED ½" APART NAILED TO FRAME

ATTACH BENCH TO FRONT & SIDE PANELS W/ ¼" BOLTS 2' O.C.

2 x 2 SUPPORT @ MIDSPAN. SUPPORT ON BRICK OR STONE

FRONT PANEL

CRUSHED STONE FLOOR 2 x 4 PRESSURE TREATED SILL (TO PREVENT ROT)

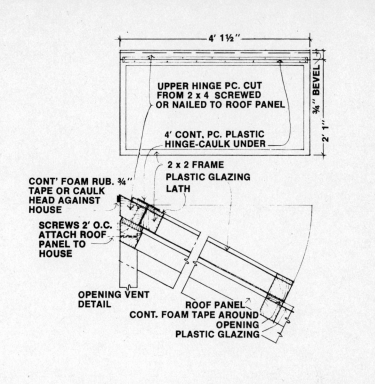

UPPER HINGE PC. CUT FROM 2 x 4 SCREWED OR NAILED TO ROOF PANEL

4' CONT. PC. PLASTIC HINGE-CAULK UNDER

2 x 2 FRAME PLASTIC GLAZING LATH

CONT' FOAM RUB. ¾" TAPE OR CAULK HEAD AGAINST HOUSE

SCREWS 2' O.C. ATTACH ROOF PANEL TO HOUSE

OPENING VENT DETAIL

ROOF PANEL CONT. FOAM TAPE AROUND OPENING PLASTIC GLAZING

each end fitting over nails driven partway into the vent and roof framing (see drawing). Hang the door on butt hinges. Add pull and hook eye.

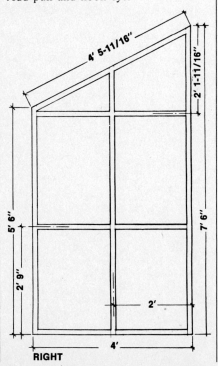

RIGHT

To build the freestanding Double Unit, make three "right" side frames (without a door) and one "left." Bolt two rights and a right and left together to form the sides. Cut two 6"-long 2x3s, and bolt one to each side frame, 5½" below the peak. Cut a 7'9" length of 2x6 for the ridge. Bevel both top edges approximately 28 degrees.

Erect the four walls, having a helper hold them temporarily upright until the structure is bolted together. Set the ridge beam on the supports bolted to the sides; secure it with lag bolts (two at each end) driven through predrilled holes in the sides.

Lift the roof panels into position and support them temporarily while drilling bolt holes through the top members of each frame. Bolt together.

Other construction details and anchoring of the double unit are the same as for the shed unit.

BAR/COFFEE TABLE

(page 51)

MATERIALS: All lumber used is ponderosa pine in nominal dimensions indicated: 1x10x4', two 1x6x8', 1x6x10', 1x4x4', 1x3x4', eight 1x2x8', 1x1x3'; 2' of ¾" dowel; 3' of ⅜" dowel; white glue; 6d finishing nails; forty 1¼" No. 10 flathead wood screws; ½ pt. each of oak and walnut stain; 1 pt. satin finish varnish.

DIRECTIONS Cutting: Six 1x6x24" side pieces (A); six 1x6x22½" partition pieces (B); two 1x10x22½" shelves (C); exactly

¾"x4"x21" bin bottom (D—rip from 1x-6); two 1x3x22" base pieces (E); two 1x-2x22½" top rails (F); four 1x1x6¾" drawer slides (G); thirty 1x2x24"* top pieces (H—*add a saw kerf, the width of a saw cut, to the 24" dimension); two 1x 4x21" top stiffeners (J); sixteen ⅜"x2" dowels (K); eight ¾"x3½" dowels (L). Assembly: Assemble sides and partitions by edge-gluing, with ⅜" dowel peg reinforcements (K) 1" in from each end of mating pieces. Clamp while glue dries. Notch partition bottoms to fit over base pieces. Assemble partitions, bin bottom, base, shelves and sides with glue, nails and screws. Countersink exposed screw heads and plug holes with ⅜" dowels cut off flush with the surface and sanded. Attach drawer slides G and top rails F, 1½" below the top edge of the sides. For cutouts in the sides, drill ⅞" holes, centered ¾" below the top edge and 2⅜" and 6½" from the ends. Cut between the holes with a saber saw or compass saw (see illustration on page 102). Sand inside the cutout. Stain the assembly.

Laminate top pieces H together and clamp until glue is dry. Attach stiffeners J to underside of top, 4½" in from each end. Plane any uneven pieces on top. Cut top in half. Sand and stain.

Set top on table unit in closed position at inner ends of cutouts in sides; drill 2¼"-deep blind holes for ¾" dowels L. Bevel ends of dowels with sandpaper; stain and glue in place. Move top to open position, flush with the partitions. Drill blind holes for dowels at outer ends of cutouts and insert dowels. To finish table, give it a coat of varnish.

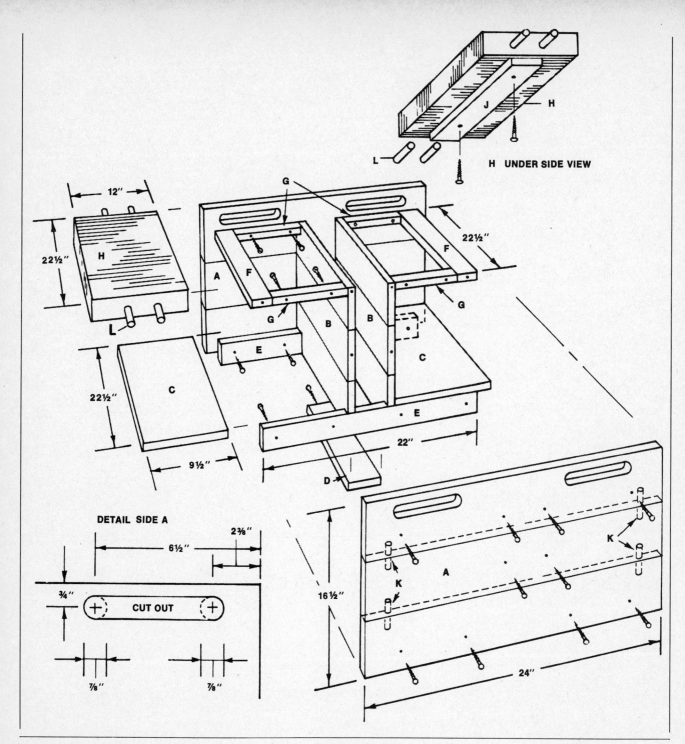

H UNDER SIDE VIEW

DETAIL SIDE A

CUT OUT

HOME OFFICE

(page 51)

Closed, this desk unit measures a tidy 21½"x40". Open the two side units to form a U shape and it's 56" across (see plan). In an L shape (as in the photo), it's 68". Fully open, it spans 80". The unit stands approximately 43" high. The writing surface and adjacent shelves are covered with tough, soil-proof plastic laminate.

MATERIALS:

Quantity	Description
2 panels	¾"x4'x8' A-B or B-B INT or MDO plywood
1 panel	⅜"x4'x8' A-B or B-B INT or MDO plywood
2 pcs.	1x4, 18⅜" long, for base (unit B)
1 pc.	1x4, 38½" long, for base (unit B)
2 pcs.	1x4, 10⅞" for base, (units A and C)
2 pcs.	1x1, 12⅝" long, for mounting desk-top bracket
4 pcs.	1x1, 6¾" long, for cleats (shelves A5, C5)
4 pcs.	1x1, 8" long, for cleats, (tops A4, C4)
2 pcs.	1x1, 3" long, for cleats, (shelves A6, C6)
2 pcs.	1x1, 7¼" long, for cleats (shelves A6, C6)
4 pcs.	1x1, 7¼" long, for cleats (shelves A7, C7)
4 pcs.	½"x¾", 6½" long, for cleats (shelves A8, C8)
2 pcs.	1x1, 16⅞" long, for cleats (shelf B6)
2	8¼" full support folding shelf brackets for desk

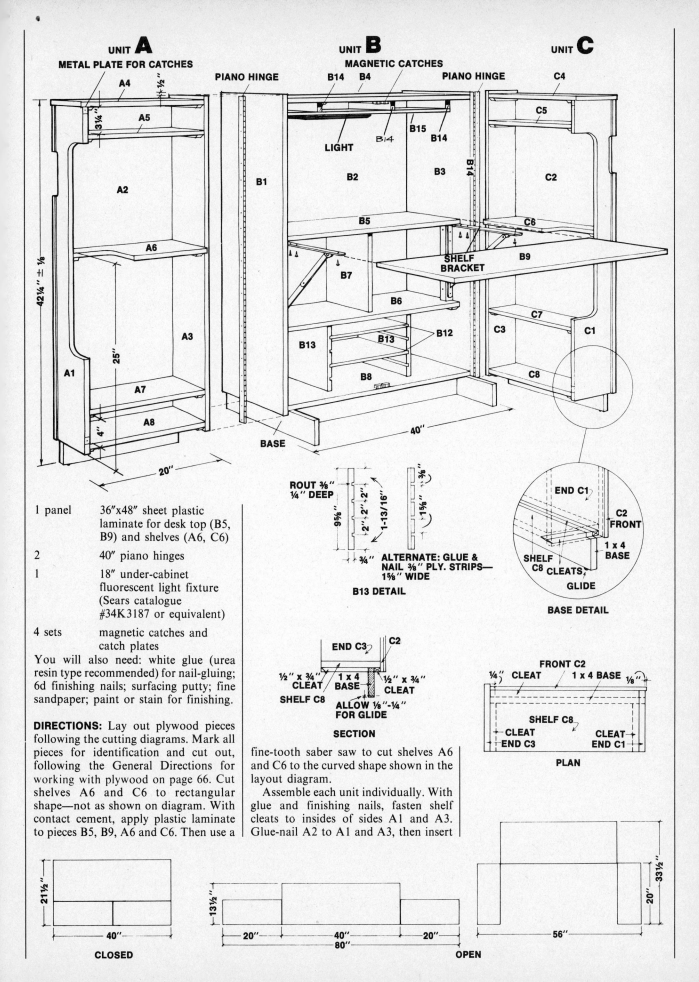

UNIT A

METAL PLATE FOR CATCHES

A4
A5
A2
A6
A3
A1
A7
A8

42¼″ ± ⅛
3¼″
½″
25″
4″
20″

UNIT B

MAGNETIC CATCHES

PIANO HINGE

B14 B4

LIGHT

B14 B15 B14

B1 B2 B3 B14

B5

B7

B6

B13 B13 B12

B8

SHELF BRACKET

B9

BASE

40″

UNIT C

PIANO HINGE

C4
C5
C2
C6
C7
C3 C1
C8

ROUT ⅜″ ¼″ DEEP

9⅝″ ¾″ 1-13/16″ 2″ 2″ 2″ ⅜″ 1⅝″

ALTERNATE: GLUE & NAIL ⅜″ PLY. STRIPS— 1⅝″ WIDE

B13 DETAIL

END C1

C2 **FRONT**

SHELF C8 CLEATS

1 x 4 **BASE**

GLIDE

BASE DETAIL

END C3 C2

½″ x ¾″ **CLEAT**   1 x 4 **BASE**   ½″ x ¾″ **CLEAT**

SHELF C8

ALLOW ⅛″-¼″ FOR GLIDE

SECTION

FRONT C2

¼″ **CLEAT**   1 x 4 **BASE**   ⅛″

SHELF C8

CLEAT **END C3**   **CLEAT** **END C1**

PLAN

---

1 panel	36″x48″ sheet plastic laminate for desk top (B5, B9) and shelves (A6, C6)
2	40″ piano hinges
1	18″ under-cabinet fluorescent light fixture (Sears catalogue #34K3187 or equivalent)
4 sets	magnetic catches and catch plates

You will also need: white glue (urea resin type recommended) for nail-gluing; 6d finishing nails; surfacing putty; fine sandpaper; paint or stain for finishing.

DIRECTIONS: Lay out plywood pieces following the cutting diagrams. Mark all pieces for identification and cut out, following the General Directions for working with plywood on page 66. Cut shelves A6 and C6 to rectangular shape—not as shown on diagram. With contact cement, apply plastic laminate to pieces B5, B9, A6 and C6. Then use a fine-tooth saber saw to cut shelves A6 and C6 to the curved shape shown in the layout diagram.

Assemble each unit individually. With glue and finishing nails, fasten shelf cleats to insides of sides A1 and A3. Glue-nail A2 to A1 and A3, then insert

21½″   40″   **CLOSED**

13½″   20″ 40″ 20″   80″   **OPEN**

33½″   20″   56″

103

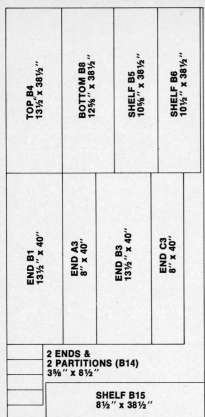

¾" x 4' x 8' APA
GRADE-TRADEMARKED PLYWOOD

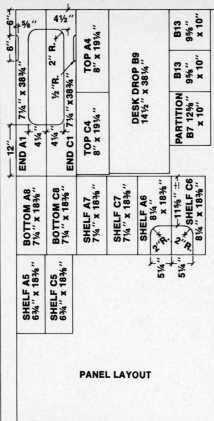

PANEL LAYOUT

¾" x 4' x 8' APA
GRADE-TRADEMARKED PLYWOOD

⅜" x 4' x 8' APA
GRADE-TRADEMARKED PLYWOOD

shelves A5, A6, A7 and A8, and top A4. Attach 1x4 base as shown in base detail. Unit C is assembled similarly.

Assemble 1x4 base for unit B, and fasten B8 to base. Fasten back B2 and sides B1 and B3 to B8; glue-nail top B4 in place. Use a router to cut ⅜"-wide, ¼"-deep slots on the insides of pieces B13, or glue-nail plywood strips to pieces B13 to support adjustable shelves B12 (see detail). Fasten partitions B13 by gluing and nailing through B8 and B2. Set shelf B6 in place and fasten. Then glue-nail B7 to B6 and B2. Fasten

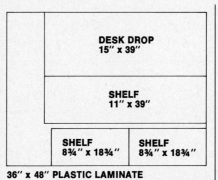

36" x 48" PLASTIC LAMINATE

1x1 shelf bracket supports to sides B1 and B3. Attach B5, gluing and nailing through sides and back, and gluing to B7. Glue-nail shelf B15 to ends and partitions B14 and fasten in place.

Fasten shelf brackets to 1x1 uprights on sides. Fasten B9 to shelf brackets. Install lighting fixture under B15. Attach units A and C to unit B with piano hinges. Fasten magnetic catches.

Countersink all visible nail heads and fill holes. Sand smooth. Finish with paint or stain. (Individual units may be finished before the final assembly.)

GAME CHEST

(page 52)

The compartmenting shown for the game chest will accommodate many favorite family games (see plan); it can be changed easily to suit your family's preferences. Only small quantities of plywood are needed for the chest; you can probably find these in your lumber dealer's odd-size or scrap pile where they are sold at bargain prices. Lattice used for drawer sides, backs and dividers and shelf edging is all ¼" thick. Various widths are indicated (see plan). If your dealer does not stock these particular widths, it is a simple matter to rip them from wider stock or to score wider lattice along a straightedge with a sharp razor blade or utility knife and break off

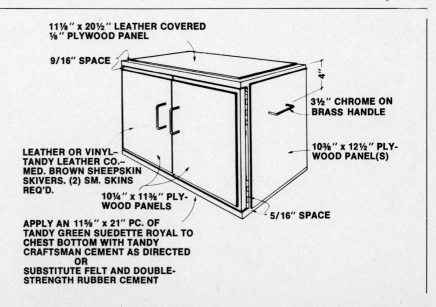

11⅛" x 20½" LEATHER COVERED ⅛" PLYWOOD PANEL

9/16" SPACE

4"

3½" CHROME ON BRASS HANDLE

10⅜" x 12½" PLYWOOD PANEL(S)

5/16" SPACE

10¼" x 11⅜" PLYWOOD PANELS

LEATHER OR VINYL—TANDY LEATHER CO.— MED. BROWN SHEEPSKIN SKIVERS. (2) SM. SKINS REQ'D.

APPLY AN 11⅝" x 21" PC. OF TANDY GREEN SUEDETTE ROYAL TO CHEST BOTTOM WITH TANDY CRAFTSMAN CEMENT AS DIRECTED OR SUBSTITUTE FELT AND DOUBLE-STRENGTH RUBBER CEMENT

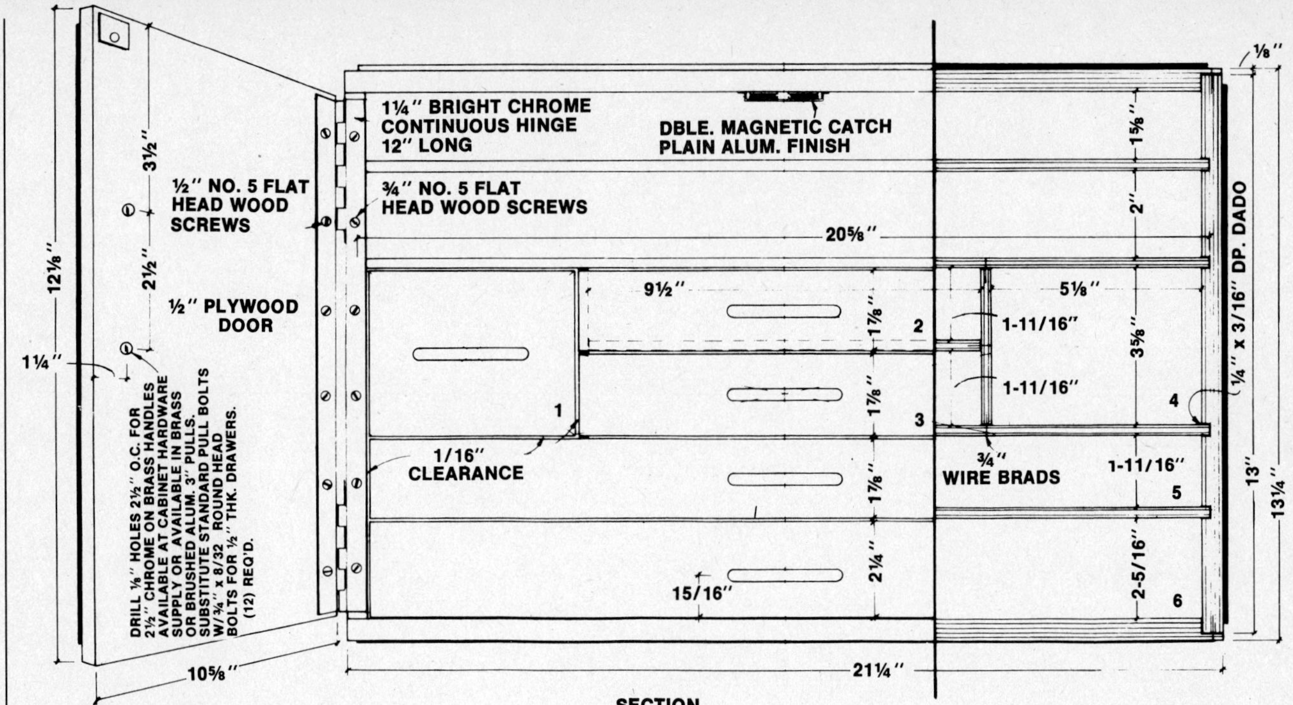
1¼" BRIGHT CHROME CONTINUOUS HINGE 12" LONG
DBLE. MAGNETIC CATCH PLAIN ALUM. FINISH
½" NO. 5 FLAT HEAD WOOD SCREWS
¾" NO. 5 FLAT HEAD WOOD SCREWS
½" PLYWOOD DOOR
DRILL ⅛" HOLES 2½" O.C. FOR 2½" CHROME ON BRASS HANDLES AVAILABLE AT CABINET HARDWARE SUPPLY OR AVAILABLE IN BRASS OR BRUSHED ALUM. 3" PULLS. SUBSTITUTE STANDARD PULL BOLTS W/¾" x 8/32 ROUND HEAD BOLTS FOR ½" THK. DRAWERS. (12) REQ'D.
1/16" CLEARANCE
¾" WIRE BRADS
¼" x 3/16" DP. DADO
12⅛"
3½"
2½"
1¼"
10⅝"
20⅝"
9½"
5⅛"
1-11/16"
1-11/16"
1-11/16"
1⅞"
1⅞"
1⅞"
2¼"
15/16"
1⅝"
2"
3⅝"
2-5/16"
⅛"
13"
13¼"
21¼"
1
2
3
4
5
6

SECTION

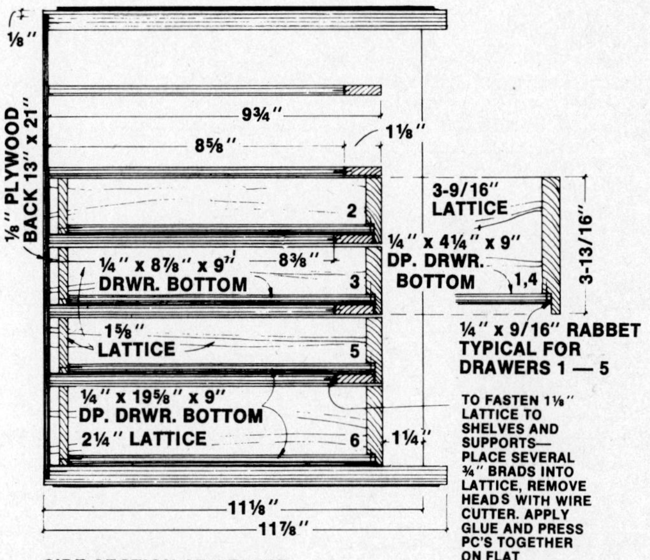
⅛"
⅛" PLYWOOD BACK 13" x 21"
9¾"
8⅝"
1⅛"
3-9/16" LATTICE
¼" x 8⅞" x 9" DRWR. BOTTOM
8⅜"
¼" x 4¼" x 9" DP. DRWR. BOTTOM
1,4
3-13/16"
1⅝" LATTICE
¼" x 9/16" RABBET TYPICAL FOR DRAWERS 1 — 5
¼" x 19⅝" x 9" DP. DRWR. BOTTOM
2¼" LATTICE
1¼"
TO FASTEN 1⅛" LATTICE TO SHELVES AND SUPPORTS— PLACE SEVERAL ¾" BRADS INTO LATTICE, REMOVE HEADS WITH WIRE CUTTER. APPLY GLUE AND PRESS PC'S TOGETHER ON FLAT SURFACE.
11⅛"
11⅞"
2
3
5
6

SIDE SECTION AT CENTER

the needed widths; plane slightly if necessary. When assembling the game chest, apply glue generously to all joints. Remove excess glue with a damp cloth. Fill all plywood edges and sand smooth before finishing.

MATERIALS: ½" plywood: two 11⅞"x-21¼" (chest top and bottom), two 11⅛"x13" sides, two 10⅝x12⅛" doors; ¼" plywood: four 8⅝"x20⅝" shelves, two 3⅝"x8⅝" upright supports, 9½"x-8⅝" shelf support, two 9"x19⅝" drawer bottoms, two 8⅞"x9" drawer bottoms, two 8⅞"x4½" drawer bottoms; ⅛" plywood: 13"x21" back, 11⅛"x20½" top panel, two 10⅜"x12½" side panels, two 10¼"x11⅜" door panels; ½x5x5' pine (rip to widths indicated on plan for drawer fronts and Monopoly drawer slotted divider); ¼"x4"x20' lattice (or various widths as noted on drawings—see above); leather (purchased by the skin—see Buyer's Guide for catalogue information) and leather cement (see Buyer's Guide), or sheet vinyl to cover top, front, back and sides; 11⅝"x21" of suedette or felt for bottom of chest; 1¼" brads; ¾" brads; white glue; wood filler; double magnetic catch; two chrome 12" continuous hinges; eight chrome or aluminum 2½" handles; satin white enamel; clear finish.

DIRECTIONS for Chest Assembly: Cut chest sides, dado for 9¾" deep shelves, dado for 9½" drawer supports. Cut chest top and bottom. Rabbet ends for ½" sides. Rabbet for back panel. Cut ⅛" back panel. Assemble chest with 1¼" brads. Set back panel in place to check square. (Do not fasten back panel.) Fill and sand edges and corner joints. Cut doors, fill and sand edges. Finish chest and doors with several coats of satin white enamel. Avoid finishing surfaces to be covered with leather or felt. Cut ¼" plywood and 1⅛" lattice for shelves and drawer supports. Pin edges to ¼" plywood. Fasten 9½" drawer support to upright supports 1$^{11}/_{16}$" down from top with ¾" brads. Mark upper 20⅝" long drawer support top and lower shelf bottom 4¾" from centers of each. Fasten above to center supports with ¼" plywood edges flush at back. Finish shelves, supports and chest back panel with several coats of high gloss varnish as directed. Sand edges where gluing will occur. Apply glue to dados and slide all shelves and supports into place. Fasten back panel with ¾" nails.

Drawer Assembly: Before starting drawers, double check dimensions of chest and vary drawer size if necessary. Cut drawer fronts from ½" pine stock. Rabbet ends ¼"x¼" for lattice sides. Rabbet drawers 1 through 5, ¼"x$^9/_{16}$" for drawer bottoms and lip. Rabbet drawer 6 ¼"x$^5/_{16}$" for drawer bottom only. Drill for handles. Cut lattice and ¼" plywood. Fasten bottom to front with ¾" brads with ends ¼" in from front ends. Fasten lattice drawer back to ¼" plywood $^1/_{16}$" from edge with ends flush. Fasten sides. Compartment drawers by cutting lengths shown dimensioned on plan first. Glue in place and fit remaining lattice as required. Check fit of

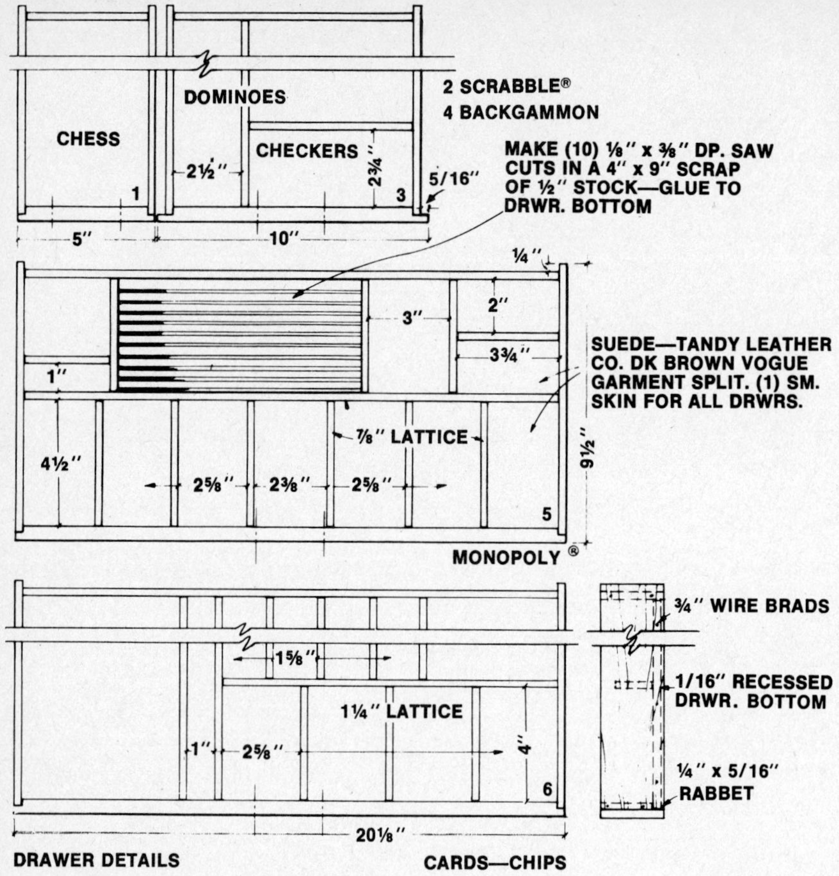
CHESS
DOMINOES
CHECKERS
2 SCRABBLE®
4 BACKGAMMON
2½″
2¾″
1
3
5/16″
MAKE (10) ⅛″ x ⅜″ DP. SAW CUTS IN A 4″ x 9″ SCRAP OF ½″ STOCK—GLUE TO DRWR. BOTTOM
5″
10″
¼″
3″
2″
3¾″
1″
SUEDE—TANDY LEATHER CO. DK BROWN VOGUE GARMENT SPLIT. (1) SM. SKIN FOR ALL DRWRS.
⅞″ LATTICE
4½″
2⅝″
2⅜″
2⅝″
9½″
5
MONOPOLY ®
¾″ WIRE BRADS
1⅝″
1/16″ RECESSED DRWR. BOTTOM
1¼″ LATTICE
1″
2⅝″
4″
¼″ x 5/16″ RABBET
6
20⅛″
DRAWER DETAILS
CARDS—CHIPS

drawers. Sand lightly. Finish similarly to shelves. Fasten handles. Cut suede insert for each drawer compartment.

Leather Panelation: Cut (5) ⅛″ plywood panels. Lay panels on leather. Mark leather with pen approximately 1½″ larger than each panel on all four sides. Cut leather and cement to top of each panel with Tandy Craftsman cement as directed. Cut leather at corners (see detail). Cement corner tabs to underside.

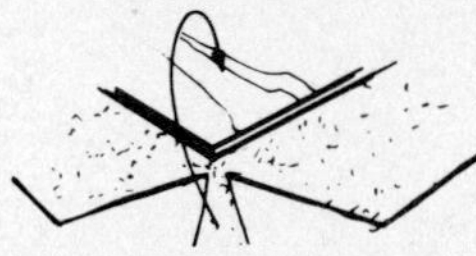

Cement remaining leather starting at center and working toward corners. Fasten completed panels to chest with Craftsman cement. Turn chest over and cement suedette to bottom.

Final Assembly: Mark handle bolt locations on doors and sides. Cut leather away, then drill ⅛″ holes. Fasten handles. Hinge doors to chest. Predrill for No. 5 screws. Fasten hinge with four screws at center. Check alignment. Complete predrilling for remaining screws. Fasten double magnetic catch to top at center. Fasten plates to doors. Touch up with white enamel. Place drawers in chest.

STORAGE SHED

(page 52)

MATERIALS:

Quantity	Description	Use
6	⅜″x4′x8′ panels of rough-sawn 303 APA grade-trade-marked plywood	front, sides, back, roof
2	2x3s, 7′9″ long redwood or treated wood	front and back sills
2	2x3s, 4′ long redwood or treated wood	side sills
4	2x2s, 5′½″ long	door framing
2	2x2s, 3′ long	door framing
2	2x2s, 2′9″ long	door framing
2	2x4s, 3′ long	door-mounted tool hangers
2	2x2s, 4′ long	rear side framing
2	2x2s, 5′3″ long	center side framing
2	2x2s, 6′4″ long	front side framing
2	2x2s, 4′ long	bottom side framing
2	2x2s, 4′9″ long	top side framing
1	2x2, 7′9″ long	upper back framing
3	2x2s, 3′11½″ long	vertical back framing
2	2x2s, 3′1¾″ long	vertical back framing
2	2x2s, 3′9¾″ long	back horizontal framing
2	2x4s, 7′9″ long	longitudinal roof framing, ripped to fit (see details 3 and 4)
3	2x4s, 4′3″ long	roof joists, cut at angles to fit (see details 3 and 4)
2	2x2s, 6′3″ long	front framing
1	2x4, 7′6″ long	door header
2	2x2s, 5′2″ long	hinge strips
1	2x2, 8″ long	joint above door
1	2x2, 7′9″ long	top front framing
4	¾″x12″ steel pipe	anchor posts
4	No. 8x2½″ flat head wood screws	door-mounted tool hangers
2	magnetic door catches	door closing
4	door hinges	door closing
2	wood door knobs	door closing

14	$5/_{16}''$x4''	sides
	carriage bolts	
	with wing nuts	
4	$5/_{16}''$x3''	
	carriage bolts	
	with wing nuts	
		sill-pipe
		fastening
20	$5/_{16}''$x2½''	(see details
	carriage bolts	3, 4 and 5)
	with wing nuts	

You will also need: 6d aluminum or galvanized box nails; drain gravel to layer 2″ deep; silicone caulk to seal all joints; glue (resorcinol is recommended); paint or stain; 4′8″x8′ roofing paper.

DIRECTIONS: Cut all plywood pieces, following panel layout diagrams and General Directions for working with plywood on page 66. Cut lumber to lengths shown on Materials list. Unless redwood (which is highly decay-resistant) is used for the 2x3 sills, treat the sills with pentachlorophenol or other wood preservative. This is best done by immersing them in the preservative and letting them soak, but if this is impractical, the preservative may be applied with a brush. Make sure the end grain is thoroughly treated.

With glue and aluminum or galvanized nails, fasten framing to the inside of the front, back, sides and doors, following the elevation drawings. Sills should extend 1″ below the plywood. Top side framing pieces should be cut at angles at both ends to make a tight fit. Cut and glue roofing paper to the underside of the roof, then fasten framing to roof, ripping the front and back framing

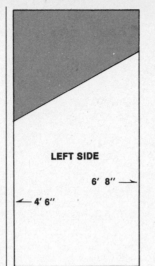
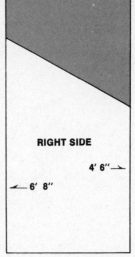
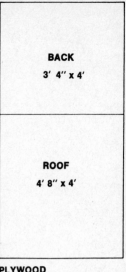

LEFT SIDE

6′ 8″ →

← 4′ 6″

RIGHT SIDE

4′ 6″ →

← 6′ 8″

BACK

3′ 4″ x 4′

ROOF

4′ 8″ x 4′

PANEL LAYOUT   ⅜″ x 4′ x 8′ ROUGH-SAWN PLYWOOD

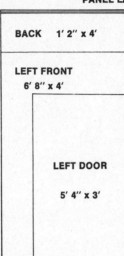
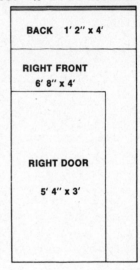
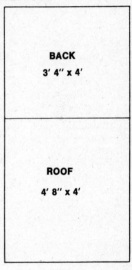

BACK   1′ 2″ x 4′

LEFT FRONT
6′ 8″ x 4′

LEFT DOOR

5′ 4″ x 3′

BACK   1′ 2″ x 4′

RIGHT FRONT
6′ 8″ x 4′

RIGHT DOOR

5′ 4″ x 3′

BACK

3′ 4″ x 4′

ROOF

4′ 8″ x 4′

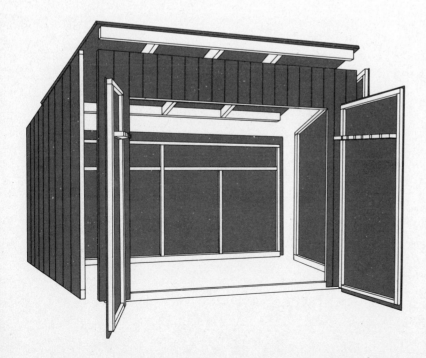

pieces to follow the roof contour (No.'s 3, 4, p. 108), cut the intermediate pieces at angles to make a tight fit.

Excavate the area where the shed is to be located to a depth of 2″. Fill the excavation with a level bed of medium to fine gravel. Set back in position and run a bead of caulking down the 2x2 end frames, then fasten sides by drilling holes and inserting bolts and tightening wing nuts (see No. 1). Similarly fasten front. Drive steel pipes into ground inside the shed flush with the tops of the sills; make sure the sills are even and level, and bolt through sills and pipes (No. 2). With a helper, lift the roof into place and fasten as in No.'s 3, 4 and 5.

Cut slots in 2x4 tool hangers (No. 6) and mount on doors. Hang doors, either flush-mounting hinges or mortising them (see detail). Install magnetic catches and doorknobs. Use leftover plywood to make shelves as needed in the shed. (You may also wish to install panels of Peg-Board for hanging sharp tools out of children's reach.) Plywood can be stained or left to weather naturally.

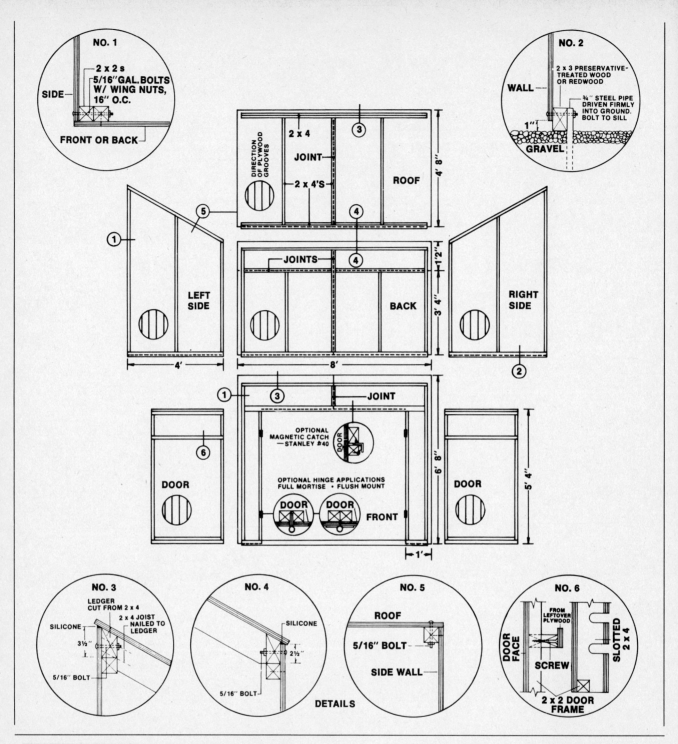

SEWING CENTER

(page 54)

This compact sewing center expands into a combination sewing cabinet with drop-in well for the machine and 20"x 30" work surface. At one end of the unit, five drawers hold everything from notions to patterns; at the other end there's storage space for the machine, plus one deep shelf for fabric and other sewing paraphernalia. Plastic laminate covers the work surfaces.

Note: Cabinet well can be cut to fit your particular machine.

MATERIALS:

Quantity	Description
2 panels	¾"x4'x8' A-A, A-B or MDO plywood
1 panel	⅜"x4'x8' A-A, A-B or MDO plywood
11 lin. ft.	½"x1" lumber for drawer slides
11 lin. ft.	1x4 lumber for drawer glides
6 lin. ft.	½"x¾" lumber cleats for pull-outs
4 lin. ft.	1"-diameter dowel
3 lin. ft.	1x2 lumber for stretcher
¼ sheet	⅛" plastic laminate for
30"x72"	notion drawer dividers laminate for contemporary unit
15	No. 10 (2") flat head wood screws
24	No. 10 (1¼") flat head wood screws
4	3" rigid casters
1	24" continuous hinge (cut to size) with screws
1 pr.	¾" wrap-around door hinges
1	magnetic catch

You will also need: miscellaneous finishing nails; glue (urea-resin type is

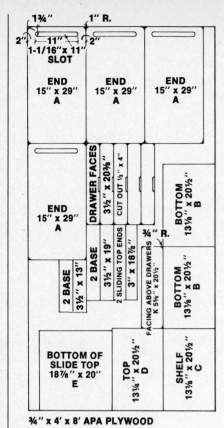

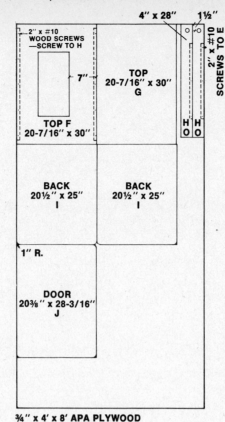

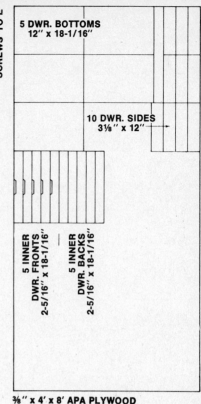

¾″ x 4′ x 8′ APA PLYWOOD   **¾″ x 4′ x 8′ APA PLYWOOD**   **⅜″ x 4′ x 8′ APA PLYWOOD**

recommended); surfacing putty; fine sandpaper; paint or stain as desired.

DIRECTIONS: Cut all plywood parts following the panel layouts and the General Directions for working with plywood on page 66. Cut a rectangular hole in top F to fit your sewing machine; use a self-starting saber saw or drill starter holes in the corners, then insert a keyhole saw to make the cut. Cut slots in ends A (see panel layout), drilling 1¹⁄₁₆″-diameter holes at each end and then us-

ing a saber saw or keyhole saw. Notch the inner drawer fronts and drawer faces, ½″ deep and 4″ long. Round all corners of the drawer faces, facing K, ends A and door J, and the bottom corners of backs I. Drill 1″-diameter holes 1½″ from each end of pieces H. Cut slots for stretchers in backs I.

Assemble base for stationary cabinet, using glue and finishing nails. Glue-nail bottom B to base. Rip drawer glides to sizes shown in side cutaway and fasten to two sides A with glue and 1¼″ wood

screws driven through pilot holes predrilled in the slides. Fasten 1x1 slides to support pullout, 4⁹⁄₁₆″ below tops of pieces A. Assemble base, back I and sides A; attach shelf D and facing K.

Assemble the other side unit, first fastening shelf cleats to sides A, then attaching back I and sides A to shelves B and C. Attach casters under shelf B. Hang door I on unit.

Screw and glue slide sides H to piece E, and top F to sides H. Fasten a stretcher stop to one end of the 1x2

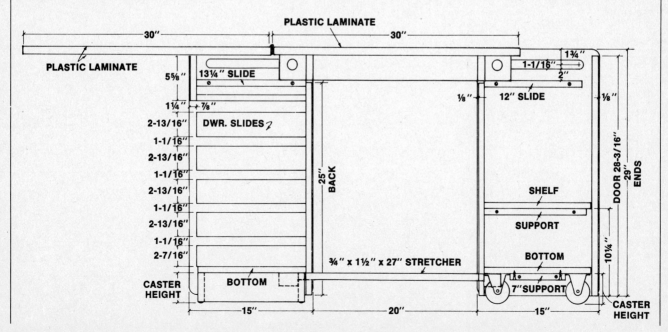

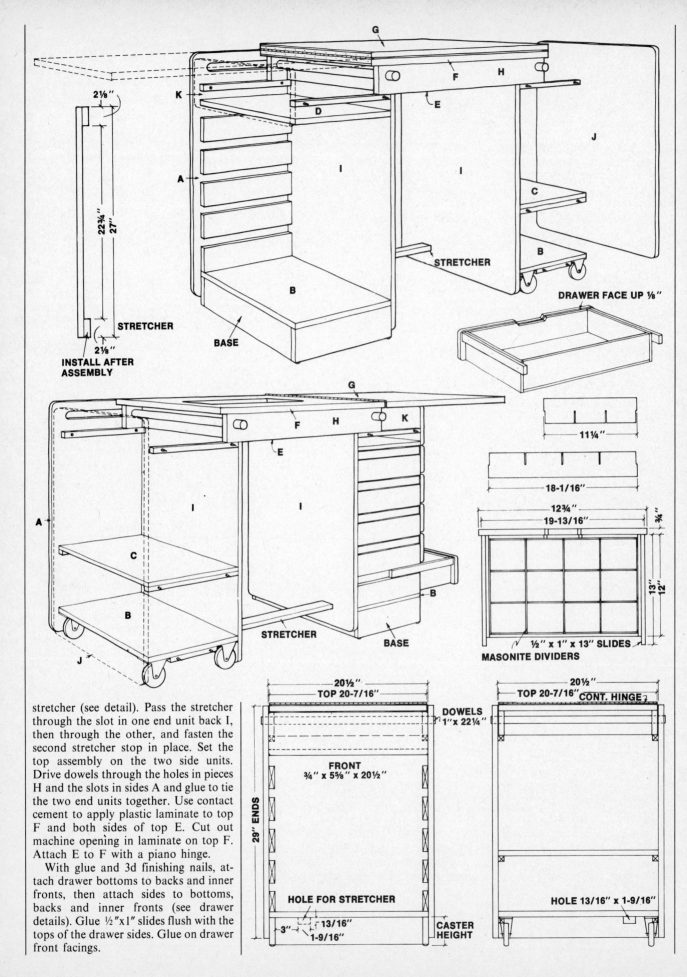

2⅛"

22¾"
27"

STRETCHER

2⅛"

**INSTALL AFTER
ASSEMBLY**

K

D

A

B

BASE

STRETCHER

G

F

H

E

J

C

B

STRETCHER

DRAWER FACE UP ⅛"

G

F H K

E

A

I I

C

B

J

B

STRETCHER

BASE

11¼"

18-1/16"

12¾"
19-13/16"
¾"

13"
12"

½" x 1" x 13" SLIDES

MASONITE DIVIDERS

20½"
TOP 20-7/16"

DOWELS
1" x 22¼"

FRONT
¾" x 5⅝" x 20½"

29" ENDS

HOLE FOR STRETCHER

3"
13/16"
1-9/16"

**CASTER
HEIGHT**

20½"
TOP 20-7/16" CONT. HINGE

HOLE 13/16" x 1-9/16"

stretcher (see detail). Pass the stretcher through the slot in one end unit back I, then through the other, and fasten the second stretcher stop in place. Set the top assembly on the two side units. Drive dowels through the holes in pieces H and the slots in sides A and glue to tie the two end units together. Use contact cement to apply plastic laminate to top F and both sides of top E. Cut out machine opening in laminate on top F. Attach E to F with a piano hinge.

With glue and 3d finishing nails, attach drawer bottoms to backs and inner fronts, then attach sides to bottoms, backs and inner fronts (see drawer details). Glue ½"x1" slides flush with the tops of the drawer sides. Glue on drawer front facings.

Cut and notch plastic laminate for dividers in notion drawers (see drawer detail). Assemble and insert in drawers.

Sand the unit smooth and finish with paint or stain as desired.

STORAGE BUNK BED

(page 56)

MATERIALS: Five 4' x 8' panels of ¾" MDO plywood, cut as follows: 40½" x 67½" (A—round all corners to 3" radius), 39" x 75" (D), two 40½" x 35" (E), three 16½" x 35" (F), three 3" x 35" (G), 2¼" x 35" (H), 10½" x 75" (J—round all corners to 3" radius), for B, C, K and two pieces L, see cutting diagram,

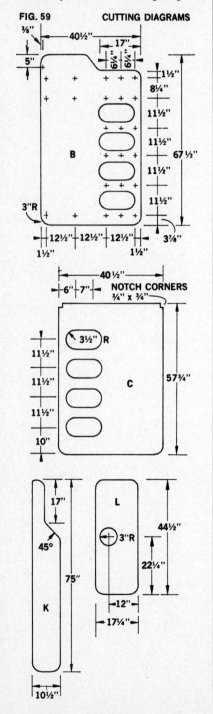

FIG. 59   CUTTING DIAGRAMS

NOTCH CORNERS
¾" x ¾"

Fig. 59; two 2x4x35" fir (M); 1½"x35" clothes rod (N) with rod brackets; 32 1½" No. 8 oval head wood screws with countersunk washers; 6d finishing nails; white glue; four butt hinges; two magnetic catches; wood filler.

DIRECTIONS: Cut plywood pieces B, C, K and L to shape. Measure and mark all screw locations piece B (Fig. 59) and drill pilot holes for screws. Use a saber saw or compass saw to cut oval holes in pieces B and C and round holes in both pieces L (Fig. 59). Round the edges of the large holes with a rasp and medium sandpaper; fill the plywood edges with wood filler and sand smooth (Fig. 59A).

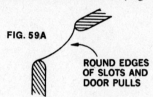

FIG. 59A

ROUND EDGES OF SLOTS AND DOOR PULLS

Begin assembly with pieces on their back edges on the floor. With five oval head screws and washers, fasten end B to platform D, with D centered ¾" in from each edge and its surface 9" below top of B. Fasten end A to D with six screws and washers driven through equally spaced pilot holes. With glue and nails driven through D, attach partition C to D, allowing 35" between C and B (Fig. 59B).

With glue and nails, fasten three shelf fronts G to shelves F. Fasten shelves F

in place, spaced as in Fig. 59B, gluing and nailing through partition C and screwing into the shelves through end B. Fasten upper shelf E between C and B, with its top 7½" below the bottom of platform D. Set the unit upright.

Fasten base pieces M, 3" in from front and back of bottom shelf E, using glue and nails. Glue and nail shelf front H to the top of bottom shelf E, 16½" from the back edge of E. Fasten bottom shelf E in place, nailing through C and screwing through side B. Nail through both C and B into base pieces M.

Fasten front and back upper side panels J and K flush with the top edges of ends A and B, nailing into platform D and screwing in place through the ends.

Mount rod brackets inside B and C, centered 10" from the front edges of B and C and 2½" below upper shelf E. Insert clothes rod. Hang doors L, with hinges centered approximately 6" from tops and bottoms of the doors, and allowing a ½" gap between doors and top and bottom shelves E. Attach magnetic catches to doors and to underside of top shelf E.

Countersink all exposed nailheads and fill the holes with wood filler. Sand smooth and apply finish.

The bed platform is designed to accommodate a standard twin (39"x75") mattress; the space beneath will accommodate a standard twin bed placed perpendicular to the bunk unit (as shown in photo on page 56).

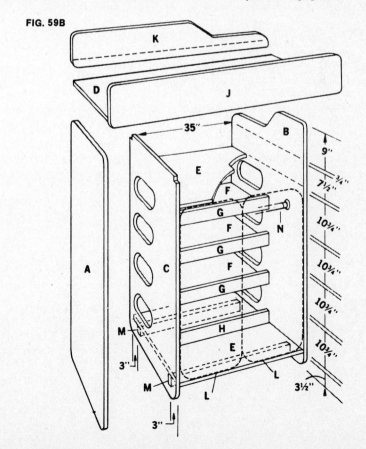

FIG. 59B

DUTCH BUFFET

(page 57)

The plywood recommended is A-A, A-B or B-B Interior or MDO APA grade-trademarked plywood.

MATERIALS:

Quantity	Description
3 panels	¾"x4'x8' plywood for parts A through E, H through K, KK, L, D1 and D2
1 panel	½"x4'x8' plywood for parts M, N, D4, T2, T4, T5
2 pcs.	⅜" plywood 20¾"x25¾" for D3
3 pcs.	½"x¾"x48" lumber strip for edging F
1 pc.	2½"x6' cove molding cut each end and mitered to fit for G1
1 pc.	46½" molding fo G2; see detail for configuration
2 pcs.	1x1x46½" lumber for screw strips O
2 pcs.	1x1x15" lumber for screw strips P
4 pcs.	23⅝" molding (24" lengths cut to fit, mitered at corners) for D5; see detail for configuration
4 pcs.	18⅝" molding (19" lengths cut to fit, mitered at corners) for D6; see detail for configuration
4 pcs.	19" molding (20" lengths cut to fit, mitered at corners) for D7; see detail for configuration
4 pcs.	14" molding (15" lengths cut to fit, mitered at corners) for D8; see detail for configuration
8 pcs.	¼"x ½"x15¾" lumber strips for gliders T3
1 pc.	1¹⁄₁₆"x2¼"x16½" lumber strips for center guides T6
2 pcs.	1¹⁄₁₆"x2⁹⁄₁₆"x16½" lumber for side guides T7
2	4" mending plates, screws
4 pair	offset hinges, decorative cabinet type
2	ceramic knobs
24	No. 10 1¼" flat head wood screws
2 pair	magnetic catches

You will also need: 6d finishing nails; glue (urea resin type recommended); surfacing putty; fine sandpaper; paint or stain for finishing.

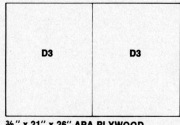

⅜" x 21" x 26" APA PLYWOOD

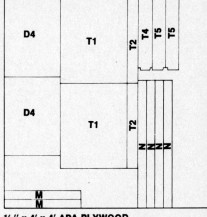

½" x 4' x 4' APA PLYWOOD

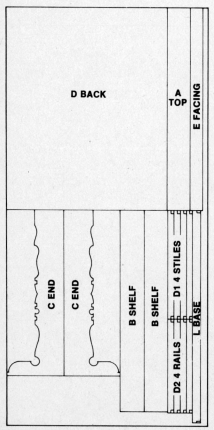

¾" x 4' x 8' APA PLYWOOD

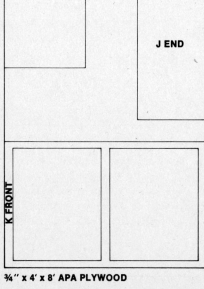

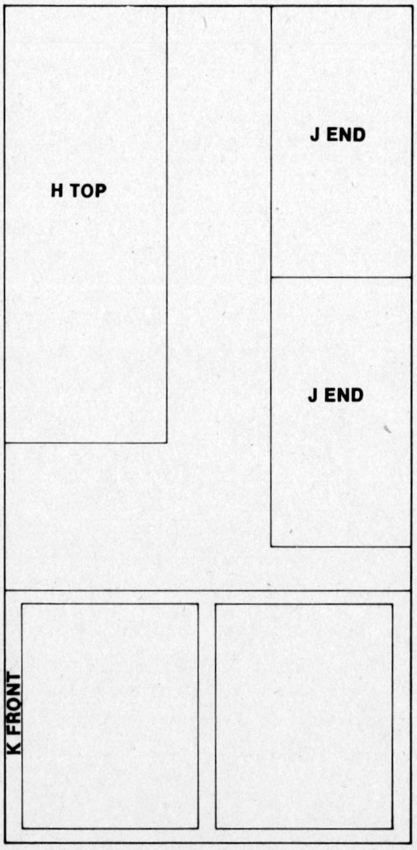

¾" x 4' x 8' APA PLYWOOD

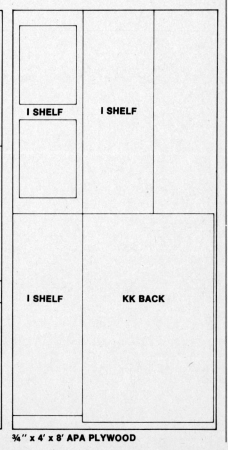

¾" x 4' x 8' APA PLYWOOD

DIRECTIONS For Cutting: Cut plywood and lumber in the following sizes, referring to panel layout diagrams.

UPPER CABINET
A—Top 1 pc. ¾"x5½"x46½"
B—Shelves 2 pcs. ¾"x5¾"x46½"
C—Ends 2 pcs. ¾"x13½"x38¼"
D—Back 1 pc. ¾"x38¼"x46½"
E—Facing 1 pc. ¾"x3"x46½"
F—Edgings 3 pcs. 45"x¾"x48"
G1—Crown Molding 1 pc. 2½" 6' (miter to fit)
G2—Molding 1 pc. 46½"

LOWER CABINET
H—Top 1 pc. ¾"x19½"x50"
I—Shelves 3 pcs. ¾"x16½"x46½"
J—Ends 2 pcs. ¾"x16½"x31"
K—Front 1 pc. ¾"x29"x48"
DOOR OPENING—21" wide x 26" high
KK—Back 1 pc. ¾"x31"x48"
L—Base 1 pc. ¾"x2"x49"
M—Base 2 pcs. ½"x2"x18"
N—End trim 4 pcs. ½"x2"x29"
O—Screw strips 2 pcs. ¾"x¾"x46½"
P—Screw strips 2 pcs. ¾"x¾"x15"

DOORS
D1—Stiles 4 pcs. ¾"x1½"x25⅛"
D2—Rails 4 pcs. ¾"x1½"x21⅝"
D3—Panel 2 pcs. ⅜"x20¾"x25¾"
D4—Panel 2 pcs. ½"x13"x18"
D5—Moldings 4 pcs. (miter to fit)
D6—Moldings 4 pcs. (miter to fit)
D7—Moldings 4 pcs. (miter to fit)
D8—Moldings 4 pcs. (miter to fit)

SILVER TRAYS
T1—Bottoms 2 pcs. ½"x15¾"x19½"
T2—Fronts 2 pcs. ½"x2½"x19½"
T3—Gliders 8 pcs. ¼"x½"x15¾"
T4—Center guide 1 pc. ½"x3¼"x16½"
T5—Side guide 2 pcs. ½"x3¹/₁₆"x16½"
T6—Center guide 1 pc. 1¹/₁₆"x2¼"x16½"
T7—Side guide 2 pcs. 1¹/₁₆"x2⁹/₁₆"x16½"

Cut openings in front K and top shelf I, following the dimensions given in the exploded drawing. First drill pilot holes in the corners of the openings, then cut out with a saber saw or keyhole saw. Notch corners of base L, stiles D1 and rails D2, and guides T4 and T5, following panel layout and dimensions in exploded drawing. Cut two pieces C as rectangles, then clamp or tack them together. Following directions in box on page 66, transfer scrollwork pattern from layout grid to plywood. Cut out with a jig saw or coping saw.

Directions: Fasten glue blocks to inside of base L. Fasten bottom shelf I to L and back KK, using glue and finishing nails. Attach ends J, middle shelf I and cut-out top shelf I, then glue-nail cut-out front K in place. Install tray guides T4

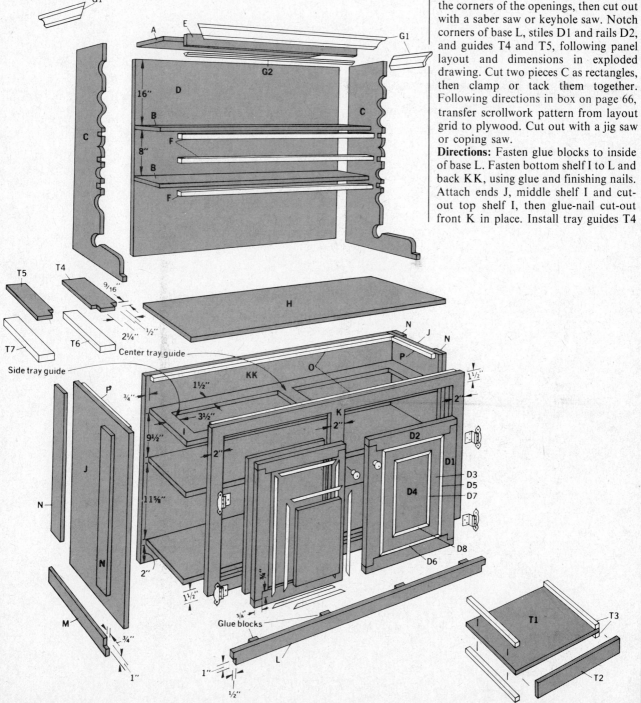

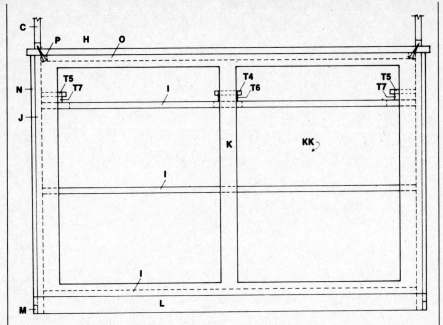

TILT-OUT SINK FRONT AND VENTILATED VEGETABLE DRAWER

MATERIALS: Two 3"x3"x⅛" Masonite sides (A); two 4"x15"x⅛" Masonite (B), for bottom of tilt-out; two 1' continuous hinges; drill with 1" bit; router.

DIRECTIONS:

1. Using a crosscut saw, cut the stationary front panel along the full length of the line marked X in Fig. 61, to separate the top portion from the bottom portion of the panel.

2. Recess lower portion of cabinet (we went back about 6½") and screw to side of surrounding cabinet.

Note: If your under-sink cabinet has a floor of its own, it should also be recessed to accommodate the door recess.

To Ventilate Vegetable Drawers

3. Now that the doors have been recessed, the side of the cabinet that houses the vegetable drawers is exposed. Drill 1" holes in the cabinet side, centering them in the airspace between the drawers, using Fig. 61A as guide for placement. Sand holes; match stain, if desired.

Tilt-Out Sink Storage

4. Remove stationary panels from cabinet front top portion. Set router at ¼" depth. Cut a groove ¼" from side edges on back of each panel, using a ⅛" straight-face cutter.

5. Cut A squares in half diagonally to make side pieces for tilt-out.

6. Glue side panels A to short edges of bottom panels B and secure with ½" brads spaced 1" apart.

7. Glue assembly sides into panel grooves (do not nail).

8. When assembly is completely dry, attach 1' continuous hinge to cabinet crossmember and bottom of tilt-out, so hinge does not show when tilt-out is in closed position.

KNIFE RACK

MATERIALS: Two 1"x5"x½" oak for ends (A); two 1"x19½"x½" oak for front and back (B); one 6"x19½"x½" oak for top (C); ¼" bit and drill; coping saw; oak stain for wood.

DIRECTIONS:

Note: Most cabinets have sufficient clearance for knife blades behind closed drawers. However, you should check your space with a yardstick before making this project.

1. Nail and glue A and B pieces together, as shown in Fig. 61B.

2. Nail and glue C piece on top of assembly, edges flush.

3. On C, draw two pencil lines, spaced as shown in Fig. 61B. Drill ¼" holes at

---

through T7, and fasten strips O to K and KK and strips P to ends J. Set top H in place. Glue on base M and trim N.

Glue-nail upper unit ends C to back D. Add shelves B and top A. Fasten upper unit to lower unit with mending plates screwed to backs D and KK, and by toenailing through predrilled pilot holes in the front edges of ends C into top H. Drive screws at 12" intervals through predrilled holes in backs D and KK into all shelves.

Glue gliders T3 to tops and bottoms of tray bottoms T1. Glue on fronts T2. Assemble door panels, rails and stiles as shown in exploded drawing. Hang doors on offset hinges. (Add knobs and catches after finishing buffet.) Glue-nail molding and trim strips as shown in exploded drawing.

Set all visible nails below the wood surface and fill holes with wood putty. Sand smooth. Finish the buffet with paint or stain, as desired.

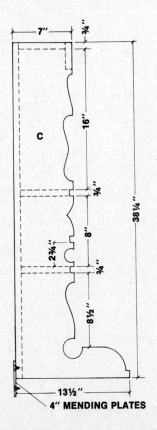

4" MENDING PLATES

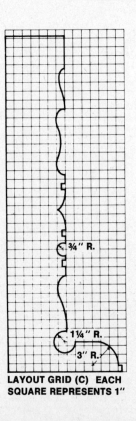

LAYOUT GRID (C) EACH SQUARE REPRESENTS 1"

FIG. 61   TILT-OUT SINK FRONT AND VENTILATED VEGETABLE DRAWERS

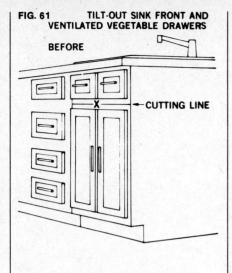

BEFORE

— CUTTING LINE

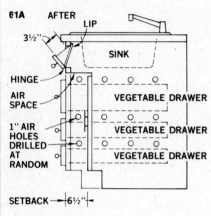

61A   AFTER

3½" LIP

SINK

HINGE

AIR SPACE

VEGETABLE DRAWER

1" AIR HOLES DRILLED AT RANDOM

VEGETABLE DRAWER

VEGETABLE DRAWER

SETBACK — 6½"

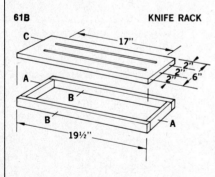

61B   KNIFE RACK

C

17"

2"

2"

6"

A

B

B

A

19½"

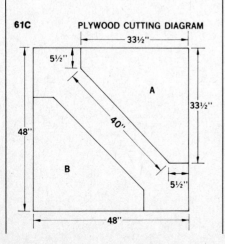

61C   PLYWOOD CUTTING DIAGRAM

33½"

5½"

A

40"

33½"

48"

B

5½"

48"

---

ends of each line. To make ¼" slots, cut on each line between holes, using a saber saw or ¼" dado blade.

4. Sand; stain oak, if desired.

5. Trace rack on countertop, flush with backsplash. Draw another rectangle 1" inside the traced line. Using a crosscut saw, cut through countertop on inside pencil line.

6. Glue rack to counter, aligning it with traced pencil lines.

FOOD WRAP BINS

MATERIALS: 4'x4'x½" INT plywood, four 4"x6"x½" for rear support (C) and sides, left and right (D); two ½"x½"x-42¼" pine trim strip (F); ½"x½"x4" pine trim strip (G); ⅛" Masonite for dividers (E); one 4½"x30"x⅛" Masonite; router with ⅛" straight-face cutter.

DIRECTIONS:

1. Mark and cut bin top piece (A) and bottom piece (B) from plywood, using Fig. 61C as a pattern.

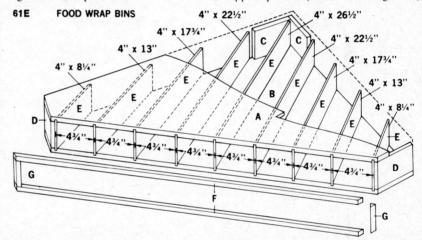

61E   FOOD WRAP BINS

4" x 22½" 4" x 26½"
4" x 17¾"
4" x 13"   4" x 22½"
4" x 8¼"   4" x 17¾"
4" x 13"
4" x 8¼"
C C
E E E
E
E B
E   A   E
D   E
E
D
G
4¾" 4¾" 4¾" 4¾" 4¾" 4¾" 4¾" 4¾"
F
G

2. Place A and B unfinished sides up, front edges aligned; clamp together and secure to work table.

3. Using a straightedge, draw center lines for dividers E (shown in Fig. 61E) straight across both surfaces.

4. Set router for ¼" depth and cut grooves on center lines.

5. From plywood waste cut C and D.

6. Nail and glue A and B to short side pieces C and D, as shown in Fig. 61E.

7. From ⅛" Masonite cut dividers E in lengths indicated in Fig. 61E. Slide dividers into assembly grooves.

8. Nail and glue trim strip pieces F and G to front. Trim angles at front.

9. Sand; prime; paint with semi-gloss latex.

APPLIANCE CENTER

MATERIALS: ½" INT plywood: two 7½"x42" for top (A) and bottom (B), three 7½"x16½" for three sides (C), one 4"x17½" for electric plug stile—front and one 3"x16½"x½" rear (D), one 5"x 10" support for Dazey Seal-a-Meal bag sealer (E, optional); two ½"x½"x38" pine trim strips for front edges (F) and

---

one ½"x½"x16½" for side edge (G); two duplex receptacles with chrome plate covers; two electrical boxes; electrical wiring as needed.

DIRECTIONS:

1. Nail and glue A, B and C pieces together as shown in Fig. 61D to form assembly with butt joints.

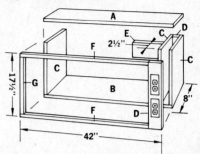

61D   APPLIANCE CENTER

A
E C D
F 2½" C
C
C B
G 8"
F D
42"
17½"

2. If you intend to install an electric bag sealer, you will need to add optional support piece E (as shown in Fig. 61D), nailing and gluing through A and C pieces. Mount sealer on E, using hardware provided.

3. Cut openings in D stile for electrical boxes at convenient placement for your appliances. Nail and glue D piece in place; insert electrical boxes and wire. Note: Electrical parts used here are available at hardware and electrical supply stores and are listed by Underwriters' Laboratories.

Important: Before you plug in any electrical equipment, have it tested by a licensed electrician.

4. Nail and glue trim strip pieces F and G to assembly front, overlapping edges.

5. Sand; prime; paint with semi-gloss.

PULL-OUT PEG BOARD STORAGE

MATERIALS: One 18"x20"x⅛" Peg-Board (A); one 1x3x23¼" pine runner for top (B); two ½"x½"x17" pine runners for bottom (C).

DIRECTIONS:

1. Cut out center stile of existing 2-door cabinet base; sand.

2. Draw line down center back of stile. Set router for ⅜″ depth. Cut stile on line using ⅛″ straight-face cutter.
3. Cut center on top runner B with router, as you did for stile.
4. Nail and glue B at center top inside cabinet, flush with front crossmember (see Fig. 61F).

61F PULL-OUT PEGBOARD STORAGE

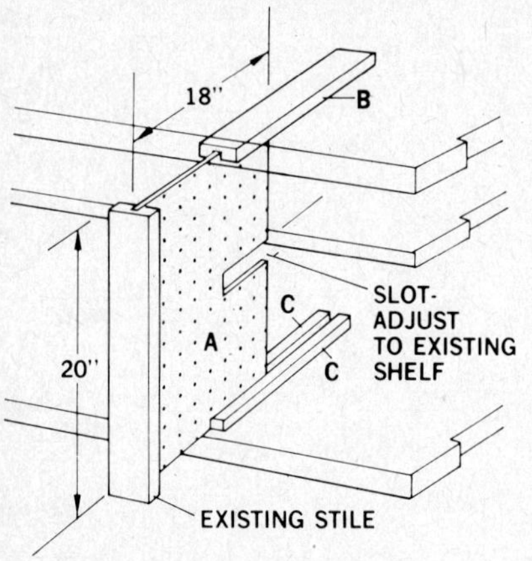

18"
B
C
SLOT-
ADJUST
TO EXISTING
SHELF
A
C
20"
EXISTING STILE

5. Slide Peg-Board into cabinet in top runner; mark a 1″ notch where board hits the existing shelf; cut 6½″-deep notch out of Peg-Board. Glue opposite edge into groove on stile.
6. Slide pull-out into runner, making sure it is plumb.
7. Mark cabinet floor with pencil lines at both sides of Peg-Board.
8. Nail and glue runners C to cabinet floor, aligning runners with pencil lines.
9. Slide pull-out into runners.

WINE RACK

MATERIALS: ½″ INT grade plywood: Two 11½″x36″ for top (A) and bottom (B), two 11½″x17″ for sides (C and D); two ½″x½″x36″ pine trim strips for top and bottom front edges (E) and two ½″x½″x17″ for side front edges (F); sixteen 28″x⅜″-diameter dowels for crossmembers.

61G WINE RACK

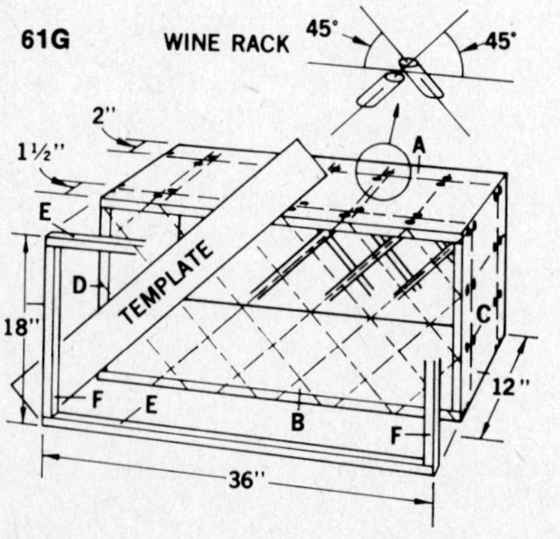

45°
45°
2"
1½"
A
E
D
TEMPLATE
C
18"
F
E
B
F
12"
36"

DIRECTIONS:
Note: Wine rack can be made larger or smaller. If you adjust our figures, make sure that the width of your rack is double to height so that the dowels can be inserted at 45-degree angles.
1. Nail and glue together pieces A, B, C and D to form the framework for the rack, butt-joining as shown.
2. Nail and glue trim strips E and F to front of assembly, butting at ends.
3. Cut a 4½″x36″ piece of Masonite or lumber to make a template.
4. Lay framework on its back. Find and mark the exact center on top and bottom strips E (see Fig. 61G).
5. Place template on frame, with bottom edge of template aligned at top center mark on top strip and the corner diagonally opposite. Mark the top and side edges on the strips where the top edge of the template crosses (Fig. 61G).
6. Reposition template at these new marks and mark strips again where template crosses at top and side. When diagonal lines have been marked completely across the framework, turn template and mark opposite diagonals.
7. To mark positions for dowel holes, draw lines perpendicular to all marks on the trim strips, straight across framework to the back edges.
8. Using a T-square draw a line 2″ in from the front and back edges of framework (see Fig. 61G).
9. Drill ⅜″ holes slowly and accurately at 45° angle from left to right where the 2″ lines cross the perpendicular (see detail with Fig. 61G). Using a T-square, draw another line 2½″ from front and rear edges. Drill ⅜″ holes as before, angling from right to left.
10. Slide dowels into place through the holes. Cut off excess as close to surface as possible, using a sharp wood chisel. File with a wood rasp or an 8″ mill bastard.
11. Sand; prime; paint with semi-gloss.

STEMWARE RACK

MATERIALS: For 6′-long, 15″-deep rack attached to the underside of wall-hung cabinet or from the bottom shelf of a pass-through or room divider you will need interior-grade plywood and lath strips in the following amounts: One 15″x72″x½″ plywood for top (A); forty-four 15″x1⅝″x¼″ lath strips (B).

DIRECTIONS:
1. Nail and glue A to underside of unit from which stemware will be suspended.
2. Draw a pencil line crosswise at center of A.
3. Nail and glue B strip 1¾″ to the right of center line; nail six more to the right, spaced 3½″ apart.

61H STEMWARE RACK

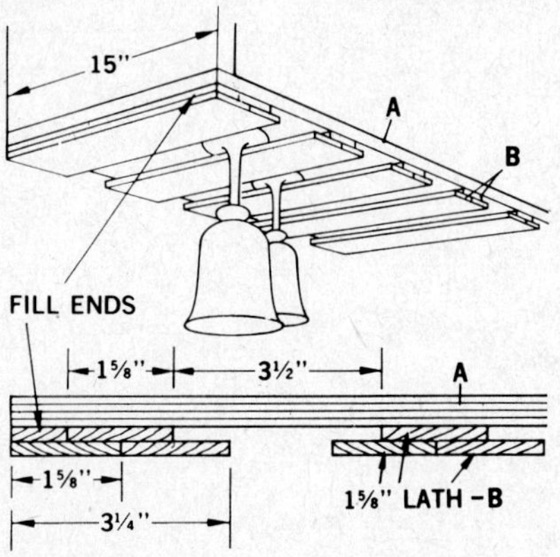

15"
A
B
FILL ENDS
1⅝"
3½"
A
1⅝"
3¼"
1⅝" LATH -B

4. Repeat to left of center mark for a total of 14 strips.
5. Nail and glue remaining lath strips in pairs that butt over an invisible center line down the middle of the previously nailed B strips (see Fig. 61H).
6. Sand; prime; paint with semi-gloss. latex. Suspend stemware as shown.

PIGEONHOLE STORAGE

MATERIALS: ½″ INT plywood: Two 8″x31″ for top (A) and bottom (B), two 8″x7¼″ for sides (C and D); two ½″x½″x31″ pine trim strips for top (E) and bottom (F) edges; two ½″x½″x7¼″ pine trim strips for side edges (G and H); eight 7¾″x7½″x⅛″ Masonite for dividers (J); one 7¼″x30″x½″ for back (K); router with ⅛″ straight-face cutter.

DIRECTIONS:
1. Place A and B, unfinished sides up and long edges butting; clamp together and secure to work table.
2. Using straightedge, draw center lines straight across both surfaces spaced as shown for dividers J (see Fig. 61I).

61I PIGEONHOLE STORAGE

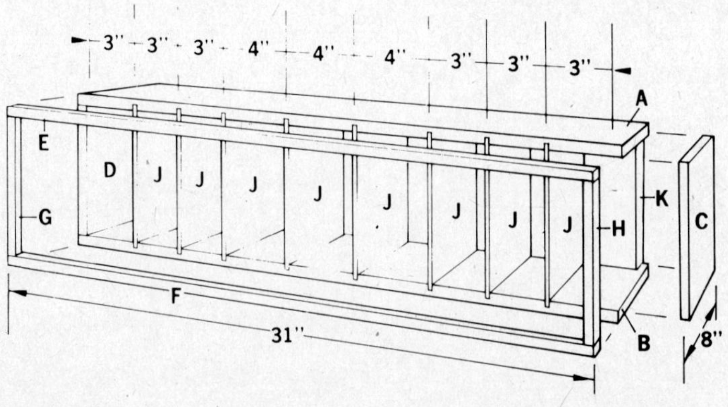

3"
3"
3"
4"
4"
4"
3"
3"
3"
A
E
D
J
J
J
J
J
J
J
J
G
K
H
C
F
31"
B
8"

3. Set router for ¼″ depth and cut grooves on center lines with ⅛″ straight-face cutter.

4. Nail and glue A, B, C and D together to form frame, butting at ends.

5. Slip dividers J into grooves.

6. Nail and glue trim strips E, F, G and H to assembly front, butting at corners.

7. Nail and glue back K in place.

8. Sand; prime; paint with semi-gloss.

POOL TABLE

(page 60)

Designed to fit into the average family room, the pool table measures 44″x88″. Its wing-support base is hinged to the top so that the entire unit folds flat for storage. The two-section regulation-size table-tennis top fastens together with two bolts and wing nuts. It rests on top of the pool table, steadied by the inner framework on its underside.

MATERIALS:

Quantity	Description
3 panels	¾″x4′x8′ plywood for pool table top and supports
2 panels	¼″x4′x8′ plywood for table tennis top
2	piano hinges, 20″ long
2	piano hinges, 42″ long
1	Pool Table Kit FC-73 (or equivalent) containing billiard cloth, extruded rubber cushion, leveling legs, drop pockets, spots and pearl sights (see Buyer's Guide)

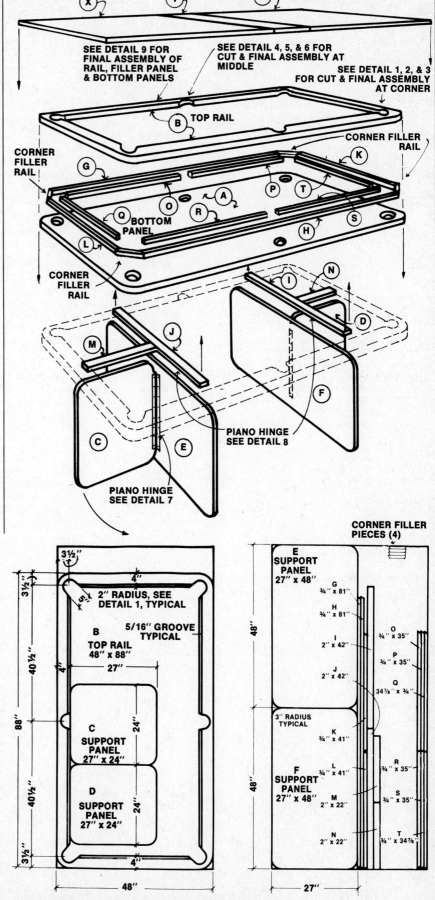

SEE DETAIL 9 FOR FINAL ASSEMBLY OF RAIL, FILLER PANEL & BOTTOM PANELS

SEE DETAIL 4, 5, & 6 FOR CUT & FINAL ASSEMBLY AT MIDDLE

SEE DETAIL 1, 2, & 3 FOR CUT & FINAL ASSEMBLY AT CORNER

B TOP RAIL

CORNER FILLER RAIL

CORNER FILLER RAIL

BOTTOM PANEL

CORNER FILLER RAIL

PIANO HINGE SEE DETAIL 8

PIANO HINGE SEE DETAIL 7

POOL TABLE PANEL LAYOUT   ¾″ x 4′ x 8′ APA PLYWOOD

3½″ RADIUS ALL CORNERS TYPICAL. SEE DETAIL 3

2½″ RADIUS HOLE, SEE DETAIL 3. TYPICAL

CENTER LINE OF BOTTOM PANEL

2½″ RADIUS HOLE SEE DETAIL 6. TYPICAL

A BOTTOM PANEL 48″ x 88″

2½″ RADIUS HOLE, SEE DETAIL 3. TYPICAL

3½″ RADIUS HOLE, TYPICAL

3½″ RADIUS

2″ RADIUS, SEE DETAIL 1, TYPICAL

5/16″ GROOVE TYPICAL

B TOP RAIL 48″ x 88″

C SUPPORT PANEL 27″ x 24″

D SUPPORT PANEL 27″ x 24″

E SUPPORT PANEL 27″ x 48″

G ¾″ x 81″
H ¾″ x 81″
I 2″ x 42″
J 2″ x 42″

3″ RADIUS TYPICAL

K ¾″ x 41″
L ¾″ x 41″
M 2″ x 22″
N 2″ x 22″

F SUPPORT PANEL 27″ x 48″

O ¾″ x 35″
P ¾″ x 35″
Q 34⅞″ x ¾″
R ¾″ x 35″
S ¾″ x 35″
T ¾″ x 34⅞″

CORNER FILLER PIECES (4)

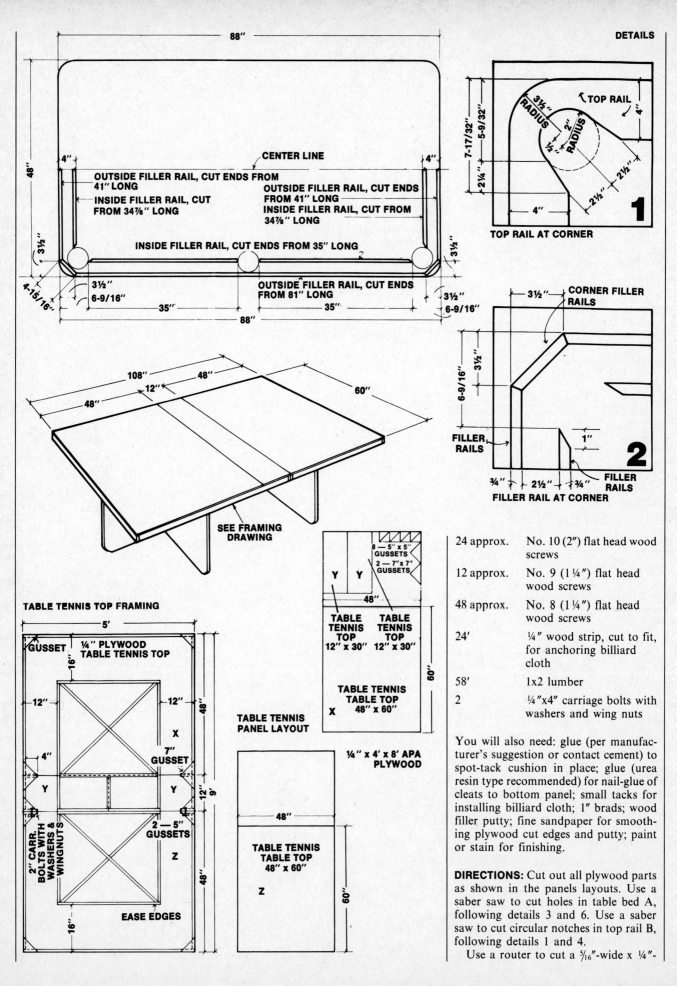

88″

CENTER LINE

OUTSIDE FILLER RAIL, CUT ENDS FROM
41″ LONG

INSIDE FILLER RAIL, CUT
FROM 34⅞″ LONG

OUTSIDE FILLER RAIL, CUT ENDS
FROM 41″ LONG

INSIDE FILLER RAIL, CUT FROM
34⅞″ LONG

INSIDE FILLER RAIL, CUT ENDS FROM 35″ LONG

4″

4″

48″

3½″

3½″

4-15/16″

3½″
6-9/16″

OUTSIDE FILLER RAIL, CUT ENDS
FROM 81″ LONG

3½″
6-9/16″

35″

35″

88″

TOP RAIL AT CORNER — 1

7-17/32″
5-9/32″
2¼″
3½″ RADIUS
2″ RADIUS
½″
TOP RAIL
4″
4″
2½″
2½″
2½″

1

FILLER RAIL AT CORNER — 2

3½″
CORNER FILLER RAILS
3½″
6-9/16″
FILLER RAILS
FILLER RAILS
1″
¾″   2½″   ¾″

2

108″
48″
12″
48″
60″

SEE FRAMING
DRAWING

TABLE TENNIS TOP FRAMING

5′
GUSSET
¼″ PLYWOOD
TABLE TENNIS TOP
16″
12″
12″
48″
4″
7″ GUSSET
X
Y
Y
2 — 5″ GUSSETS
Z
48″
9′
12″
2″ CARR. BOLTS WITH WASHERS & WINGNUTS
16″
EASE EDGES

TABLE TENNIS PANEL LAYOUT

8 — 5″ x 5″ GUSSETS
2 — 7″ x 7″ GUSSETS
48″
Y   Y
TABLE TENNIS TOP 12″ x 30″
TABLE TENNIS TOP 12″ x 30″
60″
TABLE TENNIS TABLE TOP 48″ x 60″
X

¼″ x 4′ x 8′ APA PLYWOOD

48″
TABLE TENNIS TABLE TOP 48″ x 60″
Z
60″

24 approx.	No. 10 (2″) flat head wood screws	
12 approx.	No. 9 (1¼″) flat head wood screws	
48 approx.	No. 8 (1¼″) flat head wood screws	
24′	¼″ wood strip, cut to fit, for anchoring billiard cloth	
58′	1x2 lumber	
2	¼″x4″ carriage bolts with washers and wing nuts	

You will also need: glue (per manufacturer's suggestion or contact cement) to spot-tack cushion in place; glue (urea resin type recommended) for nail-glue of cleats to bottom panel; small tacks for installing billiard cloth; 1″ brads; wood filler putty; fine sandpaper for smoothing plywood cut edges and putty; paint or stain for finishing.

DIRECTIONS: Cut out all plywood parts as shown in the panels layouts. Use a saber saw to cut holes in table bed A, following details 3 and 6. Use a saber saw to cut circular notches in top rail B, following details 1 and 4.

Use a router to cut a ⁵⁄₁₆″-wide x ¼″-

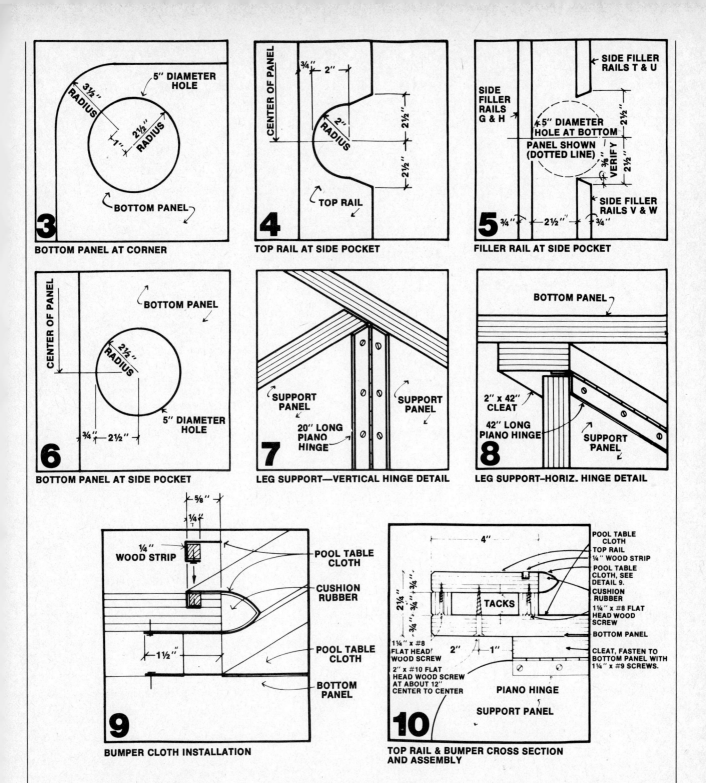

3 BOTTOM PANEL AT CORNER

5" DIAMETER HOLE
3½" RADIUS
2½" RADIUS
1"
BOTTOM PANEL

4 TOP RAIL AT SIDE POCKET

CENTER OF PANEL
¾" 2"
2" RADIUS
2½"
2½"
TOP RAIL

5 FILLER RAIL AT SIDE POCKET

SIDE FILLER RAILS T & U
SIDE FILLER RAILS G & H
5" DIAMETER HOLE AT BOTTOM PANEL SHOWN (DOTTED LINE)
2½"
2½"
⅜" VERIFY
SIDE FILLER RAILS V & W
¾" 2½" ¾"

6 BOTTOM PANEL AT SIDE POCKET

CENTER OF PANEL
BOTTOM PANEL
2½" RADIUS
5" DIAMETER HOLE
¾" 2½"

7 LEG SUPPORT—VERTICAL HINGE DETAIL

SUPPORT PANEL
SUPPORT PANEL
20" LONG PIANO HINGE

8 LEG SUPPORT–HORIZ. HINGE DETAIL

BOTTOM PANEL
2" x 42" CLEAT
42" LONG PIANO HINGE
SUPPORT PANEL

9 BUMPER CLOTH INSTALLATION

⅝"
¼"
¼" WOOD STRIP
POOL TABLE CLOTH
CUSHION RUBBER
POOL TABLE CLOTH
1½"
BOTTOM PANEL

10 TOP RAIL & BUMPER CROSS SECTION AND ASSEMBLY

4"
POOL TABLE CLOTH
TOP RAIL
¼" WOOD STRIP
POOL TABLE CLOTH, SEE DETAIL 9.
CUSHION RUBBER
2¼"
¾" ¾" ¾"
TACKS
1¼" x #8 FLAT HEAD WOOD SCREW
BOTTOM PANEL
1¼" x #8 FLAT HEAD WOOD SCREW
2" 1"
CLEAT, FASTEN TO BOTTOM PANEL WITH 1¼" x #9 SCREWS.
2" x #10 FLAT HEAD WOOD SCREW AT ABOUT 12" CENTER TO CENTER
PIANO HINGE
SUPPORT PANEL

deep groove in top rail B (detail 9).

To install billiard cloth over cushion rail, tack it at close intervals, first to the ¼" wood strip. Insert the wood strip in routed-out groove in top rail B, then turn panel over. Pull cloth taut around cushion and tack it at close intervals to bottom surface of top rail panel.

With glue and 1¼" No. 8 flat head screws driven through predrilled pilot holes, fasten inside filler rails O, P, Q, R, S and T to underside of top rail B, flush with the inner edge of B (see exploded drawing and detail 10). Similarly fasten

outside filler rails G, H, L and K to B. Add corner filler pieces to B (see exploded drawing and detail 2).

To install billiard cloth on bottom panel A, tack it securely along one side, except at pockets. On other side, pull cloth very tight, avoiding puckers (having a helper to pull and smooth makes the job easier) and tack in place. Cut out circles for pockets, making the cutouts ¾" smaller than the holes for the pockets. Carefully moisten the cut edge just enough to allow it to stretch. Then stretch it gently, shaping it down into the

pocket. Glue in place. If the cloth will not stretch sufficiently, you may find it necessary to clip it, not quite to the pocket edge, in several places for a smooth, even fit.

Fasten table bed A to rail assembly with 2" screws driven through A into B (detail 10). With glue and No. 9 1¼" screws, attach cleats I, J, M and N to the underside of A. Fasten support pieces E and F to cleats I and J with piano hinges (detail 8). Fasten fold-out supports C and D to E and F with piano hinges (refer to detail 7).

TABLE TENNIS TOP

Cut plywood top pieces and gussets following panel layouts. Cut outside framing pieces of 1x2 lumber. With glue and 1″ brads, fasten plywood top pieces to framing. Use glue and brads to fasten gussets at outside corners. Similarly fasten inside framing to top pieces (see framing detail). Use a block plane or sandpaper to ease the edges of the inside framing so that they will not damage the cushion cloth on the pool table. Drill ¼″ holes through adjoining 1x2 framing pieces for bolts that hold the two sections together.

Sand the plywood top before applying flat green paint. Finish the table base with paint or stain.

REMODELED BASEMENT

(pages 62-63)

PRELIMINARY DESIGN CONSIDERATIONS: Prepare scale drawings to incorporate your ideas and adapt our features to suit your particular needs and tastes. 2x3s may be used for most framing, instead of 2x4s, to save space and money.

Use your scale drawing to get help from your local utility, or electrical contractor experienced in electric heat installations, to calculate the heat loss and the number and location of the radiant electric heat panels and thermostats. You may wish to get help with the lighting design from your electric utility or electrical contractor to be sure the levels of illumination will be adequate in your adaptation of these plans.

Include provision in your ceiling design for access to water valves and cleanouts. This may be done in several ways: Make a simple push-up or hinged trap door of the ceiling material or use a 6″-round electrical junction box cover.

I-beams make natural locations for partitions. Be sure that the partition framing does not touch the steel beam. If it does, the doors, partition and beam will act in concert to transmit sounds throughout the house. Two-inch-thick insulation stapled between the floor joists provides additional floor-to-floor sound-proofing.

Before starting construction, take whatever steps may be necessary to assure dry foundation walls and floor. Inspect and correct any water or moisture problems. Fill any foundation cracks with waterproof crack filler and sealer, and moisture-proof the walls if necessary. Check local codes for compliance and permits.

FURRING, FRAMING AND INSULATING

MATERIALS: 1x2 No. 1 common lumber; 1x3 No. 1 common lumber; 2x2s; 2x3s or 2x4s; one bundle of cedar shims; 8d, 10d and 12d common nails; Masonite Brand General Purpose Adhesive; 1¼″ and 2″ masonry nails; ¼″x 3½″ carriage bolts; urethane foam insulation with vapor barrier or 6-mill visqueen vapor barrier; 4″ fiberglass bats.

DIRECTIONS: Start construction by furring out the foundation walls. Install 1x2s horizontally top and bottom, and vertically 16″ on center, plus two at each corner. In addition, frame the windows. Use Masonite Brand General Purpose Adhesive or Goodrich PL200. Test the foundation wall for high and low spots with a chalk line and shim. Drive nails in the 1x2s only at the high spots.

Fill the spaces between the furring with ¾″ thick, foil-backed urethane foam glued in place. It may be necessary to tack 1x2 battens across the furring strips to hold the insulation in place for 24 hours while the adhesive dries. If urethane foam is not used, cover the entire wall by stapling 6-mill visqueen on the 1x2 studding.

Next, carefully mark the location of interior walls on the floor. A 9H pencil holds its point when marking the critical cross marks on concrete. Then join the pencil lines with a snapped chalk line. Use a plumb bob to transfer these lines accurately to the joists above.

Use double top plates and single sole plates in the partitioning. First nail the upper top plate to the joists with 12d common nails. Then cut and nail the partitions together on the floor by driving two 12d nails through the top plate into the studs and two through the sole plate into the studs. Apply adhesive to the floor, and lift the partition into place. Nail the top plate into the plate nailed to the joists. Drive a few 2″ masonry nails through the sole plate to hold partition in place until glue sets.

Ceiling framing for the fluorescent light grids and heating units is next. The inside dimensions of the blocking for both light grids are 4′¼″x8′¼″. Block the opening for the light grid with 1x3s and 1x2s. Use 1x3s to block for the electric heat panels so they will be flush with the finished ceiling. Specific pattern and directions to fur out the heating units are included with the units.

The 2x2 ceiling panel blocking runs 90 degrees to the joists and 16″ on center. Additional blocking is required parallel to all panel edges. The blocking lowers the ceiling below electrical junction boxes, wiring and most water pipes.

The straight staircase was made interesting by turning the bottom two stairs. The two old treads were removed and the new design framed with 2x8s ripped to size. The frame was faced with ¾″-thick kick plates and surfaced with 2x10 treads nailed parallel to the kick plates. Evenly space the treads ⅛″ apart by using scraps of tile between each tread while nailing it down.

The pass-through partition at the foot of the stairs was designed specifically to hide a cast iron sewer pipe. It also created a foyer area and enclosed the food service area, while allowing long boards and 4x8 panels to be brought downstairs. Frame the pass-through as shown in Fig. 63B.

ELECTRICAL (Fig. 63C, p. 123)

MATERIALS: Wiring, junction boxes, switches, etc., as required; light grid: six 40W fluorescent strips, Sears Cat. No. 34J3126C; 6 sheets milk white plastic, Sears Cat. No. 64H83751N; double-strength aluminum foil; 1x2 and ¼″x¾″ clear pine; 1″ brads and 6d finishing nails; white glue; black foam; ¼″x2¼″ lag bolts and washers; 500 watt electrical radiant heat panels, Federal Pacific RCP 50012 with line voltage thermostats.

DIRECTIONS: After the ceiling blocking and framing are in place, staple aluminum foil into all fluorescent strip

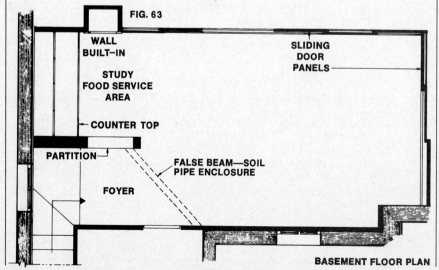

FIG. 63

WALL BUILT-IN

STUDY FOOD SERVICE AREA

SLIDING DOOR PANELS

← COUNTER TOP

PARTITION→

FALSE BEAM—SOIL PIPE ENCLOSURE

FOYER

BASEMENT FLOOR PLAN

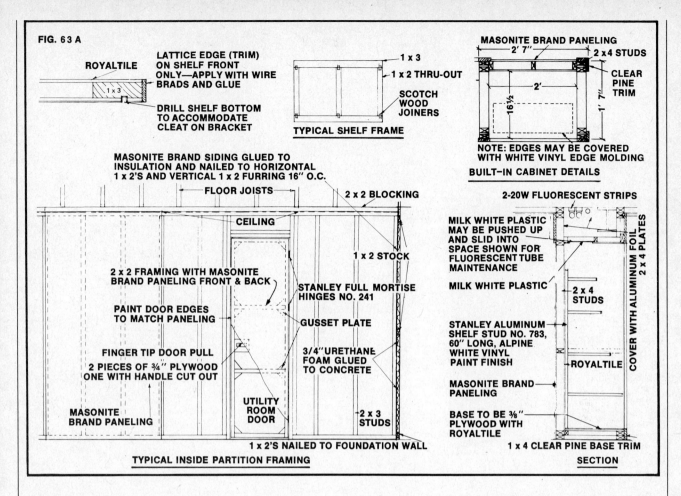

FIG. 63 A

ROYALTILE

LATTICE EDGE (TRIM) ON SHELF FRONT ONLY—APPLY WITH WIRE BRADS AND GLUE

1 x 3

DRILL SHELF BOTTOM TO ACCOMMODATE CLEAT ON BRACKET

1 x 3

1 x 2 THRU-OUT

SCOTCH WOOD JOINERS

TYPICAL SHELF FRAME

MASONITE BRAND PANELING

2' 7"

2 x 4 STUDS

CLEAR PINE TRIM

2'

16½

1' 7"

NOTE: EDGES MAY BE COVERED WITH WHITE VINYL EDGE MOLDING

BUILT—IN CABINET DETAILS

MASONITE BRAND SIDING GLUED TO INSULATION TO HORIZONTAL 1 x 2'S AND VERTICAL 1 x 2 FURRING 16" O.C.

FLOOR JOISTS

2 x 2 BLOCKING

CEILING

1 x 2 STOCK

2 x 2 FRAMING WITH MASONITE BRAND PANELING FRONT & BACK

STANLEY FULL MORTISE HINGES NO. 241

PAINT DOOR EDGES TO MATCH PANELING

GUSSET PLATE

FINGER TIP DOOR PULL

3/4" URETHANE FOAM GLUED TO CONCRETE

2 PIECES OF ¾" PLYWOOD ONE WITH HANDLE CUT OUT

MASONITE BRAND PANELING

UTILITY ROOM DOOR

2 x 3 STUDS

1 x 2'S NAILED TO FOUNDATION WALL

TYPICAL INSIDE PARTITION FRAMING

2-20W FLUORESCENT STRIPS

MILK WHITE PLASTIC MAY BE PUSHED UP AND SLID INTO SPACE SHOWN FOR FLUORESCENT TUBE MAINTENANCE

MILK WHITE PLASTIC

2 x 4 STUDS

STANLEY ALUMINUM SHELF STUD NO. 783, 60" LONG, ALPINE WHITE VINYL PAINT FINISH

ROYALTILE

MASONITE BRAND PANELING

BASE TO BE ⅜" PLYWOOD WITH ROYALTILE

COVER WITH ALUMINUM FOIL

2 x 4 PLATES

1 x 4 CLEAR PINE BASE TRIM

SECTION

cavities. Obtain the services of a competent electrician to prewire and install the light, power and heat. Use your scale drawings to get bids.

A 4'x8' lighting grid is built into the ceiling of the basement room. The 4' dimension in the grid runs parallel to the joists. Six 4' light fixtures are fastened between the seven joists in this unit.

Cut the 1x2 grid frame pieces to size. Assemble on the floor with 6d finishing nails and glue. Cut the ½"x¾" pieces of parting strip to length. Fasten to the 1x2 frame with nails and glue while using scrap milk white plastic on the floor to hold the parting strip about 1⁄16" above the bottom edge of the 1x2 frame. Paint the grid black or stain it. Use a utility knife to cut the milk white plastic inserts to fit the grid and install. Fasten black foam (or felt) light seal in place, and install light grid with ¼" lag bolts. Install warm white fluorescent tubes to blend with the color of incandescent light.

FLOORING

The flooring shown in the photos is Congoleum Industries' Spring pattern Shinyl Vinyl cushion tile. It comes in rolls 6' wide and is best laid professionally.

It is best to have the flooring installed after the framing, electrical and ceiling paneling and trim are in, but before the wall paneling and trim. Use your scale drawing to obtain bids for installing the flooring and sealing the seams with SU 91 sealer.

Protect the flooring during the remaining construction with building paper secured from your local lumber dealer. Use 2"-wide masking tape to hold the paper down neatly—about 1" from the studding so it won't interfere with installing the paneling and trim.

PANELING

MATERIALS: Masonite Brand Surfstone (ceiling); Masonite Brand Coach House, White (walls); Masonite Brand Royaltile, Arctic White; Masonite Brand General Purpose Adhesive; Match-Stix; waterproof caulk.

DIRECTIONS: Masonite Brand Coach House White paneling is shown in the photographs. Saw off both the top and bottom so the paneling fits the height of your walls. Cut the baseboard of the Coach House to a uniform width— about 5½"—to match the pine baseboard of the sliding doors when they are hung and so the middle rail of this paneling blends well with other architectural features. Also, plan for the location of the vertical stile in this paneling, or saw it off so the stile does not butt against a vertical trim board.

Use 2x3s laid on a saw horse to support the 4'x8' paneling while sawing it.

If a portable circular saw is used, set the depth of cut about ⅜". Use a factory edge of a 10"-wide piece of ¾"-thick particleboard as a straight rip fence. Hold the rip fence in position with clamps at both ends.

Follow the installation directions printed on the protective covering of each panel. Three joint treatments may be used where the paneling joins the trim: 1. Butt the paneling against the architectural trim board; 2. Butt the panels together and cover the joint with a trim board; 3. Cut a ¼"x¼" rabbet in the trim board to cover the edge of the paneling.

The inside corner joints of the Royaltile in the closet are 90-degree butts. Therefore, measure and cut carefully. You can "fudge" on these joints a little by running a fine bead of white silicone tub caulk, smoothed with your index finger, along the joint. Use nails sparingly—rely on the panel adhesive. Wherever possible, place nails so they will be hidden behind shelf standards.

Cut the ceiling panels to fit your plan. Do not butt the panels tightly; leave an expansion gap. Cut access holes wherever electrical junction boxes occur. (Cover these holes with 6"-diameter junction box covers painted to blend with the ceiling materials.) Also cut access holes for water valves, clean-outs.

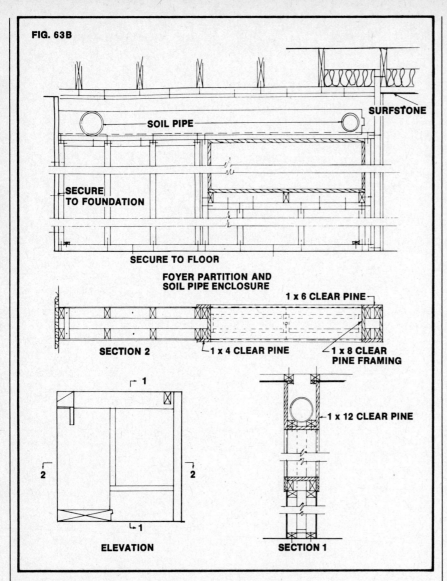

SURFSTONE

SOIL PIPE

SECURE
TO FOUNDATION

SECURE TO FLOOR

FOYER PARTITION AND
SOIL PIPE ENCLOSURE

1 x 6 CLEAR PINE

SECTION 2 — 1 x 4 CLEAR PINE — 1 x 8 CLEAR
PINE FRAMING

1 x 12 CLEAR PINE

ELEVATION

SECTION 1

Fasten paneling to the ceilng blocking with adhesive applied generously, and 1" colored nails spaced every 4".

ARCHITECTURAL TRIM
MATERIALS (for finishing trim): Sherwin Williams A-48N Pecan, Water Rinsable Stain; Sherwin Williams Beauty-Lok Satin Varnish; spackle; mineral spirits; dry color (brown and yellow).

DIRECTIONS: Trim the ceiling, then the walls. As you cut each piece of ceiling or wall trim to size, sand out the planer ripple marks and erase pencil marks. Remove dents by applying a wet rag on the depression and pressing it with a soldering iron. The steam created will bring out the dent. Stain the board. (See Finishing text.) Then, fasten the board in place with 6d or 8d finishing nails and set them. The false beams hide drain pipes and are simple boxes nailed and glued together and fastened to the ceiling blocking. Cut clear pine to fit between the window trim boards and the furring and install. Miter the 1x3 trim around

the light grid.
Finishing: Plastic resin glue is recommended whenever you glue pine components that will be stained. Use a hot, wet rag to wipe the excess glue that squeezes out. That part will accept stain whereas white glue often coats the area and affects the even absorption of stain. Dilute stain with 1/3 mineral spirits and apply generously with an old brush. Experiment with the amount of mineral spirits to add to get the desired shade. Wipe off the excess stain promptly with a rag to achieve the even shade desired. When dry, varnish.

Fill nail holes after the first coat of varnish has dried with precolored wood putty. Sand lightly.

Moisten a small amount of the colored spackle to putty consistency. Use your index finger to apply it. You do not have to be too careful when applying, because after 24 hours, you can quickly remove the excess spackle and smooth by wiping clean with a damp rag. No sanding the spackle. After 24 hours, apply a second coat of varnish.

FOOD SERVICE/HOBBY/STUDY AREA

SLIDE-AWAY TABLES
MATERIALS: 4 pieces 2"x2"(full)x8' clear white pine; 3'x5' panel Masonite Brand Royaltile, Arctic White; 3'x5'x¾" particleboard; 3 pieces 1x2x8' clear pine; two 3'x⅜" dowel rods; 6d finishing nails; white glue; plastic resin glue; 8 nylon furniture glides, 1" diameter, ¼" thick.

DIRECTIONS: Design these tables to fit under the counters with about 1" clearance at all sides. Start construction by cutting the 1¼"x2" notches in the particleboard for the legs. The clear white pine stock for the trestle should be a full 2"x2". Plane or smooth as necessary. Then cut the legs and H frame stretchers to length (Fig. 63D, page 124).

Assemble the H frame by using the notched particleboard top as a pattern. Clamp the two end pieces of the frame to the particleboard surface so they line up with the edges of their respective notches. Bore the double dowel holes through each end and 1" deep into the cross bar. Cut four dowel pins 3¼" long. Coat the holes with plastic resin glue and drive in the dowels. Wipe off excess glue with a wet rag. (The dowels should protrude ¼"; cut them flush later.) Keep the H frame stretcher clamped in position for 24 hours until the glue sets.

Cut the legs and the ¾"x1½" tenons to length. Bore two ⅜" holes through the legs and 1" into the ends of the H frame. Cut the ⅜" dowel pins 3¼" long and assemble the trestle dry.

Cut the Royaltile next. Apply panel adhesive to the particleboard, place the Royaltile on it, and weight down. When dry, turn the table upside down, and fasten thc legs in their notches with 6d finishing nails and plastic resin glue. Put the same glue in the holes in the legs and drive in the dowels. While the table is upside down, use bar clamps if necessary to assure that the two corner-to-opposite-corner distances between legs are equal and, therefore, square. Also, use a framing square to be sure that all legs are 90 degrees to the top. When the glue has set, turn the table over. Cut the mitered 1x2 edge border and fasten with 6d nails and plastic resin glue.

Saw off the dowels to within 1/16" of the leg surfaces. Then pare the dowels flush to the surface with a sharp ½" chisel. As you pare, tap the chisel toward the center of the dowel. Drive nylon furniture glides into each leg. Sand and finish table.

COUNTER
MATERIALS: Electrical: wiring, junction boxes, switches, quad convenience outlet, etc.; three 150W incandescent fixtures with drop lens (Sears Cat. No.

34H3287). For Counter: 2x2s; ½"-thick A-C plywood; 1x3 clear pine; Masonite Brand Royaltile, Arctic White; 10d common nails; 6d finishing nails; ¼"x2¼" lag screws.

DIRECTIONS: Install incandescent ceiling lighting, with wall switch above counter so the center line of the drop lens is plumb with the front edge of the counter. If the joists don't permit this optimum location, move the fixtures toward the wall the minimum necessary. Install quad convenience outlet 8" above counter.

Cut the pieces of 2x2 framework to fit your designed space, and assemble with 10d common nails. Then fasten the ½"-thick plywood to the frame with white glue and 6d common nails. Next, saw the Royaltile paneling to size and glue to the plywood with panel adhesive.

Locate the wall studs, then bore the ¼" lag holes in the frame accordingly. Level the counter 32" above the floor, so the slide-away tables will fit under the 1x3 facing when it is in place, and so the

bottom of the 1x3 is along top line of the middle rail of the Coach House paneling. Bore the ⁵⁄₃₂" pilot holes into the wall studs. Screw the counter to the paneled wall. Cut the 1x3 pine trim to length; stain and fasten to the counter front with 6d finishing nails and white glue. Sink nails and finish.

CABINET

MATERIALS: ⅝" particleboard; Masonite Brand Royaltile, Arctic White; Masonite Brand General Purpose Panel Adhesive. Lumber: 1x3 No. 1 common, 1x1, 1x2 clear pine, 1x3 clear pine; ⅜" dowel pins; ¼"x¾" lattice; eight cabinet pivot hinges, satin aluminum finish (Stanley No. 332); two double magnetic catches (Stanley No. 45); 1½" No. 8 wood screws; ¼"x4¼" lag screws; 6d and 1" finishing nails.

DIRECTIONS: Start by constructing a five-sided box long enough to fit your designed space. Cut the members to size from ⅝" particleboard and assemble with 6d common nails and white glue. Cut the center divider to size and nail

and glue into place. Brace, or clamp, as necessary, to insure the box is square while the glue dries. Then, nail and glue the 1x1 stringers along the front and back of the cabinet as shown. Nail and glue the 1x3 to the back (Fig. 63D).

When the glue has dried, locate the studs in the back and sides. Use large flat head wood screws or lag screws to hang the cabinet. Butt the top of the cabinet against the bottom of the 1x12 top trim, or about 76" from the floor.

Next, make the facer frame from clear 1x3s for the top and bottom rails, a 1x2 for the center stile and 1x1 for the end stiles. The end stiles may be wider (for filler) if desired. The glued butt joints in the facer may be strengthened with screws or dowels. Nail to the front of the cabinet with 6d finishing nails.

Make the doors of Royaltile laminated to ⅝" particleboard. To do this, cut out a piece of particleboard 21½" wide and 8' long, and a piece of Royaltile the same size. Glue the pieces together with panel adhesive. When dry, cut off the four door pieces to fit your cabinet,

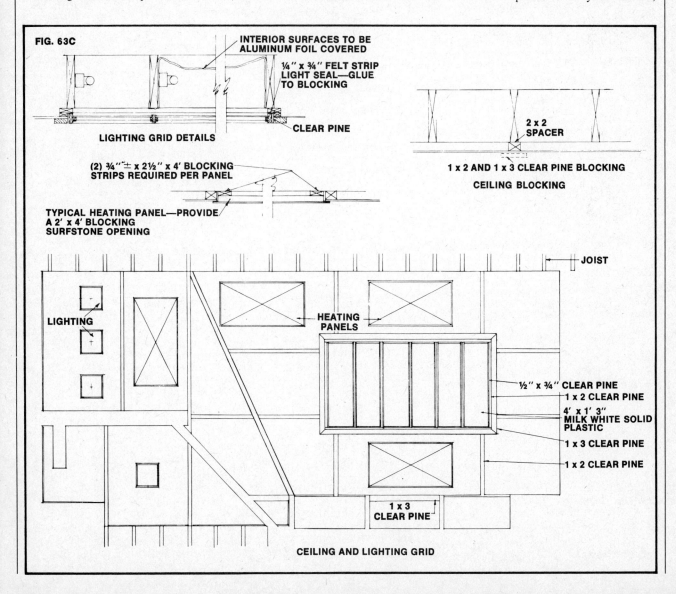

FIG. 63C

INTERIOR SURFACES TO BE ALUMINUM FOIL COVERED

¼" x ¾" FELT STRIP LIGHT SEAL—GLUE TO BLOCKING

CLEAR PINE

LIGHTING GRID DETAILS

2 x 2 SPACER

1 x 2 AND 1 x 3 CLEAR PINE BLOCKING

CEILING BLOCKING

(2) ¾"± x 2½" x 4' BLOCKING STRIPS REQUIRED PER PANEL

TYPICAL HEATING PANEL—PROVIDE A 2' x 4' BLOCKING SURFSTONE OPENING

JOIST

LIGHTING

HEATING PANELS

½" x ¾" CLEAR PINE
1 x 2 CLEAR PINE
4' X 1' 3" MILK WHITE SOLID PLASTIC
1 x 3 CLEAR PINE
1 x 2 CLEAR PINE

1 x 3 CLEAR PINE

CEILING AND LIGHTING GRID

allowing ¼″ for the lattice plus ⅛″ clearance on either side of each door. Band the doors with ¾″-wide lattice nailed and glued. Carve the cutaway hand grip with a router or dado. Hang the doors with pivot hinges. Install double magnetic catches on the bottom of the cabinet centered on each pair of doors. Stain and varnish the pine trim and door banding; varnish the particleboard. Or you may prefer to paint the cabinets as part of an overall decorating scheme for your basement.

SLIDING BARN DOORS

MATERIALS: Clear pine in the following sizes: 1x4, 1x6, ½x3, ½x6; ¾″x¼″ lattice; 1x2 birch threshold; Masonite Brand Coach House White; Masonite Brand General Purpose Panel Adhesive; white glue; plastic resin glue; epoxy glue; ⅜″x1½″ lag screws with washers; 6d

finishing nails; Stanley Sliding Door Hardware: aluminum track for bypassing doors up to 150 lbs. (lengths to suit) No.T2840, trolley assembly with link bolt (2 per door) No.2844-1, hanger assembly (2 per door) No.2844-2, bottom door guide, zinc-plated (2 per door) No.2670 BG, mortise door guide track (floor—lengths to suit) No.2670MG; ¼″x1½″ flat head bolts with lead anchors.

DIRECTIONS: Two examples of framing for the sliding door track are illustrated: parallel to the I-beam; parallel to the joists. There is one lap joint in the frames to accommodate the offset of the joists on either side of the I-beam. Be sure that the 1x12 top will cover your framing design. Modify the design to suit so there will be frames 16″ on center. Prepare a jig or pattern from scrap Masonite paneling.

Cut the 2x3s and 2x2s to size and assemble them on your pattern with nails and plastic resin glue. Also, saw out gussets from scrap Masonite paneling or Peg-Board, and nail and glue to reinforce the notched butt joint.

After the glue has set 24 hours, fasten frames to the joists, or ceiling blocking, with ¼″x3½″ carriage bolts and white glue. Mark the location of the first and last frames and fasten them in place. Then tie four taut strings between the two frames (top and bottom each side) to guide location of intermediate frames.

When the framing is up and the glue has set, use white glue and 8d finishing nails to fasten the trim boards to the frames. Start with the bottom boards (if there is not a partition); the width of the frame may require two boards. Then install the three boards that form the track channel.

Barn Doors: Panel both sides of doors that divide two living areas. Panel only the face of doors closing off storage or utility areas. Paint the panel backs of the latter doors with off-white enamel. The horizontal rails in the front of the barn doors fit between the stiles; they do not go across the width of the door. The back of the door is constructed just the opposite; the rails do go across the width of the door.

Determine the size of the doors for your opening. Cut the clear pine boards to size per plan and stain them before fabricating. If Coach House paneling is used, make the middle rail 3⅞″ wide to cover the rail pattern in that paneling. If door is double face, cut a rabbet ¼″ deep and ½″ wide for the paneling on the interior side to fit into. For these doors, the middle rail on the back is ½″-thick stock. If there are three sliding doors to cover an area, omit the single cross piece in the front side of the upper section of the middle door. (Cross buck members not necessary on door backs.)

Cut the paneling to size: 1″ narrower than the door or to fit in the rabbeted stiles. Assemble the doors with panel adhesive and ⅜″ lags/washers. Use 6d finishing nails as required to clamp the 1x4 framing together.

Fill the ¼″ gap between 1x4s by gluing in lattice and planing it flush later, when dry. Stack the doors on a flat surface for 24 hours until the glue sets. Finish wood trim.

Hanging Doors: Install the upper and lower hardware on the doors. Turn the hardware slightly so the screws are driven into wood and do not wedge the frames apart.

Screw the upper track to the center of the track channel. Drop a plumb bob from the center of the inside track at each end to establish the center line of that track on the floor. Snap a chalk line on the floor. Hang the doors that go on

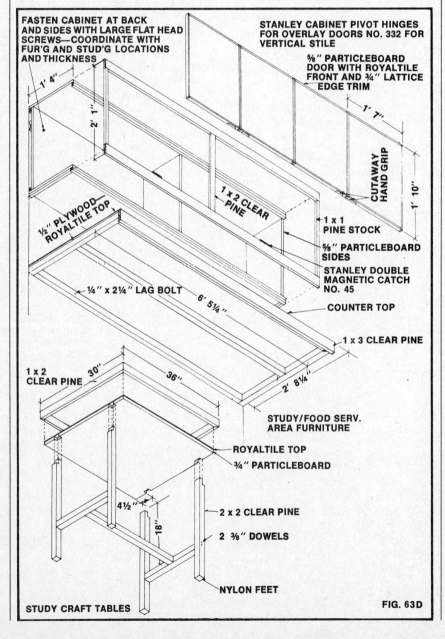

FASTEN CABINET AT BACK AND SIDES WITH LARGE FLAT HEAD SCREWS—COORDINATE WITH FUR'G AND STUD'G LOCATIONS AND THICKNESS

STANLEY CABINET PIVOT HINGES FOR OVERLAY DOORS NO. 332 FOR VERTICAL STILE

⅝″ PARTICLEBOARD DOOR WITH ROYALTILE FRONT AND ¾″ LATTICE EDGE TRIM

1' 4"
2' 1"
1' 7"

½″ PLYWOOD ROYALTILE TOP

1 x 2 CLEAR PINE

CUTAWAY HAND GRIP

1' 10"

1 x 1 PINE STOCK

⅝″ PARTICLEBOARD SIDES

STANLEY DOUBLE MAGNETIC CATCH NO. 45

¼″ x 2¼″ LAG BOLT

6' 5¼"

COUNTER TOP

1 x 3 CLEAR PINE

1 x 2 CLEAR PINE
30"
36"
2' 8¼"

STUDY/FOOD SERV. AREA FURNITURE

ROYALTILE TOP
¾″ PARTICLEBOARD

4½"
18"

2 x 2 CLEAR PINE

2 ⅜″ DOWELS

NYLON FEET

STUDY CRAFT TABLES

FIG. 63D

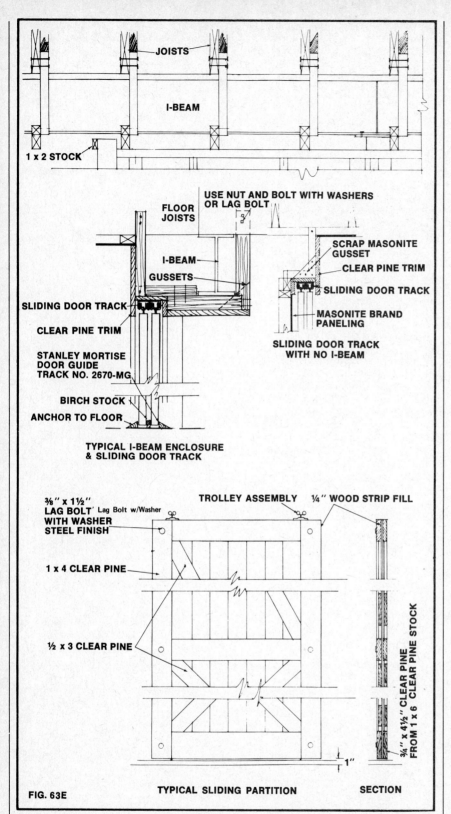

JOISTS

I-BEAM

1 x 2 STOCK

USE NUT AND BOLT WITH WASHERS
OR LAG BOLT

FLOOR JOISTS

I-BEAM

GUSSETS

SLIDING DOOR TRACK

CLEAR PINE TRIM

STANLEY MORTISE
DOOR GUIDE
TRACK NO. 2670-MG

BIRCH STOCK

ANCHOR TO FLOOR

SCRAP MASONITE GUSSET

CLEAR PINE TRIM

SLIDING DOOR TRACK

MASONITE BRAND PANELING

SLIDING DOOR TRACK
WITH NO I-BEAM

TYPICAL I-BEAM ENCLOSURE
& SLIDING DOOR TRACK

3/8" x 1½"
LAG BOLT Lag Bolt w/Washer
WITH WASHER
STEEL FINISH

TROLLEY ASSEMBLY   ¼" WOOD STRIP FILL

1 x 4 CLEAR PINE

½ x 3 CLEAR PINE

¾" x 4½" CLEAR PINE
FROM 1 x 6 CLEAR PINE STOCK

1"

FIG. 63E

TYPICAL SLIDING PARTITION   SECTION

the inside track. Slide the U-shaped mortise door guide track in place, and center the holes over the chalk line. Mark the locations of the holes. Drill and bolt U tracks down with lead anchors spaced at least every 24". Cut the 1½"x¾" center strip of birch threshold to length; stain it and cement it down with panel adhesive. Hang the outer door and slide the U channel into

place. Hold outer channel tight against the center birch strip and mark the bolt holes. Install lead anchors and bolt down. Chamfer both outer pieces of 1x2 birch threshold. Stain and fasten in place with epoxy glue.

Adjust leveling screws so the doors match in height and are plumb. Fill nail holes and varnish. (Door details are shown in Fig. 63E, above.)

(continued from page 29)

3. Fill with walnut filler and rub off excess across grain.

4. Scuff with medium sandpaper.

5. Brush on thinned shellac. Dry four hours.

6. Steel-wool with #3/0 steel wool.

7. Brush on another coat of thinned shellac. Dry overnight.

8. Steel-wool again. Wax, let dry 20 minutes, buff.

Natural Oak Finish

1. Scuff with medium sandpaper.

2. Flow on thinned shellac with brush. Let dry four hours.

3. Scuff again as in step one. Coat with thinned shellac and dry overnight.

4. Rub with medium waterproof sandpaper, lubricate with mixture 8 parts Savasol No. 5 and 1 part light rubbing oil or thin mineral spirits.

5. Wax with good paste wax, let dry and buff.

Natural Korina Finish

1. Sand smooth to touch with fine sandpaper. Dust.

2. Apply red or brown mahogany alcohol or water stain to shade desired, according to manufacturer's instructions. Dry overnight.

3. Brush on thinned solution of shellac and denatured alcohol. Allow to dry for three hours.

4. Steel-wool lightly and dust. Apply a second coat of shellac and dry overnight.

5. With a fine Wet-or-Dry sandpaper, lubricated with light machine oil, rub with the grain. Wax and allow to dry for 20 minutes; buff to high luster.

Gray Birch Finish

1. Brush stain mixture, ½ teaspoon No. 8 Behlen's to ½ gallon water, add small amount of No. 96 orange. Dry for four hours.

2. Brush on thinned coat of shellac. Let dry for four hours.

3. Scuff with medium sandpaper, coat with shellac and dry overnight.

4. Rub with waterproof sandpaper, lubricate with mixture 8 parts Savasol No. 5 and 1 part light rubbing oil. Rub again with fine waterproof sandpaper and lubricate again as in step 4, "Natural Oak Finish." Wax and polish.

Ebonized Mahogany Finish

1. Stain furniture with water stain mixture of 8 tablespoons of No. 8 Behlen to ½ gallon of water. Dry 1½ hours.

2. Scuff with medium sandpaper. Brush on coat of thinned shellac and let dry for four hours.

3. Steel-wool with #3/0 and flow on another coat of thinned shellac. Dry overnight. Steel-wool again.

(continued on page 128)

LARGE AND SMALL BRICK BARBECUES AND TABLE/BENCH

Note: For basic procedure (bricklaying and concrete) on all three brick projects, see the General Directions below.

GENERAL DIRECTIONS: Building the brick units consists of two operations: the construction of a concrete base and the bricklaying.

Concrete base: "Ready-mix" concrete may be used, or the concrete may be mixed on the site. If the concrete is to be mixed at the site, a recommmended mix is 1 part portland cement, 2 parts clean dry sand and 2½ parts gravel or crushed stone, by volume.

First, dig the footings and construct the form for the base. If the holes are dug accurately to the required depth of 24 inches, forms may not be necessary, for the earth will provide its own form. If the surface of the base is to be above the existing ground level, it will be necessary to build a wood form in the shape of the base. In either case, the surface of the concrete should be finished flat and level.

The concrete may be mixed in a wheelbarrow with a garden hoe. Ingredients should be thoroughly blended, as directed above, before adding water. No more than six gallons of water per bag of cement should be used. In estimating, it can be assumed that the yield of concrete will be approximately equal to the quantity of gravel used. The concrete should begin to set within one-half hour and should be covered with burlap or plastic for the first 48 hours.

Bricklaying: Bricklaying tools include a hammer, mason's string, a few 10d nails, a trowel, a spirit level, a hand level, a piece of carpenter's chalk and a broad-bladed cold chisel. The chisel, called a brick set, is used for cutting brick. A tap on the chisel with a hammer will score the brick along the line of the cut. This is done on two surfaces of the brick. Then, pointing the chisel inward, strike a sharp blow with the hammer; a clean break should result.

Brick should not be laid bone dry. They should be damp, but not wet. A thorough spraying with a hose 15 minutes before using will usually suffice.

Before using any mortar, make a 'dry run." Draw the outline of the barbecue with chalk on the foundation slab, about 2 inches in from the edge. Keep this in mind when laying out the dimensions of the slab. Allow for ½-inch mortar joints.

Lay up the first two courses (layers) dry, to make sure that the bond or pattern will work out. If it does, the actual walls will be accurate.

For mortar, use 1 part portland cement, ¼ part hydrated lime, and 3 parts fine clean sand by volume. Add enough water to get the consistency of soft mud. It's about right when it slides from the shovel easily, but does not run. Mix small batches—by the shovelful, not the bagful (i.e., 1 shovelful of cement, ¼ shovelful lime, 3 shovelsful sand). No more mortar should be mixed than can be used up in 2 hours. Should the mortar lose its plasticity before being used, temper it by remixing with a little fresh water.

Spread a bed (horizontal) joint first to the proper thickness for not more than three bricks at a time. Roughen the surface of the mortar by making a shallow furrow with the point of the trowel. The head (vertical) joint is applied by spreading one end of the brick with mortar. Make sure that all joints are completely filled with mortar—to insure a watertight structure.

Build the corners first, going three or four courses high, then filling in the wall from corner to corner. Be sure to lay the bottom course on mortar to bond it to the slab. Frequent use of a hand level will help keep the wall plumb and the courses level. Make all mortar joints even at ½ inch.

Excess mortar can be clipped off every 2 or 3 courses with the trowel. Tooling is done at the same time to seal the joints. For tooling, a short length of pipe, slightly larger in diameter than the thickness of the joints, can be used, working first vertically and then horizontally to achieve a concave joint. NOTE: A secret of good brickwork is not to move a brick once it is in place; consequently, care in placing the brick in mortar pays off.

Weights for concrete and mortar materials per cubic foot are as follows:
Portland cement = 94 pounds (1 bag)
Hydrated lime = 40 pounds (1 bag)
Sand (damp, loose) = 87 pounds
Gravel (damp) = 105 pounds

SMALL BARBECUE
(page 55)

MATERIALS: 525 solid, uncored bricks (3¾"x2¼"x8"); 10⅝ bags portland cement (8⅝ for concrete, 2 for mortar); ½ bag hydrated lime; 22¾ cubic feet of damp, loose sand (16¾ for concrete. 6 for mortar); 21 cubic feet of crushed stone or gravel; steel reinforcing rod (#3 or ⅜" diameter): two 32", six 18", twelve 4"; two 20½" x 36" cast iron or steel grills. Before mixing concrete for the foundation, set aside the following materials for the hearth slab: 40 pounds cement; 72 pounds sand; 109 pounds crushed stone.

DIRECTIONS: Lay up the first four courses of brick for both outer and inner walls. Allow mortar to set thoroughly. Fill the hearth cavity with gravel or crushed stone to within 4" of the top course of brick. Mix and pour 2" of concrete on top of the gravel. Embed reinforcing rods in the concrete, on 8"

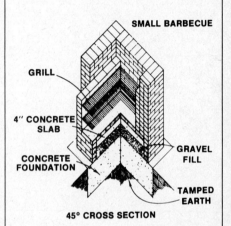

SMALL BARBECUE
GRILL
4" CONCRETE SLAB
GRAVEL FILL
CONCRETE FOUNDATION
TAMPED EARTH
45° CROSS SECTION

centers in both directions. Finish pouring concrete level with the top of the brick. Allow concrete to cure for several days, keeping it covered with damp burlap or plastic for at least the first 48 hours.

Lay the hearth course of brick, then continue building up the outer and inner walls. Between the eighth and ninth courses of the inner wall, place three 4" lengths of reinforcing rod in the mortar

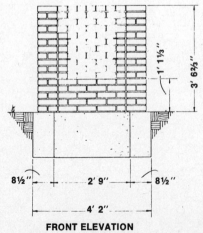

1' 1⅓"
3' 6⅔"
8½"   2' 9"   8½"
4' 2"

FRONT ELEVATION

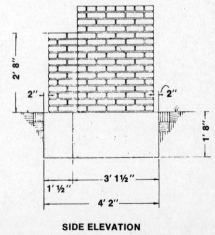

2' 8"
2"   2"
1' 8"
1½"   3' 1½"
4' 2"

SIDE ELEVATION

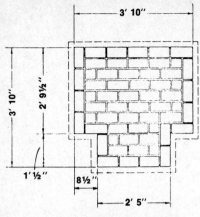

3' 10"
2' 9½"
3' 10"
1' 1½"
8½"
2' 5"

HEARTH PLAN VIEW

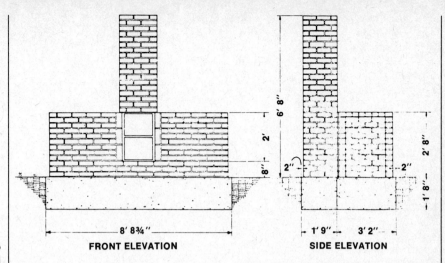

8' 8¾"

FRONT ELEVATION

6' 8"
2'
8"
2"
2"
2' 8"
1' 8"
1' 9"
3' 2"

SIDE ELEVATION

bed on each side, allowing them to protrude 1″ as supports for the charcoal grill. Similarly emplace support pins for the cooking grill between the eleventh and twelfth courses.

tion, set aside these materials for the hearth slab: 48 pounds portland cement (about ½ bag); 86 pounds sand; 129 pounds crushed stone.

of brick, and the chimney. Before laying top course, set steel plates on walls. Lay top course and finish chimney.

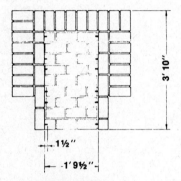

3' 10"
1½"
1' 9½"

PLAN VIEW TOP COURSE AND HEARTH

LARGE BARBECUE
(page 64)

MATERIALS: 684 solid, uncored bricks (3¾″x2¼x8″); 18 bags portland cement (15½ for concrete, 2½ for mortar); ⅝ bag hydrated lime; 38 cubic feet of damp, loose sand (30½ for concrete, 7½ for mortar); 37¾ cubic feet of crushed stone or gravel; two ¼″ steel plates, 2'8″ x 3'4″; prefabricated charcoal grill unit. Before mixing concrete for the founda-

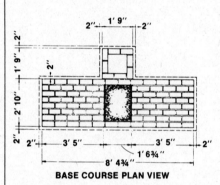

2" 1' 9" 2"
2"
1' 9"
2"
2' 10"
2"
2" 3' 5" 3' 5" 2"
1' 6¾"
8' 4¾"

BASE COURSE PLAN VIEW

DIRECTIONS: Lay the base course of brick (see plan view). Lay up two more courses in front and back and alongside the hearth (see charcoal grill course plan view). Mix and pour concrete level with the top of the brick. Let concrete cure.

Set prefabricated grill unit in place. Build up front, back and inner courses

TABLE/BENCH
(page 64)

MATERIALS: 1,346 solid, uncored brick units (3¾″x2¼″x8″); 36 bags portland ce-

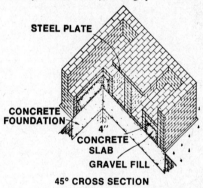

STEEL PLATE
CONCRETE FOUNDATION
CONCRETE SLAB
GRAVEL FILL
4"

45° CROSS SECTION

ment (5 bags for mortar, 31 bags for concrete); 1¼ bags hydrated lime (for mortar); 75½ cubic feet damp, loose sand (15 cubic feet for mortar, 60½ cubic feet for concrete); 75½ cubic feet crushed stone (for concrete); reinforcing steel, #3 or ⅜″ diameter: four 70″ pieces and eighteen 16″ pieces; ½-inch-thick steel plate, 3'5″x6'11½″. Im-

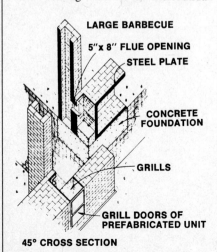

LARGE BARBECUE
5″ x 8″ FLUE OPENING
STEEL PLATE
CONCRETE FOUNDATION
GRILLS
GRILL DOORS OF PREFABRICATED UNIT

45° CROSS SECTION

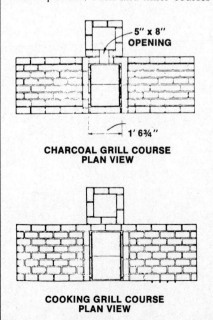

5″ x 8″ OPENING
1' 6¾"

CHARCOAL GRILL COURSE PLAN VIEW

COOKING GRILL COURSE PLAN VIEW

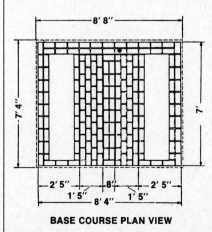

8' 8"
7' 4"
7'
2' 5" 8" 2' 5"
1' 5" 1' 5"
8' 4"

BASE COURSE PLAN VIEW

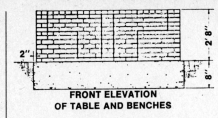

**FRONT ELEVATION
OF TABLE AND BENCHES**

portant: Set aside the following materials for the seat support slabs before mixing concrete for foundation:

127 pounds portland cement (about 1⅓ bags)
228 pounds sand
342 pounds crushed stone

DIRECTIONS: Lay up 11 double courses of brick for the outer wall of the table/bench, leaving off the top course. Lay up six single courses for the fronts and ends of the benches. Lay the brick floor, and build the table leg. Allow

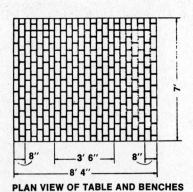

PLAN VIEW OF TABLE AND BENCHES

mortar to cure thoroughly.

Fill the bench cavities with gravel to within 4″ of the top. Mix and pour approximately 2″ of concrete on top of the gravel, then embed steel reinforcing rods in the concrete, running them in both directions on 8″ centers. Complete pouring the concrete level with the top brick courses for the bench fronts. Allow the concrete to set for several days, keeping it covered with damp burlap or plastic for the first 48 hours.

Lay the bench courses of brick on the concrete slabs. Set the steel plate on top of the table leg, extending onto the outer wall. Lay the top course of the wall and the table top.

(*continued from page 125*)

4. Wax with good paste wax, dry and buff.

Honey Color Maple Finish

1. Stain with weak walnut alcohol or water stain.
2. Dry 1½ hours.
3. Scuff with medium sandpaper.
4. Flow on thinned shellac with brush.
5. Dry four hours.
6. Cover with another coat of

thinned shellac.
7. Dry overnight.
8. Rub with medium waterproof sandpaper. Lubricate with 8 parts Savasol #5 and 1 light rubbing oil or thin mineral spirits.
9. Rub with sandpaper, lubricate again as in step 8.
10. Wax with good paste wax, let dry 20 minutes and buff.

Charred Finish

A surface charring and hardening with flame presents an interesting and easy finish for the handyman to apply to new or old furniture. Two pieces of equipment—a torch and a stiff bristle brush—are all that are needed for the project. Practice on an old plank or board first. The following steps outline the char finish:

1. The furniture to be finished must be dry and free from any paint or inflammable material.
2. Light the torch. Adjust the flame and pass the flame from the torch back and forth in smooth sweeps over the surface of the wood. This will produce an even over-all char on the surface of the wood. Be careful not to burn too deeply.
3. Inside joints and corners require a bit more care. Watch for a circle of yellow flame which indicates that you're beginning to burn too deep. Don't try to burn joint lines too deep and dark or try to match the adjacent surfaces. Brushing later will darken and even off this area.
4. After the charring operation, comes brushing. Use a stiff bristle brush to brush out the soft char. Brush lightly with the grain and blow the dust away as you work. Brush in the corners with a toothbrush or similar small brush. Brush and char alternately until you have produced the desired shade and grain effect.
5. Shellac or varnish the surface to protect the finish. Paste wax can also be used to seal the surface and repeated waxings will produce a whitish flecked surface which resembles an old worn and antique finish.

Plain Sliced Oak Pickled Stain

1. Natural paste wood filler thinned according to directions with turpentine or mineral spirits; to this mix add 15% white Firzite.
2. Apply as per directions, being sure to rub well into pores and off the surface completely. Let dry 24 hours.
3. Two or three coats Satinlac; each coat steel wooled with #3/0 steel wool, left dull.

Philippine Mahogany, Light Finish

1. Natural paste wood filler tinted with approximately 2 level teaspoons

each burnt sienna and burnt umber in oil to 1 quart of thinned natural filler.
2. Apply as per instructions. Let dry 24 hours.
3. Two or three coats Satinlac; each coat steel-wooled, left dull.

Economical Finishes

An inexpensive but pleasant blonde finish can be obtained with an easy two-step procedure. First, a coat of interior white undercoat thinned so the wood pattern shows through; the undercoat may be tinted if color is desired. Then, a coat of clear shellac, lacquer or flat varnish.

When using conventional dark stain on fir plywood, first apply clear resin sealer, followed by successive coats of stain and varnish. Sealer may be omitted if greater color contrast is desired.

Paint Finishes

Conventional wall and woodwork paints and enamels are easy to use on Douglas fir plywood. Here again, it pays to use top quality materials. Follow directions on the label regarding mixing, thinning and drying time for each coat.

Interesting textured effects can be obtained with stippling paints—either flat or gloss. This type of finish is easy to apply and covers minor imperfections. For cabinet doors or other surfaces which require cleaning, use washable paints or enamels.

Here are the basic steps to follow in painting or enameling plywood.

1. Fill open surface areas with wood putty. Sand lightly and dust clean. For additional smoothness, panel edges can be coated with surfacing putty or wood putty. Apply a thin layer and sand smooth when dry.
2. Brush on a flat paint or enamel undercoat. Cover sides and edges. If you discover any unfilled surface blemishes, fill with spackle when coat is dry. Sand lightly and dust clean.
3. Apply second coat of undercoat. For high-gloss enamel finish use undercoat mixed of equal parts flat undercoat and high-gloss enamel. For semigloss or flat finish, use undercoat tinted to approximate shade of finish coat. Sand lightly when dry.
4. Apply final coat as it comes from can. This coat as well as preceding coats may be thinned slightly with turpentine or thinner to get better brushability.

Our source is Family Circle DO-IT-YOURSELF ENCYCLOPEDIA, Vol. 8, copyright 1973, Rockville House Publishers, Inc.